# Ghost Towns & Mining Camps of California

## A HISTORY & GUIDE
## BY REMI NADEAU

CREST PUBLISHERS, SANTA BARBARA, CALIFORNIA

To Christine, Barbara and Remi

# Acknowledgments

This book has a history of nearly half a century. It first appeared in 1952 as a series of 26 articles in *Fortnight* magazine, which published it in book form in 1954. It was thoroughly revised, with much added history and guide information, under the Ward Ritchie imprint in 1965. It was revived with minor changes in 1990 by Crest Publishers, which introduced a fourth edition (1992) with major revisions, particularly in updating and expanding the "Points of Interest" sections at the ends of the chapters. This 1999 edition incorporates a number of changes based on new research.

This edition is equally valuable in bringing to life the turbulent times in the heyday of each town, and guiding the visitor to the sights that are relics of those times.

In the evolution of this book I am indebted to many. My wife, Margaret, was sporting enough to accompany me to Bodie and Aurora during our honeymoon in the Sierra in 1947, and has since ridden with me over many roads, good and bad, to other mining camps. She worked with me in recording the surviving buildings on a recent three-week trip in the gold country, and performs the myriad responsibilities of a publisher. Our children—Christine, Barbara, and Remi Robert—have more than once fought their way through sagebrush to view a few crumbling walls.

Our son-in-law, Donald DeVitt, provided invaluable technical support for this edition; among many other things, he put the 1990 edition on computer disk, thus greatly facilitating revision and word processing. Our son, Remi Robert Nadeau, made an essential contribution in using the disk to make additions and corrections, and in teaching me, with much patience, how to use the computer.

In my own childhood my father and mother, Remi and Marguerite Nadeau, took me on trails to old abandoned towns as soon as I was old enough to travel. In those years I was fortunate enough to meet such mining camp authorities as W A. Chalfant of Bishop, Jim Cain of Bodie, and John Delameter of Calico. Over many years since then I have drawn on the personal knowledge of Ed Shepherd and Mrs. Jack Gunn of Independence; Edward Elder of Lone Pine; Paul Hubbard of Randsburg; George Pipkin of Wildrose Station; Sewell "Pop" Lofink of China Lake; Douglas Mooers of Malibu (grandson of the discoverer of Randsburg); Mrs. J. S. Gorman of Moorpark; and W. J. Jenkins of Oakland. For special information I am indebted to Stephen Ginsburg of North Hollywood, an authority on Southern California ghost towns.

For this latest edition, still others have provided helpful information. They include Mary and Jerry Grimsley of Ridgecrest; Jan and Mike Hillenbrand of the Randsburg General Store; Leona Pupich and the Friends of Bodie; Nancy Thornburg, Director of the Alpine County Museum, Markleeville; William G. Hample, President, Kern County Historical Society, Bakersfield; Tim I. Purdy, Director of the Historic Uptown Susanville Association; Mary Etta Segerstrom of Sonora; Michael Hendryx of the Siskiyou County Historical Museum, Yreka; James Lenhoff of Oroville; Alberta Guiver, Butte County Historical Society, Oroville; and John Hutchinson, ranger at the Gold Discovery Park, Coloma.

Visiting the old mining towns is essential in writing about them, but to bring back the characters and events of their golden hours, one must go to the many collections of newspapers, letters, diaries and reminiscences throughout California. Those institutions and persons most helpful over many years were the U.C.L.A. Library; Los Angeles County Museum Library; San Diego Public Library; Pasadena Public Library; Santa Monica Public Library; Inyo County Free Library at Independence, California; St. Joseph Public Library, St. Joseph, Missouri; Library of Congress, Washington, D.C.; History Room of the Wells Fargo Bank, San

Francisco; Society of California Pioneers and California Historical Society, both in San Francisco; Title Insurance and Trust Co. of Los Angeles and San Diego; the George Eastman House; American Antiquarian Society, Worcester, Massachusetts; History Department of the Los Angeles Public Library; Henry E. Huntington Library in San Marino; Bancroft Library, University of California at Berkeley; California State Library at Sacramento; Stockton Public Library; and Eastern California Museum at Independence. I am also indebted to the *Inyo Register* of Bishop and to Donald Segerstrom of Sonora for permission to read their collections of mining town newspapers; to the office of the *Mariposa Gazette;* to Mr. and Mrs. Kenneth Robinson, Fred Richards, and Sylvia Winslow of China Lake; and to two other ghost town buffs, E. D. Nadeau and Douglas Nadeau.

The rare and often unique illustrations were collected and selected by Robert A. Weinstein, historian and expert on early California photographs.

Walter Clark, of Eastman Kodak's Research Laboratories, was helpful in providing rare photographs of the American River mining camps in 1856.

Burr Belden and Stephen Ginsburg generously allowed the reproduction of rare photographs from their collections.

The photograph of the stamp mill at Panamint reproduced on page 199, credited to the *Westerners Brand Book No. 11*, is from the Russ Leadabrand Collection. Also, the photograph on page 199 of Aurora, reproduced from the *Westerners Brand Book No. 11*, was taken by Burton Frasher and is used through the courtesy of Burton Frasher, Jr.

To stay within a reasonable scope it has been necessary to limit the towns covered to those originating as mining communities, and to eliminate those starting as agricultural, railroad, or oil centers. Generally, I have also restricted them to towns where metal—particularly gold, silver, and copper—was mined. Within these boundaries, I have tried to cover all those mining localities in California that were at one time large enough to be termed "towns", and today show at least some remains. Many, of course, continue as lively communities.

Remi Nadeau, 1999

---

# Preface

If you want to find the essence of American character, study the people who made the Western mining frontier. For they left the restraints of society behind them and embarked on a desperate quest against the country's toughest natural obstacles. On such a background, the American spirit was painted in caricature—at its worst, and its best.

So this excursion through the Ghost Towns and Mining Camps of California is more than a collection of anecdote and story. It is a fragment of Americana that helps to explain the whole.

As for the towns themselves, many in this book are not ghostly, but are thriving localities included here because they are essential to the story and have their own atmosphere and relics of yesteryear. Many of the ghost towns have in the past been prey to vandals and looters. Today a more conservation-minded public tends to appreciate the charmed ruins and leaves them intact for others. The true ghost town buff follows the maxim, "Take nothing but photos, leave nothing but footprints."

# Contents

# PART I. THE DISCOVERY AND THE RUSH

TODAY'S *Mother Lode explorer should be cautioned on several possible misconceptions.*

*First, the Gold Rush communities that have stayed alive and are presently well populated generally contain more old structures than the ghost towns. Occupied for generation upon generation, they were not allowed to fall into disrepair. So even though they don't appear in early-day dress, the old houses and stores are there if you can somehow get beneath the accretions of paint, stucco, and signboards. One way is to check the backs of the main street buildings from a rear alley; there you will often find the arched windows, iron shutters, or rock walls that speak of the 1850s.*

*But these buildings were preserved with an eye to the practical, not the picturesque. If you are looking for the breath of antiquity you will want to seek the enchanting ruins of towns that died. Many of them are on narrow (often dirt) roads heading into the Sierra east of Highway 49.*

*Yet one should remember that even these are not the living spirit of California mining camps, but their mortal remains. The air that hangs over these old scenes is one of sweet decay. They are fascinating, even romantic, but they give an opposite impression from the hellbent life that once surged through the same streets. This book attempts to reawaken that life—its characters, its conflicts, its laughs—for the reader.*

*Still another caution: Nearly all the oldest structures remaining in Mother Lode towns, dead or alive, date from the 1850s—generally from the middle and late '50s. The devastating fires that frequently swept the gold towns carried away the pioneer canvas, log, and board houses. Looking down most any main street, do not believe that you have caught hold of 1849. At best you are glimpsing the high tide* of the gold boom in the maturing '50s. But after all, what more could be asked by any Gold Rush buff?

To help fill the gap of 1848 and '49, the story of these events is provided in Part I.

Courtesy of California Historical Society

*Daguerreotype of the saw mill at Coloma in which James Marshall first discovered gold in 1848.*

*Miners working placer deposits near original discovery site  at Coloma, 1850-51.*

*Contemporary drawing showing a camp of Chinese miners in the early 1850's.*

*A group of young miners showing primitive equipment used in placer mining, 1853.*

*At Sardine Bar, miners turned the South Fork of the American River out of its bed to mine the gravel, 1856.*

*Daguerreotype portrait showing youthfulness
of typical miner, 1849.*

*Miners going to their lunch at Cranwell's Bar, American River, 1856.*

*Wooden water wheels in river bed provide both water and power for washing out gold-bearing gravel, 1856.*

*Forest Hill, typical mountain mining community of the Sierras, 1856.*

# Chapter 1. "Gold! Boys, Gold!"

A PIECE OF YELLOW METAL. A little flake, shimmering in the water among the granite pebbles. Along the Sierra foothills millions like it lay in the stream beds, waiting to be discovered.

On a cold January morning in 1848, a tall, bewhiskered man—his eyes shaded by a slouch hat— is looking at this little flake. Through the quiet ripples it is plainly seen—shining and urgent—fairly dancing among its fellows.

The man stoops down, thrusts his hand into the icy water, seizes the flake. Sees another, takes it, too. Examines them closely. Can this be gold? Or iron pyrite—fool's gold? He sits down on the bank, hammers a piece between two rocks. Under the blows the metal yields—spreads out, paper thin.

Back along the bank hurries James Marshall. Almost breathless, he arrives at a crude plank building—an unfinished sawmill. To the first workman he encounters Marshall shows the bright flakes in his hand.

"I have found it!" he declares, importantly.

The man looks up from his work, squints at the out-stretched palm.

"What is it?"

"Gold!"

"Oh no!" is the dull answer, "that can't be."

His word doubted, Marshall replies with authority.

"I know it to be nothing else."

California's mighty treasure is unlocked, the giant oyster unhinged.

For centuries the Indians had seen and ignored it. For eighty years the Spanish, who knew gold when they saw it, occupied California without finding it. Franciscan missions rose and faded, Spanish rule was broken by Mexican revolution, and still the glittering booty lay undiscovered.

A trace had been found in Placerita Canyon, far to the south

10

near the tiny pueblo of Los Angeles. A few other Southern California canyons had yielded a few thousand dollars in gold. But compared to the fabulous mines of Mexico and Peru, this was nothing. To the Spanish, California was only fit to produce cowhides and wine.

For twenty years a growing column of American trappers and traders had ventured across the massive Sierra into this Mexican province. Others had brought wagons and families, settling on the broad, rich valleys of the Pacific slope. Marshall himself was of this tribe—restless, dissatisfied, moving first to Oregon, then to California. All of them had passed by the very rivers that held the secret.

Still others—both Americans and Europeans—arrived by sailing vessel to take up land under the liberal policy of the Mexican governors. Typical was Captain John Augustus Sutter, a hearty Swiss who had come in 1839 by the round-about route of Missouri and the Hawaiian Islands. From his thick-walled fort on the site of present-day Sacramento he ruled a veritable wilderness kingdom within Mexican California. His empire crept to the green Sierra slopes, knocking on the treasure house.

By 1846 the incoming foreigners had broken the Mexican dam. The United States was at war with Mexico, and Yankee squadrons descended on the California coast. After sharp fighting in the south, the province fell to the Americans. For months, while the war dragged on in Mexico, California was an occupied land—its future uncertain, its government the American military headquarters at Monterey.

At this unsettled moment Captain John Sutter chose to build a flour mill. To do so he needed lumber, and up in the pine-clad Sierra was an inexhaustible supply. In the summer of 1847 he sent a party of Indians and Americans into the wilderness to build a sawmill. Among the party were several Mormons, who had come to California in the American conquest. Leading the expedition was James Marshall—by trade, a wheelwright; by disposition, sullen, moody, excitable, a mystery to his closest companions.

In the wild, roaring South Fork of the American River, Marshall set up his camp. Locating the millsite inside a bend of the river, he dug a ditch that would divert a flow of water to drive the main wheel. And in that ditch, or tailrace, he found gold on the morning of January 24, 1848.

Next morning, Marshall found more gold in the tail race. He and his companions tried it all by crude tests. At each experiment their hearts leaped higher.

Jim Marshall was now too agitated to think of anything but gold. He must hurry to Sutter with his discovery. Asking the men to keep the secret, he rode down the canyon on the 28th. That evening, in darkness and pouring rain, the anxious man arrived at the fort. There he and Sutter tested it; they found it to be what Sutter called "the finest kind of gold."

A few days later Sutter visited the discovery site and caught Marshall's enthusiasm. But he called the men around him and asked them to keep the secret for six weeks, so that he might finish his sawmill and flour mill before the excitement engulfed them all. To this they readily agreed.

But while the men went back to work, Sutter and Marshall laid new plans. As partners, the discoverer and the landlord would reap the golden harvest. Urged on by Marshall, Sutter could see mountains of gold added to his empire.

Since the captain's original grant did not include the discovery site, the first step was to secure the land. Meeting with the local Indians, Sutter arranged to lease some ten or twelve square miles in return for clothing, farm implements and the promise to grind the native grain. He then returned to the fort and dispatched one of the mill hands, Charles Bennett, to Monterey.

Sworn to secrecy, Bennett carried specimens of gold and a letter to the military governor, Col. Richard B. Mason. In it, Sutter asked for a pre-emption on the quarter section of land around the mill site. He and Marshall meant to control the gold fields with a double title.

Still, everything depended on secrecy. If the news escaped before Sutter's claim was confirmed, the treasure would lie open to every vagabond in California.

Then Sutter made his first mistake. Since the party at the mill needed provisions, he sent a wagonload by the Swiss teamster, Jacob Wittmer. When he returned to the fort Wittmer brought with him a sack of gold dust. That evening a few at the fort gathered in the blacksmith shop to see it tested. A yellow nugget was heated in the forge, then hammered on the anvil. Just as Marshall's original flake had done, it flattened under the blows—according to the nature of gold. Silence leaped into bedlam. Around the anvil the men danced—shouting, singing, laughing.

"Gold, gold, gold, it's gold, boys, it's gold!" chanted the loudest. "All of us will be rich! Three cheers for the gold!"

At this racket heads appeared at doorways all around the fort. Sutter stepped out of his room and motioned a friend to his side.

"My secret, I see, has been discovered," he said quietly, with a philosophic smile. "Since we expect to be rich, let's celebrate with a bottle of wine."

Down the Sacramento Valley in mid-February rode Sutter's secret emissary, Charles Bennett, carrying the land application to the governor. But he became instead a herald of gold to all he met, and a plague to Sutter. At the very first settlement—the board-walled village of Benicia—he poured forth the story. He showed the gold in the sprouting village of San Francisco. On down to Monterey pressed Bennett, spilling the news as he went. Into the adobe headquarters of Governor Richard B. Mason he stomped—presented Sutter's application and uncovered the gold. Mason refused the land application, but news of the gold discovery sprang through Monterey.

And so the beckoning cry resounded down the corridors of California. Gold was wealth, comfort, power. Now—almost for the first time—it could be won without a struggle. It lay in the Sierra canyons—shining and vibrant—to be picked up by the first arrivals.

This was the call, high and shrill, that broke on the frosty California air early in 1848. With the suddenness of a thunderclap, it killed a way of life, and brought forth another.

Up from Sutter's Fort in late February came the first modern Argonauts—three Mormon workmen heeding a message from a brother at the mill. At an exposed sand bar they struck far richer deposits than those in Marshall's tailrace. Back to the fort they went for supplies, and when they returned others trailed after them. Soon Mormon Island, as the sand bar was christened, became the first gold camp in California.

By this time the rumble of excitement was rising in San Francisco. The first miners were drifting in from the mountains, displaying bags of gold dust to curious street-corner crowds. Starting in mid-March the two weekly newspapers gave modest notice. Word came that miners averaged $20 to $30 per day—ten times the prevailing workman's wage. By April, San Francisco was stripped of pickaxes and crucibles as the first gold hunters headed for Sutter's Fort.

By now Marshall finished his mill and began turning out lumber. But it was a pitiful attempt at sane endeavor in a world gone mad. For within a few days came Sam Brannan, brought up from San Francisco by an urgent letter from partner George Smith at the Fort Sutter store. A confirmed opportunist, Brannan had an eye for gold in any form. He had brought a shipload of Mormon settlers to California in 1846, had founded the first newspaper in San Francisco the following year, and now operated between the bay and the fort as a merchant and trader.

Shrewdly Brannan surveyed the busy scenes at the mill and Mormon Island. Here was a rich discovery that all of California deserved to know. And as the whole country would come storming in, he would be on hand to sell the necessities of life—from blankets to shovels to whisky. Back down to the bay hurried Sam Brannan. In mid-May he was striding through the dirt streets of San Francisco, waving a quinine bottle full of yellow dust.

"Gold! Gold!" he bellowed like a town crier. "Gold from the American River!"

All at once the California Gold Rush was on. What had been an unhurried exodus now became a headlong stampede. Carpenters dropped their hammers, clerks closed their books, grocers locked their doors. With shovel and pick in hand, they headed for Sutter's Fort. At San Francisco's presidio, Yankee soldiers deserted in a body, galloping off with the officers' horses. Across the bay and up the Sacramento scooted a fleet of sailing launches, jammed with Argonauts.

Day after day that procession of sails increased. San Francisco, so recently enjoying a building boom, was left deserted and silent. The new schoolhouse, first in the city, lost its teacher. Even the magistrates and members of the Town Council left their duties. The two newspaper editors, losing their subscribers and their printers, stopped publication and joined the throng. By the end of May not a workman was left in town save one blacksmith, who was feverishly turning out pickaxes at $5 to $10 each.

The strange contagion was also spreading to the ships anchored in the harbor. Over the sides went the crews, commandeering the life boats and sailing up the Sacramento River. One captain, pleading in vain for his men to stay, finally lowered a boat and went with them. A whaling ship sailed through the Golden Gate, unaware of the discovery. Anchoring behind Sausalito in Whaleman's Harbor, the skipper sailed across the bay to San Francisco in a whale boat. There the few remaining inhabitants told him to move out quickly for the islands or lose his crew. But by the time he had returned and weighed anchor, his men had learned the news. When they found the ship heading out the Golden Gate they refused to go. The captain was forced to put into San

Francisco, where the sailors gagged the night watch, took the whale boats and raced for the mines.

By the end of May all Northern California was afire. Ripened grain was left standing in the field unharvested. The spring cattle roundups were forgotten. In Sonoma, Benicia—every settlement in the north—houses and streets were deserted. From San Jose the jailor hurried up the road, taking his prisoners with him to dig for gold. At Carquinez Straits hundreds waited to be ferried across in two small sailboats and a few flimsy rowboats. The more impatient refused to wait, and swung eastward for the treacherous crossings of the San Joaquin.

"Along the whole route," as one Forty-eighter described it, "mills were lying idle, fields of wheat were open to cattle and horses, houses were vacant and farms going to waste."

Not until the end of May did the gold fever strike the provincial capital at Monterey. Unable to believe the wondrous stories, the local *Alcalde* (magistrate) sent a messenger to the mines to find the truth. On June 20 the rider pounded back into town, and was immediately surrounded by eager citizens. Dismounting, he pulled from his pockets some nuggets and passed them around. Next moment Monterey was thrown into a panic. Soldiers and sailors deserted their posts. One boarding-house keeper ran off without collecting the bills due from her lodgers.

"All were off for the mines," noted *Alcalde* Walter Colton in his diary, "some on horses, some on carts, and some on crutches, and one went in a litter."

Within three weeks every servant in town had disappeared, leaving the *Aicalde* and the Governor of California to shift for themselves in the kitchen—"grinding coffee, toasting a herring and peeling onions!" The American consul, Thomas O. Larkin, had already dashed off for the mines, and had immediately sent back for all the spare shovels, buckets, bowls, baskets, pans and tin cups in Monterey.

Down the coast sprang the contagion. By July 18 it

reached Los Angeles, where eight American soldiers deserted and three military prisoners broke out of jail. They rode northward under a hail of bullets with a body of dragoons after them.

The story was the same in every coastal town, each of which had a company or more of the First Regiment of New York Volunteers, who were waiting to be mustered out of service and receive four months' back wages. Over 300 of them—one-third of the whole—deserted. The rest were mustered out in September and decamped immediately for the mines.

As early as June the news had flown beyond California. Members of the Mormon Battalion returning to Salt Lake after the Mexican War threw that young community into new excitement. But Brigham Young pronounced a stern warning against the California fever.

"If you elders of Israel want to go to the gold mines," he chided them, "go and be damned!"

Most of the Saints held to Brigham's counsel, though a few companies hitched up their teams and hurried to California.

"If they have a golden god in their hearts," he roared after them, "they had better stay where they are!"

Westward into the Pacific the word sailed, reaching Honolulu with the arrival of the schooner *Louise* on June 17. As ship after ship came in with wonderful tales and samples of the gold itself, the islanders caught the fever. Merchants found themselves so busy selling boots, shovels and pickaxes that they could hardly stop to count the money. Through the streets a frantic procession of boxes and bundles moved toward the wharves. On one vessel the captain and officers gave up their berths to the passengers, while others slept on the dining tables. Every ship sailing for San Francisco was crowded to the rails; one man shoved off into the Pacific in a whaleboat, propelled only by a small sail and a pair of oars.

From the islands the schooner *Honolulu* carried the news

to Oregon Territory, where American families were then carving new homes out of the wilderness. Catching the fever, the Oregonians dropped their plows, bade goodbye to wives and children, and headed southward. Throughout August pack trains were scurrying through the Willamette Valley for California. At Oregon City, Salem and other settlements, only women, children and old men were left to bring in the harvest. More than 2,000—two-thirds of the able-bodied men—left Oregon in 1848. Unable to muster a quorum, the Legislature was suspended. Both territorial newspapers stopped publication. The Attorney General, Commissary General, and judges of the territorial Supreme Court rushed off to California with pick and shovel.

Far to the south, sailing ships had also brought the news to the Pacific ports of South America by late summer of '48. Word sped through Peru of a "whole continent of gold." In Callao several vessels bound for other ports promptly set sail for California. One American schooner consigned to China turned her prow northward instead.

"Everybody here is almost crazy about it," wrote one Peruvian, "and numbers are preparing to leave Callao and pick up gold by basketfuls."

It was the same along the coast of Chile. Wrote a merchant of Valparaiso, "It is reported here that California is *all gold!*" So many clerks left Valparaiso that commerce came to a halt.

At the same time the news flew across the northern states of Mexico. Their own gold and silver mines in sad decline, the men of Sonora were ripe for the call. Soldiers, heads of government, men of wealth and position, all joined the throngs leaving Tubac and Hermosillo in the fall of '48. In parties of fifty to a hundred they came, many with their entire families, their burros packed with provisions and mining tools.

Through the summer and fall the Forty-eighters swarmed across California's central plain and into the Sierra. Like some ragtail army they came—motley, nondescript, wild-eyed. Onto the fertile plain of the Sacramento they descended—some of them breaking down fences, stealing horses, killing cattle as they chose. In their haste they left their campfires to burn along the road, setting the wheat fields aflame, so that the whole route from the bay to Sutter's Fort became a charred and smoldering waste. As they approached the mines every useful item was picked up and carried along like a leaf in the maelstrom. One landowner returned to his rancho at the junction of the Feather and Yuba Rivers to find the flooring torn up—the boards gone to make gold rockers for the mines. Upon Sutter's Fort the Argonauts fell like a horde of Goths.

"They stole the cattle and the horses," groaned Sutter, "they stole the bells from the Fort and the weights from the gates, they stole the hides, and they stole the barrels."

With one swoop the Forty-eighters conquered California—smashed its charming pastoral life, did what the invading American troops had never tried to do. The natives were almost left as bystanders in the onrushing stampede. In every pueblo they were the last to leave—and then only after the richness of the mines had been confirmed beyond doubt. In contrast to the restless Yankees they saw no point in rushing after gold when life was enjoyable enough in pastoral California. Were not the *fiesta* and the *fandango*, the roaring hearth and the welcome latch-string, paradise enough for any man? On his vast rancho bordering the north shore of San Francisco Bay, the aging Luis Peralta called his three boys about him while the world rushed past.

"My sons," he told them, gravely, "God has given this gold to the Americans. Had He desired us to have it, He would have given it to us ere now. Therefore, go not after it, but let others go. Plant your lands, and reap; these be your best gold fields."

But such wisdom was lost in this frenzied hour. Down upon the mines thundered the Forty-eighters. On almost every river where they sunk a pick, the happy miners had struck color. So much time was spent in following rumors of new strikes that most miners would have made more by remaining steadily in one spot. As fast as they explored every niche and corner of the treasure house, it yielded up more riches. A German struck a three-ounce nugget while digging a hole for a tent pole. An old man sitting on a rock was complaining of bad luck when a stranger suggested that he roll the stone over. This he did merely to humor the other—and discovered half a pound of gold! One soldier on furlough spent eight days in the mines and returned to duty at Monterey with more than five years' army wages.

So plentiful was the gold in '48 that the boys treated it recklessly, as though the supply was inexhaustible. Gold was taken so casually that it was freely loaned from one miner to another—sometimes to perfect strangers—in full confidence that it would be repaid. According to one story, a fellow was slow in returning six ounces to his tentmate, who dunned him for it at every meal. At the next reminder, the debtor rose abruptly from the table.

"Just wait ten minutes," he drawled, shouldering his pick-axe. "And *time* it."

Out into the night he stomped, and within the allotted time he was back with more than enough gold to settle the debt.

In the midst of such easy wealth, the mines were practically free of crime in '48. If a robber was caught his punishment was swift and sure. The boys dropped their picks, grabbed their rifles, formed a "miner's court" and tried him. If found guilty he was flogged or hanged, depending on the enormity of his crime. But through the first year in the mines, such justice was rarely invoked. Thousands of dollars were left in tents unguarded. A shovel or pick lying in a hole was the accepted sign of ownership, and no one thought of jumping the claim.

Yet California in '48 was no paradise. Gold digging was, in the words of one expert, "matter-of-fact, back-aching, wearisome work." Wages were not always high. When James

Carson first arrived at Mormon Island he worked some fifty pansful of dirt and recovered about fifty cents worth of gold. Complained another miner on the Stanislaus:

`I worked harder today than I ever did in my life, and all for what? Why, not more than twenty-five cents!"

Poor or rich, the Forty-eighter saw his pile diminish rapidly as he turned to buy the necessities of life at the wilderness stores of Sam Brannan, Charles Weber and other pioneer traders. Butter and cheese ran as high as $6 per pound. Blankets were $50 to $100. Shirts were $16, and were laundered but not ironed for $1 apiece. Horses were from $100 to $150 apiece, and since the miner could dig the price of a horse easier than he could feed and care for one, it was not unusual for him to pay this price for a mount, ride it to a new diggings, and then turn it loose.

Beset by hardships and extortionate prices, the miner adopted habits as rough and wild as his mountain surroundings. While carrying several thousand dollars on his person, he presented the most unwashed and beggarly appearance. He did manage to keep the Sabbath, but after his own fashion. Putting aside shovel and rocker, he spent Sunday washing his clothes, prospecting for new diggings, gambling away his week's earnings or drinking himself into a stupor. Living miles and sometimes continents away from home and family, he cast off civility with the ease of a snake shedding its skin. And although he remained honest in his dealings, he indulged in the most shameful dissipation whenever whisky found its way to the mines. Piles of bottles, purchased at $8 to $16 apiece, were commonplace sights in every populated gulch. One enterpriser hauled in a barrel of brandy and sold it by the wine glass, realizing $14,000. When a barrel of New England rum arrived on the Stanislaus the boys came running with every available container—cups, sauce pans and coffee pots—while one eager customer offered $10 to poke his straw in the bung.

Rivaling this pastime was the gaming table, which captured the miner's reckless spirit and most of his gold dust. Among the Sonorans gambling was a disease and a way of life. At their main camp on the Tuolumne, hundreds surged around the monte bank, frantically trying to lay their bets on the turn of a card. Throughout the mines poker was the favored game in '48. Bets ranged from one to six ounces, while one eyewitness reported a wager of 36 ounces, or $576. The pot was growing mightily in one game when a miner decided he needed more dust to see the last raise. Putting his pile aside, he calmly turned to a companion.

"Here, Jim," he remarked, "watch my pile until I go out and dig enough to call him."

Beginning in late summer the insufferable heat spread sickness through the mines, and the backwash of '48 began. Hordes of vagabonds descended upon Sutter's Fort, turning it into a carnival of humanity. To accommodate the traffic, Sutter had rented his stalls and shops to merchants, barkeepers and even a hotelman—so that the entire courtyard of the fort was filled with a sea of dishevelled miners, horses and wagons, piles of sacks and barrels, gaudy displays of merchandise. Here gambling and carousing raged around the clock as the wealth of the Sierra flowed in.

Nor had the high tide of gold-seekers yet appeared. Late in June Governor Mason headed for the mines to see for himself. There the miners crowded about to show their gold and tell fabulous tales of wealth. Returning to Monterey, Mason sent a letter to the War Department describing the gold excitement. There was enough gold in the new territory, he claimed, to pay for the Mexican War a hundred times over. On August 17 he sent it eastward in the hands of the trusted lieutenant, Lucien Loeser. With luck he would reach Washington in time to have the news incorporated in President James Polk's annual message to Congress.

# Chapter 2. "Ho! for California!"

IN 1848 the American frontier stood at the great bend of the Missouri River, halted there by the forbidding plains and deserts that had been set aside for the Indians as their permanent hunting grounds. For a quarter century, however, trickles of population had spilled westward—traders to Santa Fe; pioneer settlers to Texas, Oregon and Upper California; and most recently, Mormon colonists to Salt Lake. Because the war with Mexico had suddenly brought much of this territory under American rule, the California emigration of 1849 was expected to be greater than usual. But there was no reason to believe that the frontier was ready to make another major advance.

By the early fall of '48 the fantastic story of California gold was spreading through the United States. Since August the first rumors had appeared in Atlantic newspapers. Since October letters from various officials in California had kindled a flame of interest. Excitement was beginning to rise when President James K. Polk confirmed the importance of the discovery in his message to Congress on December 5. To substantiate his words, he submitted the official report from Governor Mason.

Such confirmation, printed in newspapers throughout the country, was like a torch to the tinder. Lingering skepticism gave way to complete credulity. In every home, on every street corner, California was the overriding topic. Horace Greeley's *New York Tribune* cried out exultantly: "We are on the brink of the Age of Gold."

Through December, January and February, the nation was a scene of feverish preparation. Either as individuals or in hastily formed "California mining associations", an army of gold hunters gathered provisions for the great trek. In store windows and newspaper ads, every conceivable commodity was labeled with the magic word "California". There were "California hats", "California pistols," even "California pork and beans". On doors and counters the posted notice "G. T. C." meant only one thing: "Gone to California."

Nearly everyone, in fact, had a friend or relative who had announced his departure—an act that immediately made him a home-town hero. Almost all expected to return, wealthy and admired by all, within a year.

Since the overland passage was impossible in winter, the first Argonauts chose the ocean routes. For the first time, an important advance of the American frontier was spearheaded by sea, and led by those farthest East. As the California companies arrived at the coast, every port from Boston to New Orleans was overrun. Ticket offices were jammed; at the docks, a horde of Argonauts pleaded to be taken aboard the ships. Skippers and mates were so anxious to get off that they shipped as ordinary seamen, rather than wait for their own vessels to be outfitted. The ships were jammed with "Californians", who lined the railings like some guerrilla army about to invade a hostile shore. Rifles and shotguns were slung from their backs; revolvers and Bowie knives hung from their belts. At their sides were shovels, picks, gold pans and various "gold-sifting machines".

At length, with cheer upon cheer from relatives on the wharf, the ships would cast off—sometimes accompanied by the booming of a deck cannon. But as they stood out into the Atlantic, the spirit of hilarity was over. Heavy wintry seas and the fearful tossing of the deck sent every passenger to the rails. Could all the gold in California be worth such misery?

But once the landlubbers got their sea legs, the California fever seized them once more. Standing before the mast, they took the salt spray in their faces and conjured visions of California gold.

The quickest way to the mines was *via* the Isthmus of Panama, and since monthly postal service was just being established to California over this route, the earliest emigrants rode the mail steamers. Chugging across the Caribbean Sea, the paddlewheelers landed their passengers in eight or ten days at the miserable village of Chagres, on the Atlantic side of the Isthmus. From here they pushed on up the Chagres River in canoes, propelled along by native polesmen. Through tropical forests they rode, past chattering monkeys and parakeets. A thousand miles from the states, the Isthmian jungle resounded to "O Susannah!" as the Argonauts taught the words of this Gold Rush theme song to the canoemen.

After some forty miles they stopped at one of two primitive outposts, Gorgona or Cruces. From these points, roads led over the divide to the Pacific port of Panama. Though little more than a day's muleback ride, this was the toughest stretch of the entire trip. The Cruces road had been paved years before by the Spanish gold traders, but since the South American revolutions the traffic had vanished and the road was in bad repair. Great gullies cut across it, forcing a laborious descent into defiles so narrow that when a pack mule fell, he could not be raised without removing the load. While the Argonauts stepped over bodies of dead mules, vultures flapped out of the way, to return when the party passed. As one Argonaut described the road, "It is only fit to be traveled by a mountain deer or goat. . . "

In the evening the mule trains descended into the drowsy city of Panama, which sprawled by the Pacific in quiet decay. With the great days of the South American gold trade long past, she was now suddenly aroused to play the way station on another golden trek. The lusty Americans came upon her like some raucous storm—clattering through her streets, filling her hotels, crowding her fandango halls.

But in Panama their headlong rush abruptly halted. There were not enough ships to take them up the Pacific. By the spring of '49, 3,000 angry Americans idled in this unhealthy, vice-ridden city, their money wasting away in hotel bills and gambling losses. By October they were in a state of delirium.

The arrival of a steamer was heralded by shooting of guns, shouting in the streets, and a wholesale stampede to the landing—followed by a nightlong celebration by the fortunate ticket-holders. When two new steamers were put into service, the Americans stormed the ticket office by the hundreds, breaking windows, collapsing the balustrade on the stairs, and finally fighting their way back into the street—hats crushed, clothing torn, hands clutching a precious ticket to California.

Similar problems were encountered by other emigrants crossing the continent above Panama. A few parties packed across Nicaragua, the Isthmus of Tehuantepec, and various other routes through Mexico. Except for the uncertainty of ship passage on the Pacific side, some of these proved to be simpler and safer than the beaten paths.

But the most popular sea route was the voyage round the Horn, which took from four to nine months, depending largely on the winds. In 1849 more than 15,000 Argonauts shipped *via* the Cape in what became known as the California Fleet. On this 15,000-mile trip, monotony was the chief enemy. In mid-Atlantic a sailing vessel might lie becalmed for days or even weeks while the passengers wore heavily on each other's nerves. All day long they were on deck playing whist or backgammon on the tops of barrels. Every school of porpoise was the signal for frantic unlimbering of fishing gear. Pistols were fired at sea birds and sharks, or in celebration of Independence Day or the crossing of the Equator—at any possible excuse.

As time wore on, more ingenious pastimes were devised: auction sales, debates, kangaroo courts, cotillion dances with half the men dressed as women. For such a diversion there was no lack of accompanying music. More than one ship had a complete band, which strolled along the deck blaring forth with "Yankee Doodle", "Home Sweet Home", and the inevitable "O Susannah!"

In the early spring of '49 the California army descended

upon Rio de Janiero and the smaller port of St. Catherine's Island further down the Brazilian coast. Some arrived in time to participate in the pre-Lenten carnival. Most came afterward, when the streets were shrouded in silence and decorum. In this situation the hilarious Yankees made themselves conspicuous. There were riotous parties every night at the hotels. Soldiers patrolling the corners after the curfew hour challenged the revelers as they passed down the street, but the answer, "Americanos—amigos!" became the accepted password.

The same unruly spirit wore hard on the captains of the California Fleet. Years of sea adventure never schooled them to manage this wild cargo. The passengers insisted on climbing aloft in the rigging to help the crew. When the ship was becalmed they jumped overboard for a swim and a bath. Many of them consumed fearful quantities of rum and brandy, making it nearly impossible to keep the sailors sober.

On every ship a group of sturdy, God-fearing passengers worked against this carnival atmosphere. Church services were held on deck every Sunday. On one ship a temperance pledge was circulated the day after each new orgy. But the pious passengers noted with sadness the continuing rise of drinking and profanity.

Most of all, the Californians complained. They complained about the slow passage, the water supply, and especially the food. One distraught captain warned them he would put into the nearest port and have them thrown in irons for mutinous language. Another threatened to put them on short rations unless they stopped complaining.

"I never heard such grumbling," he observed, "even from whalemen."

Real troubles awaited the Californians as they approached the Horn. Once the vessels turned full under Tierra del Fuego, the raging Cape storms were upon them. Snow and sleet whitened the rigging; mountain-high seas broke against the bow, sending foaming waves over the deck, tossing the ship until its lee rail dipped the surface. Below, crockery and hardware flew in all directions. Passengers tried to sleep while holding tight to their bunks, lest they be plunged out of bed onto the brine-washed floor. Some of them prayed for the first time in their lives.

Off Tierra del Fuego the brig *Colorado* fought to keep from being blown onto the rocks. At the height of the storm the tops of the masts were broken off, dangling crazily above the deck. Robbed of its balance, the ship lurched uncontrolled before the storm. Wave after wave broke upon the helpless vessel. Water poured below decks, where the wretched passengers were frantically manning the buckets. Above the storm they heard the dread cry: "The ship is sinking!" The captain, haggard and dripping, came into the dining saloon.

"We can do nothing more," he told the stricken faces; "if it is God's will we shall be saved."

California gold was nothing in this sickening instant. But the ship stayed afloat until dawn, when the passengers found themselves clear of the rocky shore. The crew was removing the broken rigging from the deck. They were sailing west-ward under a fair wind.

Up the Pacific pressed the Californians—for the first time pointing toward the land of gold. Catching the southeast trades, they fairly flew up the Chilean coast. A few ships pushed on without stopping; more than one Argonaut traveled from New York to San Francisco without ever seeing the mainland. But most vessels were forced by water shortage to put into the Chilean ports—perhaps to pest-ridden Talcahuano or the more inviting Valpar-aiso—where for the first time they heard later news of the California mines.

Fired anew with tales of gold, they stood out to sea again, drawing halfway to the Hawaiian Islands in their quest for an eastward wind that would blow them into San Francisco. For weeks they lay becalmed in the horse latitudes, with California scarcely a four-day run before them.

But at last, with a wind filling the sails, the ships scooted for California. With spirits bursting, all hands paraded the deck in their finest clothes, ready for the arrival. Pistols were inspected, tools sharpened for the descent upon the gold fields.

Throughout the summer of 1849 the California Fleet straggled through the rock-bound Golden Gate and into San Francisco harbor. The vanguard arrived in June; at the high point in mid-September they were coming in at the rate of ten per day. As each new ship glided among the "forest of masts" that filled the harbor, the Argonauts could hardly contain themselves. So frantic was the crew of the ship *Hopewell* that she rammed into two vessels and stove her own side.

"I expect," announced one eager arrival, "to be worth a thousand in a few days."

Since March of '49, the overland army had been assembling for the second wave of the great migration. From as far East as the Appalachians they came, taking passage on the river steamboats or driving their teams across country, converging on the point where the Missouri River leaves its westward course and bends sharply to the north. Here, the frontier town of Independence was the traditional outfitting place for westward travel. Overtaking it in popularity was St. Joseph, situated eighty miles upstream. A third outpost was Kanesville, established by the Mormons two years before at Council Bluffs, Iowa. Those who took the perilous southern route *via* the Arkansas River and Santa Fe generally outfitted at Fort Smith, Arkansas.

To these jumping-off places every steamer brought another mass of gold hunters, who filled the hotels or camped on the outskirts of town. The main streets were jammed with emigrant teams, produce wagons, auction sales, horse and mule markets. Blacksmith and harness shops were besieged with customers. Daguerreotype studios did a thriving business in "accurate likenesses" to send home to the loved ones.

General stores advertised all manner of "California fixin's". At night the gaming tables were crowded; many a well-intentioned Argonaut reached the end of his westward march in the muddy alley behind an Independence saloon.

Outside of town where the wagon trains were forming, the men were drawing up the rules of organization that would guide them across the plains. The laws were harsh and inflexible—dictated by the hazardous journey ahead. Among the typical provisions: "Members shall not be allowed to quarrel among themselves, nor shall any member be allowed to drink intoxicating liquors, gamble, use profane language, or labor on the Sabbath." Nearly every constitution sealed the bargain with a mutual vow: "If any members of this company shall be so unfortunate as to lose their teams or provisions, we pledge ourselves that we will not leave them on the plains to suffer but will take care of the unfortunate."

So with high spirits the great army gathered itself and plunged across the Missouri. All the way from St. Jo up to Council Bluffs, ferries were operating to carry the wagons to the opposite shore. With wheels creaking and chains rattling, the teams fell into line across the prairie—the white-canvassed wagons standing like a squadron of sails against the horizon. Beyond the point where the Independence and St. Joseph trails converged, 8,000 vehicles formed a continuous line across the plain.

Along the shallow Platte they rolled, across the green prairies of what would later be the states of Nebraska and Wyoming. This was Indian country, and every Argonaut expected to fight for his scalp. But in '49 most Plains Indians were more of a nuisance than an actual threat. Descending on a wagon camp at supper time, they would crowd about the campfire, getting in the cook's way and hinting for an invitation to dinner. At night they would creep into the wagon corral and run off with food, equipment and livestock.

This was also buffalo country, and the adventurers were eager for the chase. More than one old bull, panicked by his pursuers, charged through a wagon camp, scattering pots and pans, stampeding the stock and drawing a fusillade of shots. By the end of May dead buffalo lined the trail, many of them killed more for sport than necessity. At night the roasting of buffalo was the signal for a general feast. Neighboring campers were invited in, and someone was sure to produce a fiddle for a "hoe down," carried off with much clapping and yelling.

But each day as the teams were yoked up and turned into the trail, the overland route took its toll in hardship. Wagons had been piled so high with goods that the animals were wearing themselves out on the easiest stretch of the road. By the time the trains reached Fort Kearney the men were throwing away excess baggage by the armful. Chairs, stoves, trunks and other luxuries went first. Then boots, quilts, sides of bacon, bags of salt—even firearms. All the way to Fort Laramie the overland trail was paved with provisions, trappings and even pieces of wood sawed off the wagons.

Too late most Argonauts lightened their loads. Their animals were already sore and jaded from the overpowering weight. Many were dying in the harness, and soon the trail was marked by the carcasses of oxen and mules.

By contrast, trains of pack mules were hurrying past the wagons without difficulty. Impressed by this example, many Argonauts cut up their wagons into pack saddles and pressed on by mule train. They soon found themselves at the head of the migration.

From Fort Laramie west the going became tougher. The grass was shorter and scarcer; exhausted animals were further weakened by lack of food. The rivers were swifter and deeper; although crude ferries were doing a bustling business at every crossing, they were used for wagons only. Animals and men jumped into the current and paddled fiercely for the other shore. Most of these landsmen were no swimmers. More of them died by drowning than any other cause.

Sickness, too, was prevalent among the Argonauts, for the

rigors of the trail weakened the hardiest of them. Cholera followed them from the settlements. Pneumonia took its toll; drenched by prairie storms, they often slept in their wet clothes. Accidental gunshot wounds were not infrequent, for the Argonauts were armed to the hilt with rifles and pistols. Not all wounds were accidental; as misery heightened and tempers grew short, conflict was inevitable.

One by one the high avowals of their company constitutions were forgotten in the overpowering realities of the trail. At first the assembled companies voted whether or not to travel on Sundays; later they pushed on through the Sabbath as a matter of course. Loyalty to one's own company was lost in the headlong race to California. Men moved from one wagon train to another if they thought they could gain speed, until the entire trail was one common community on wheels.

Beyond the Continental Divide, crossed by most emigrants at historic South Pass, lay the final test. Some swung southward to Fort Bridger and to welcome asylum in the new Mormon settlement at Salt Lake. Others pushed directly westward over Sublette's Cut-off, dropping into Bear River Valley by lowering wagons with ropes down the cliffs.

Either way, the terror of the Great Salt Desert lay ahead. Over this sterile route the wisest men carried grass along for their animals, hiring an Indian or half-breed guide to show the way and warn against poisonous water holes.

Animals were dying in great numbers now. Indians skulked along the trail, shooting arrows into the oxen so as to retrieve them for beef after they were abandoned. Partial relief was offered by the winding Humboldt River. But beyond it lay fifty miles of waterless desert before reaching the cool streams flowing out of the Sierra.

Through this barren inferno the gold fever was forgotten; survival was everything. One emigrant counted 100 wagons and 500 animals left along the trail. Those who reached water first carried some back to relieve others who had fallen along the way.

"I gave an old man a drink from my canteen," wrote one diarist, "which seemed to have done him more good than a purse of gold."

Still worse was the route to the south taken by those reaching Salt Lake too late to cross the Sierra before the snows. Among these was Louis Nusbaumer, a German-American who spent Christmas day in the southwestern desert throwing away his worldly possessions to lighten the load. With three oxen packed with food, he and his companion pushed across alkali wastes in the vicinity of Death Valley. Nearly crazed with thirst, the doughty German tried to drink salt water at a desert spring. Overtaking a wagon party which had a supply of water, he offered to exchange his coat and two shirts for a drink. The man in charge refused. But when the latter had to abandon an ox, Louis and his friend shot the animal and caught its blood in a drinking cup.

Compared to the desert passage, the Sierra crossing was almost anticlimax. It was laborious, especially for wagon parties, but in these soaring granite peaks was ample water and relief from merciless heat. Through several gaps in the mountains, from Goose Lake down to Carson Pass, the emigrants poured over the crest and down the western slope.

As the early arrivals brought tales of suffering on the trail, California moved quickly to claim its own. From San Francisco to the mines, the people poured $100,000 into a relief fund for the emigrants. Military authorities sent parties loaded with provisions and fresh animals over the Sierra. To the stragglers foundering in the desert, these merciful troopers were God-sent. Women and children were mounted on the fastest animals and escorted into the settlements. By October's end the migration of 1849 was safely in.

Then down the broad and fertile Sacramento Valley they rolled, past ranch houses, herds of horses and cattle. Here, once more, was civilization, however primitive and remote. Into riotous Sacramento City they thronged, meeting their seaborne comrades who had arrived by launch and schooner up the river from San Francisco. Some never got to the settlements, but with shovel and gold pan had struck color on the upper reaches of the Feather and Yuba Rivers.

The rush of '49 was over. For many it was hard disappointment. Back-breaking work and an ounce of gold per day were the miner's lot in '49, with diminishing fortune in the years that followed. But by sheer force of energy the Forty-niners tore the American frontier loose from its Missouri River moorings and sent it leaping to the Pacific; gave the West Coast a powerful momentum that has never faded; and showed a world of kings and dictators that individuals, acting on their own, could make history.

# PART II. THE CENTRAL MINES

HISTORY'S *greatest gold rush brought more than population to California. Within a few tumultuous years it brought steamboats, railroads, telegraph lines, commerce, finance, agriculture, industry, churches, schools—all the trappings of civilization. But in the first years after Jim Marshall's discovery, life was simple, primitive, and in many ways charmingly naive. Civilized men, flung suddenly into a wilderness, had to start a new society from scratch.*

*Mostly, this act in the California drama took place first in what were called the Central Mines. Here the golden treasure was first opened; here was the earliest stamping ground of the Forty-eighters—those who preceded the deluge of 'Forty-nine. Here is the effective birthplace of American society in California.*

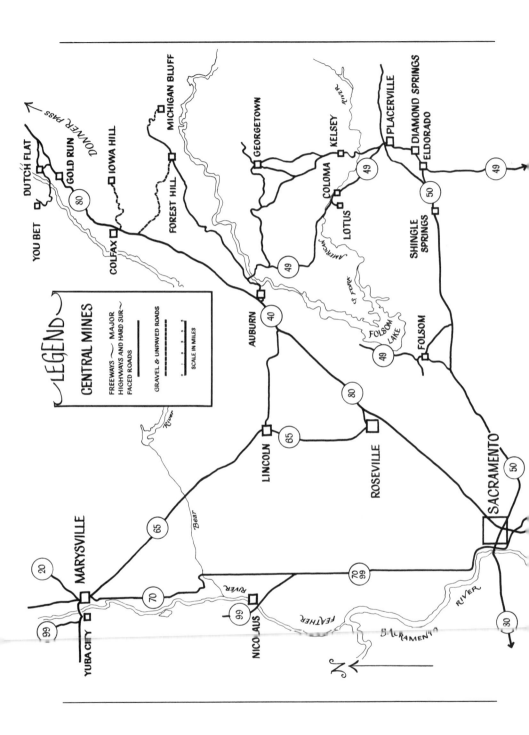

*Rocker designed for separating gold from gravel
in use by young miner.*

*Coloma, on the South Fork of the American River, 1856.*

*Miners demonstrating the long tom for a photographer on a Sunday afternoon near Auburn, 1852.*

*Woman visitor from Sacramento or San Francisco watches Auburn miners operating double long tom, 1852.*

*Chinese and American miners operating sluice box at Auburn, 1852.*

*Typical construction of Sierra mountain town
at Yank's Station (Meyers).*

*Early railroad town of Cisco shows the bustle of
mountain freighting traffic.*

*Panama straws, sailors' jackets, and tall beaver hats. A great confusion of dress was always in evidence at the mines, 1856.*

*Miners using hydraulic monitor at Michigan Bluff, 1854.*

# Chapter 3. Coloma: Where Gold Began

IN THE FIRST WEEKS of the rush, Sutter's vanity exceeded his caution. One had but to announce himself as a titled dignitary, and the hospitable Swiss would accompany the whole party to the millsite on the South Fork of the American.

"These gentlemen have come to see the gold mines, Mr. Marshall," he would proudly declare on arrival. And Marshall, making no attempt to hide his displeasure at the interlopers, gave them the same treatment he gave to all the rest who inquired about the gold.

"You'll find it anywhere you've a mind to dig for it down there," he snapped, jerking his arm in the direction of the river.

Following Marshall's whimsy, the tenderfeet were almost sure to strike color wherever they happened to turn the earth. Word soon spread that the famed discoverer had an uncanny sense in finding gold. Men followed him everywhere, knocked on his cabin door at all hours, begging him to lift his finger and point the way. In desperation he turned more into his lonely self, tried to shut out the multitude crowding in upon him.

At first the gold-seekers settled along the banks of the South Fork, between Sutter's Mill and Mormon Island. Scarcely a stone's throw from the discovery site sprang the town of Coloma, first important mining town in the Gold Rush. Shunning the initial tent-and-canvas phase that would mark the birth of other mining towns, Coloma sprang full grown from lumber cut at Sutter's Mill (and sold at $500 a thousand feet). By the summer of 1848 Coloma had about 300 frame buildings and a big hotel under construction. Along the main street they bore the false fronts and wooden awnings that set the style in mining camps for the next half century.

The remote boom town also established the tradition of outrageous prices. Almost any commodity—flour, pork, sugar, coffee—sold at the flat rate of a dollar a pound. Shovels and picks were at least $50 each, butcher knives between $10 and $25, boots $25 to $50 a pair, wool shirts $50 each. Since the dollar was worth at least 100 times more than it is today, these prices were outrageous. The Sierra Indians were bewildered by the white man's frenzied interest in the yellow metal, and at one point on the South Fork were giving a handful of gold dust for a handkerchief or shirt.

In Coloma one woman took in laundering at a dollar an item. When her husband came back from the mines after four weeks' work, she laughed at his hard-earned pile. In the same time she had earned double the amount washing shirts.

Since coin was scarce in the remote Sierra, gold dust quickly became Coloma's currency—with a pinch of dust supposed to equal one dollar. One South Fork storekeeper insisted on doing the pinching himself; wetting his thumb and forefinger, he would plunge his hand in the miner's sack and come out with from four to eight dollars' worth. But in early '48 gold was so plentiful that the miners passed this off as a huge joke.

One day a popular miner died on the South Fork, and the boys resolved to give him a proper funeral. The grave was dug in a flat nearby, and the ceremony was performed by a one-time preacher who had given up the Gospel for the call of gold. When he launched into a long prayer some of the boys grew restless and began fingering the dirt from the grave. They found it "lousy with gold." In a moment the ex-preacher sensed the distraction and opened one eye.

"Boys, what's that?" One glimpse was enough. "Gold, by God!"

Solemnly raising his hand, he dismissed the congregation and led the rush for pick and pan. As for the body of the miner, it was later consigned to ground that was more hallowed—and less rich.

By June there were 2,000 men in and around Coloma. The creak and rattle of their rockers provided a tune from dawn to dusk.

It was soon apparent that Marshall's chance discovery was far from the richest. Mountaineers who visited Sutter's Mill remembered similar ground elsewhere and went back to make their own strikes. Up and down the river new diggings were abandoned when they no longer yielded two or three ounces per day per man.

As elsewhere in the mines of 1848, the Coloma region knew almost no crime. Tools and equipment were left lying about without the slightest fear of robbery. At Mormon Island one mining party piled all its equipment and provisions in an open place, leaving them unguarded and unmolested for days at a time.

The few cases of outlawry were summarily dealt with by traditional miners' justice. In the summer of 1848 one rascal stole a sack of gold; when captured, he refused in spite of threats to tell where it was hidden. The miners gave him 30 lashes, but still he defied them. Exasperated, they tried more subtle torture. He was tied to a tree with his back laid bare to the mosquitoes that abounded on the South Fork in July. After three hours of this attention, he surrendered.

"Untie me," he moaned. "I will tell."

"Tell first," was the miners' demand. And while some of them shooed the insects off his back, others followed his directions and found the gold. Then they washed his back, cut him loose and helped him dress. That was Forty-eighter justice.

But while the first year of gold has been called "the Age of Innocence," 1849 was different. With the flood tide of the gold rush came a motley crew of cutthroats and thieves. Miners' courts were improvised to cope with the crime wave, and since there was a scarcity of jails, punishment often

47

included such grim procedures as ear-cropping and branding. Whisky flowed freely in the courtrooms, with the bill customarily paid by the defendant.

But Coloma's hectic days were numbered. She had won her population and excitement on the strength of Marshall's original discovery, not on inherent wealth. Richer localities up and down the Mother Lode were soon drawing the restless gold-hunters. In late 1851 a visitor called Coloma "the dullest mining town in the whole country."

By 1870 Coloma—the "Queen City of the Mines"—was reduced to 200 residents. It was a place of quiet serenity, of flower gardens and shaded lanes. The throbbing pulse of a stormier hour returned only once a day—when the Concord stage whirled in and lurched to a stop at the Wells Fargo office.

As for Marshall, his life paralleled that of his discovery spot. Unwilling to join in the headlong rush he had launched, he tried to capitalize on his now-famous name. At first he exacted half the earnings of the Mormon diggers at the sawmill. When this failed he went up the South Fork of the American with another prospector to make a new strike. Three miles northward they picked up a cupful of gold from a sand bar.

"Now, James," said his companion, "suppose we divide this gold."

"No," returned Marshall, "I don't divide. You are a hired man."

"That ends our contract," cried the other.

And the lonely Marshall went his way, holding himself above the miner's lot by virtue of his discovery, and gaining nothing.

A similar fate met John Sutter. Joining the gold-seekers, he stumbled through the Sierra foothills with his little army of Indian diggers. But the doughty Swiss was no better at mining gold than keeping its secret. On the South Fork of the American his camp was invaded by a wave of miners who quickly stripped the diggings. Sutter then moved his caravan south of the Cosumnes River and founded a new camp—Sutter Creek. Here gold clinked into his coffers until several saloons were established nearby. Then, according to his own account, the workers drank and gambled away their day's earnings, forcing him to give up and break camp.

But the master himself was example for the slave. On the day of departure, with the entire outfit packed up and ready to mount, Sutter was too inebriated to climb aboard his mule. Instead he swayed unsteadily before the whole company, regaling the Indians with his military triumphs in Switzerland.

Unsaddling, the party remained for three more days until the jolly captain was ready to move. Then, with a flourish, the comic caravan of John Sutter jolted its way out of Sutter Creek and out of the California mines.

Marshall and Sutter—tragic pair! Having put the roaring flood in motion, they were spewed like driftwood upon the shore. Unequal to their historic role, they became silent and disgruntled bystanders in a world gone mad.

### POINTS OF INTEREST

COLOMA. The discovery site is a state park, with appropriate historical markers and an extensive museum. The principal point of interest is the replica of John Sutter's sawmill, which is about 100 yards upstream from its original site.

One of the stone ruins marks the Coloma jail, built in 1856. Two brick buildings are the Robert Bell Store (1855) and Frank Bekeart's gun shop (1854). Two Chinese stores, originally operated by Man Lee and Wah Hop, are also preserved from about 1856.

Until the Coloma site was acquired by the state in 1942 it was for many years part of the estate of the Monroes, a black pioneer family whose matriarch, Nancy Gooch, came as a slave in 1849.

Of the frame buildings in the area, some were originally

built of lumber from Sutter's sawmill. Among these are the Emmanuel Episcopal Church, built in 1855, and St. John's Catholic Church, 1858. On the hill overlooking the town are the grave and statue of James Marshall. Near the statue is a restoration of his cabin, where he lived for some 20 years after the discovery.

LOTUS. Here are the remains of a small town, originally named Marshall after the gold discoverer, and then Uniontown. Still standing are the red brick Adam Lohry store and his family's brick home, both constructed in 1859.

GEORGETOWN. Originally bearing the remarkable name of Growlersburg, Georgetown was ravaged in 1856 by a fire that swept away all its earliest buildings except the Masonic Hall. Rebuilt almost entirely of brick, the town has a number of structures dating to the 1850s, including the former Wells Fargo office and the old Balzar House, which served first as a hotel, then a theater, and later as a lodge meeting house. Georgetown is one of the few sizable settlements still bearing the look of the mining frontier, principally because it is located (Hwy 193) off the beaten track of Highway 49.

---

# Chapter 4. Placerville: Hangtown & Horace Greeley

NO SERIOUS VISITOR is allowed to leave Placerville without hearing two stories—how it got its early name of Hangtown, and how Horace Greeley arrived after his wild stage ride over the Sierra. But these are only a part, and a small one at that, of the heritage of rare old Placerville. Its narrow and winding streets, nestled in a pine-clad fold of the

Sierra foothills, saw the ebb and flow of California history for two uproarious decades. It was, by turn, the first big gold camp after the discovery at Coloma; the hell-roaring gateway to California for the overland Argonauts; and depot for the stampede back across the Sierra to the Comstock Lode.

Its story began in June 1848, when Indians carried word along the forks of the American of a new placer that was yielding six ounces ($96) per man per day. In a twinkling another stampede was on to the new camp below the South Fork. Over hill and across canyon tumbled the boys, leaving rich diggings behind for the rumor of something richer. Within a week the old placers were depopulated and close to a thousand were crowding into the new ground. After the river level fell in midsummer the men were forced to carry their ore several hundred yards to water. But even with this time-consuming delay they still made two to four ounces per day. Frequently someone would strike a *bonanza*, or rich pocket, and others would scramble in shoulder to shoulder, many reaping several hundred dollars in a day.

Through the summer of '48 Dry Diggings, as it was called, was the great rendezvous for all the Argonauts—be they American backwoodsmen, native Californians, or deserters from army and navy. Ragged, dirty, bewhiskered—they were yet, in the words of one, "the happiest set of men on earth."

By autumn it was a thriving camp, composed first of tents and log cabins, then of board and shingle stores, muddy streets and surging traffic. By the winter of 1849 gold was still plentiful, but not plentiful enough to prevent the rise of crime. In January five men broke into a gambler's room and while one of them held a pistol at his head, rifled his belongings. They were immediately captured, tried by a vigilance court of 200 irate miners, and given 35 lashes each. Then three of them were charged with robbery and attempted murder on the Stanislaus River. A miner's jury found them guilty again.

"What shall be done with them?" demanded the acting

judge.

"Hang them!" someone shouted. And though one miner mounted a stump and pleaded against lynch law, the three men were placed in a wagon, driven under a tree on Main Street, and each fitted with a noose. At a signal, the wagon was driven out from under them.

Since this was the first recorded lynching on the Mother Lode, the place quickly got its second name—Hangtown.

The event and the name had a civilizing influence. Bad men were on their good behavior in this strict camp. And as the mines prospered, the town went metropolitan. Regular stages arrived in 1851, bringing passengers to several hotels offering such luxuries as tablecloths and silver service. In fact, the place was becoming famous abroad for other things besides lynch law. An imaginative cook put together eggs, bacon, oysters and other grease-loving ingredients in what became known as a "Hangtown Fry". The concoction appealed to hardy stomachs, and was soon a celebrated dish up and down the Mother Lode. Leading restaurants in San Francisco had to put it on the menu to satisfy visiting miners.

As whole families moved in to replace the strictly male population, Hangtown became positively genteel. It got so the young ladies parading along the streets in their fine hoop skirts were unapproachable. "They're dreadful shy of Forty-niners, turn their noses up at miners," ran a rousing Gold Rush song called "Hangtown Gals". And when Hangtown acquired a temperance league and a Methodist church, the seal was placed on her lawless days. Agitation began for a less morbid name.

Besides, the hangman's tree was no longer the town's most distinctive feature. Gold had been discovered in the neighboring creek, and on the approaches to town groups of men were working feverishly at the business of placer mining. Standing barefooted in icy mountain water, they were shoveling sand into long toms—wooden troughs with cleats that caught the gold as the dirt washed through. In fact, one eager prospector struck pay dirt in the center of town, and the boys descended on it with pick and shovel. A visitor found parties of energetic miners digging holes and operating long toms right in the middle of Main Street and even in some of the houses.

"There was a continual noise and clatter," he reported, "as mud, dirt, stones and water were thrown about in all directions."

Yes, old Hangtown had changed, and the people began clamoring for a more fitting name—Placerville. In 1850 the Legislature gave it the new title, though the disagreeable "Hangtown" persisted in popular usage for some years. But as Placerville it was incorporated in 1854, and as Placerville it supplanted Coloma as the seat of El Dorado County three years later.

By this time the placers that had given it a name were fading, but the town lived high through the '50s as the roistering terminus of the Overland Trail. Earliest gold hunters had gone over Truckee Pass and into California by way of the Yuba and Feather Rivers. But in the early '50s most of the wagons dropped below Lake Tahoe, down the South Fork of the American River and into Placerville.

Through the high tide of the Gold Rush, this was the hoped-for haven after a 2,300-mile trek across the American desert and over the lofty Sierra. One weary wagon train, with its chains jingling and mules snorting as they had every day since leaving the bend of the Missouri, was drawing near Placerville when an almost-forgotten noise split the air. A rooster had crowed! Without a signal, the wagons halted and the men let out a yell. Here, at last, was civilization.

The town at the end of that covered wagon trail was not a pretentious sight. One arrival called it "one long straggling street of clapboard houses and log cabins." Through this narrow thoroughfare, blocked with miner's diggings and knee-deep mud puddles, sloshed bearded Argonauts, six-horse stages, plodding ox and mule teams. The only paving was a litter of "old boots, hats, and shirts, old sardine boxes, empty tins of preserved oysters, empty bottles, worn-out pots and kettles, old ham-bones, broken picks and shovels."

The unique institution of the town was its general stores, which served as combination saloon, grocer's, hardware shop and social hall. Behind the counter, which was also a bar, were stacked whisky bottles, canned fish, bottled pickles, and every conceivable item. And prices? An ounce of gold dust ($16) bought a pound of gunpowder, a chicken or a bottle of champagne. Business was thriving, but conducted with pure informality. The storekeeper customarily sat with miners at a rude table, playing seven-up for "the drinks".

In snowy weather, a customer could comfortably spend a whole day in one of these retreats, provided his credit was good. Witness, for example, the story told by one page of a daybook from an old Placerville store: "Mr. Boyer 6.25–2 drinks, .50; 1 ditto, .25; 1 lug tobacco, .50; 2 drinks, .50; 1/2 pie, .50; 1 drink, .25; 5 drinks, 1.25; 1/4 pie, .25; 1 drink, .25; 1/2 pie, .50; 2 drinks, .50; 1 ditto, .25; 1 drink, .25." There is no record of a final necessity: 1 stretcher.

Probably it was such a grocery store as this that Mark Hopkins started in 1849; here he launched on a career that made him one of the Big Four rail builders, the first to span the Sierra with tracks. The one item that the stores did not carry was meat; this was handled exclusively by butchers, and one of these was Philip D. Armour, who began here his upward climb in the meat packing business. Still another Placerville pioneer was John M. Studebaker, who made wheelbarrows for the miners and saved the $4,000 with which he started his wagon-building business in South Bend, Indiana. Today, autos descended from his Studebakers roll over Placerville streets once trod by the original, one-wheel model.

Meanwhile Placerville was taking on a permanent air. Stone and brick buildings were lining her winding streets. A decline in mining and a devastating fire gave Placerville a double blow in 1856, but her greatest days were yet to come.

It was in June 1857 that Jared B. Crandall, one of California's stagecoach kings, drove his Concord out of Placerville and into the Sierra pines. In the next few days, accompanied by directors of his company, he prodded his six horses over rocky ledges and steep ravines, across Johnson Pass and down into the Mormon village of Genoa, in what would later be Nevada Territory. Then they fought their way back, to a hilarious greeting at Placerville by a shouting, shooting crowd.

It was the first stage over the Sierra between California and the Carson Valley. While state officials talked of surveys and road appropriations, Crandall had proven that the route was feasible—with no road but the primitive emigrant trail. After that, Crandall's stages ran biweekly over the great barrier, soon connecting with another stage line spanning the Utah desert to bring California into direct communication with the Atlantic. Placerville was a major milestone on the path of empire.

But the line had its disadvantages. Those six-horse stages careened along precipitous mountain roads that defied gravity and paled the tenderfoot passenger. In winter the coaches were withdrawn, leaving it to that intrepid postman, Snowshoe Thompson, to carry the mail on 10-foot skis between Placerville and the Carson Valley.

But by 1859 the route was becoming almost civilized. Such furious whips as Hank Monk would take their coaches through in several hours, with never a quiver, though perhaps they had brushed death a dozen times. In that year, along came Horace Greeley, America's great publisher and crusader, who was just then interested in a transcontinental Western railroad. On the bouncing stage ride from Missouri he'd already been spilled on the prairie when a herd of buffalo stampeded the stage horses and overturned the coach; dumped into the Laramie River when the vehicle capsized again; plunged once more into the Sweetwater River, where he lost a trunk full of manuscripts; and generally shaken up and beaten down by the incessant bumping and swaying of a three-week stage ride.

At the foot of the Sierra he encountered the incomparable Hank Monk, whose coach promptly whirled him out of the desert and into the clouds. Over hair-tingling Sierra roads lurched the stage, as Horace himself wrote, "just as fast as four wild California horses, whom two men could scarcely harness, could draw it." When they clattered into Placerville, a dishevelled and discomposed Greeley emerged from the coach and before the crowd could capture him, made his way to the Carey House bar. The Placerville crowd that had turned out for a grand welcome found him there, and escorted him to a waiting banquet table. There, in response to ringing toasts, the poor man arose—not from a chair, according to press accounts, but from a couch. Whether or not he said so then, he later admitted:

"I cannot conscientiously recommend the route I have traveled to summer tourists in quest of pleasure, but it is a balm for many bruises to know that I am at last in California."

This much is fact. But Placerville, delighted at this priceless joke on Horace, blew it into something more. Within a few months every journalist and storyteller who came to California was repeating it—with embellishments. Artemus Ward, the great prankster of the 19th Century, passed through Placerville shortly after and dressed up the story like this:

When Greeley was put aboard Monk's stagecoach, the driver was ordered to deliver him in Placerville for a speaking engagement at seven o'clock. Off dashed the coach with such furious speed and fearful bouncing that Greeley soon decided he wasn't in such a hurry, after all.

"Sir," he told Monk out the window, "I don't care if we don't get there at seven!"

"I have got my orders," retorted the driver, and urged the horses to a faster pace. Finally Horace poked his head out again.

"I don't care," he pleaded, "if we don't get there at all."

"I've got my orders," shouted Hank, and went madly on. Then a jarring bump sent Greeley's head crashing through the roof of the coach. "Keep your seat, Horace," ordered the unruffled Hank Monk.

Just outside of Placerville, a welcoming committee, complete with brass band, stopped the stage to take Greeley and carry him in honor to the city, but Hank whipped up the team and scattered the crowd with the cry, "I've got my orders!"

When Mark Twain came along in 1861, he first heard the story from a stage driver at the Platte River. Out of Denver a passenger related it in identical words. A cavalry sergeant from Fort Bridger repeated the exact yarn, followed by a Mormon preacher who got on at Salt Lake. Along the Carson River they picked up a half-dead wanderer who launched into the same story.

Mark Twain then rebelled. "Suffering stranger," he warned, "proceed at your peril." The man stopped, but as Twain claimed, "In trying to retain the anecdote in his system he strained himself and died in our arms."

Over his next six years in California and Nevada the humorist heard that "deathless incident 81 or 82 times"—from drivers and passengers, Chinese and Indians, flavored with every aroma including "whisky, brandy, beer, cologne, sozodont, tobacco, garlic, onions, grasshoppers. . ." Mark Twain has been spared the thousands of retellings since then, and today any Placerville patriot believes that Horace Greeley came whirling into town on Hank Monk's stage with his head sticking through the top.

It was in the same year of Greeley's trip that Placerville swung into its final, furious hour.

The fabulous Comstock Lode had been discovered in the Washoe country (soon to be part of the new state of Nevada). As the tide of humanity swung back over the Sierra, Placerville became the main outfitting point for the Washoe silver mines. It was suddenly so overwhelmed with business that there were not enough wagons or mules in the country-side to keep the stampede moving. The hills above town were piled with boxes of merchandise while their owners vainly offered fantastic freight fees for hauling them over the Sierra. Stagecoaches and mule trains were booked up days in advance. Streets and hotels, saloons and restaurants, were thronged with a noisy crowd of expectant millionaires.

Recharged by the Nevada excitement, Placerville even aspired to become a railroad center when work began on the "Placerville and Sacramento Valley Railroad". But the rails stopped at Shingle Springs a few miles short of town, and the rival Central Pacific line of the Big Four pushed on over the Sierra. After 1867 Placerville lost her traffic to the rail-roaders.

But the quaint old camp, its streets still following the original mule paths, thrives today as the center of a lumber, mineral and vineyard country. And the town that once changed its name to Placerville out of civic pride, today insists on telling everybody (for the same reason) that its name used to be Hangtown.

### POINTS OF INTEREST

PLACERVILLE. Modern Placerville is charmingly nestled in the Sierra foothills, with the distinctive atmosphere of a mountain town. But though most of its buildings have modern façades, the visitor can get information on them by starting at the Placerville Museum at 524 Main St. Some of those dating from the Golden Fifties are: Cyrus Bales Building (1853) at 248 Main St.; Adams Express office (1856) at 435 Main; Wells Fargo office (1856), 437 Main; Smith & Nash hardware (1856), 441 Main; the Nuss Building (about 1854), 524 Main; and the Pearson Soda Works (1859), 594 Main. The site of the Carey House where Horace Greeley landed after his wild ride over the Sierra was at 300 Main. Only the site remains of the old Hanging Tree that gave Hangtown its name. The air of the 19th Century is best absorbed among the homes on the back streets. The visitor can tour a gold mine at Bedford Park a mile or so north of town.

EL DORADO. Once called Mud Springs, El Dorado was founded as a way station at the foot of the Carson Pass emigrant route. In the 1850s it boomed as a mining camp. Among the buildings remaining from the gold days are the brick Wells Fargo office (now a restaurant and bar) and three other stone and brick structures.

DIAMOND SPRINGS. Among the few remaining buildings in this once-flourishing camp are the Wells Fargo office, built in 1854 on the west side of Main St., Louis Lepetit's store (1856) and the Odd Fellows Hall (1852). Several other stone and brick structures, some with the familiar iron shutters, also remain.

SHINGLE SPRINGS. Begun as a stopping place on the road from Sacramento to Placerville, it blossomed as a mining town when gold was discovered nearby in 1850. On the west side of town the Wells Fargo office and what was originally called the Shingle Springs House both date from the 1850s.

---

# Chapter 5. Auburn: Three-Story Town

THERE IS A PLEASANT LEGEND that Auburn was never one of the wild towns of the Mother Lode. Unlike her raucous neighbors, she was at least moderate in her sins.

Perhaps this harmless tale grows out of her sylvan setting. Could this quaint and rustic place, nestled in the tree-shaded Sierra foothills, have been a rendezvous of bad men and a scene of violence? Or maybe it is her innocent name, recalling her English namesake of Goldsmith's lines: "Sweet Auburn! loveliest village of the plain."

Auburn today is California's unique "three story town". At the lower level is the scene of her first gold strike in May 1848, when hundreds of miners poured in from the discovery site at Sutter's Mill and points south. Known at first as Rich Dry Diggings, the new locality produced as much as $1,500 a day for a lucky few. Of this original site little is left today save some half-hidden foundations.

By 1850 Auburn numbered 1,500 persons, and the more permanent gold town mushroomed on its second location a little further up the hill. Town lots were laid out around a Spanish-style plaza, with one parcel to go to each citizen. One "sooner"—an enterprising barkeeper—moved in on one of the choicest lots and started his building. The aroused populace held a mass meeting and sent a rider to the county seat at Nicolaus for an injunction. By the time he got back the crisis was over. The building was finished and the barkeep was placating everybody with free drinks.

It is this middle location around the plaza that is Auburn's picturesque "Old Town". On its narrow and winding streets stand old-time buildings of false fronts and wooden canopies. Some are ghosts, some are occupied; only a few go back to the 1850s. But all of them carry the frontier flavor that makes "Old Town" Auburn one of the most colorful of Sierra mining camps.

A short distance higher lies the modern city— as lively and progressive a town as California boasts. As the seat of Placer County, she is the capital of a territory rich in agricultural and mining products. From her highest point a panoramic view of the American River Valley is unsurpassed. Quiet and orderly is the modern town of Auburn. But in her younger days?

Auburn's first lynching occurred on Christmas Day, 1850, when one citizen killed another and gave himself up to the sheriff. An outraged mob captured him, tried him by miners court and hanged him to an oak tree handily situated in the middle of town. Despite this grim lesson, another Auburnite committed murder soon after—resulting in another seizure, another rump court, another lynching. But, of course, Auburn was a quiet town.

In the spring of 1850 Auburn decided that she ought to be the seat of Sutter County, which then included much of Northern California. So she secured an election on the issue, in rivalry with the existing county seat of Nicolaus. To the polls inside her biggest general store she brought not only Auburnites, but voters from as far away as Coloma, in El Dorado County. With the lure of free "refreshments" she captured a majority larger than the county's whole population. This so impressed her rivals that next year when the new Placer County was formed, she remained the seat of government without a contest.

Auburn was, after all, a quiet and orderly town.

Then in 1855 California's Gold Rush struck the rocks in a financial panic. Surface mining had passed its peak, and for months the lagging gold supply had forced the banks to withdraw money from circulation to meet the needs of business. California was vulnerable to the slightest financial setback. It came in January 1855, when the St. Louis bank of Page and Bacon Company closed its doors. As soon as the news reached California a run was started on the San Francisco branch. By February 23 nearly all the banks in the state had locked their doors. Californians were clamoring for their funds. In Auburn's neighboring towns of Nevada City, Coloma, Placerville and Sacramento the crowds collected outside the banks and discussed how they could recover their deposits. But what happened in Auburn? An armed crew forced the bankers to open the safe and pass out the money to the depositors. On the whole, though, Auburn was a quiet town.

Outlawry came early to Placer County. By April 1852 the gold country's first important stage holdup occurred a few miles north of Auburn near Illinoistown. Reelfoot Williams and his gang stopped a coach and made off with $7,500 from the express box. A posse from Marysville caught up with them on the Yuba River and in a short battle put the Williams gang out of business.

Throughout the middle 1850s two bandits ranged through the mines—and made the country around Auburn their general headquarters. One of these was "Rattlesnake Dick" Barter, who won his wicked name not from personal ferocity but because he first settled at Rattlesnake Bar. Dick had been an honest miner until he was twice falsely accused of thefts. Each time he was exonerated. But with his reputation smirched, he changed his name, left Rattlesnake Bar and settled in the northern town of Shasta.

Before long a former neighbor came through camp and, catching sight of Dick, dealt him another foul blow by telling of his suspect character. At this final injustice, Dick broke down and took to the road to fulfill his reputation. One night near Shasta he robbed a lone traveler and vanished with the melodramatic news that he was "Rattlesnake Dick, the Pirate of the Placers."

Quickly Dick returned to the Auburn country and took up the highwayman's trade in earnest. For six years he plundered the highroads from Nevada City to Folsom. Many times he was captured and lodged in the local calaboose to await trial, but as many times the slippery outlaw made his escape. One chronicler insists that "he broke out of every jail in Placer and Nevada Counties."

Once Dick and a companion showed themselves on the streets of Nevada City and calmly took seats on the south-bound stage. Hearing this news, a deputy sheriff of Placer County decided to carry the burlesque still further by waylaying the stage at Harmon Hill. But the two bandits were unimpressed, and boldly demanded to see the officer's warrant. When he stopped to produce it, they sent a bullet barrage through the stage windows. The deputy bravely returned the fire with a one-shot derringer. No one was hurt, and before the officer could reload the robbers coolly left the stage and with some rude remarks, bade the bewildered deputy goodbye.

In the end, Dick carried his boldness too far. One night in July 1859 he and a fellow bandit rode openly through the main street of Auburn. The town could not let this insult pass, and a three-man posse caught up with the pair before they had gone a mile. The leader called on them to halt.

"Who are you, and what do you want?" Dick demanded, and ended the brief conversation with a blast of gunfire. One posseman was killed, but the other two fired back. Dick lurched in the saddle, then righted himself and rode off with his comrade. He didn't go far. Next morning his body was found by the roadside and carried back into town on the Auburn stage.

This was an unusually exciting moment in a camp that was always quiet and orderly.

A very different type from Rattlesnake Dick was Auburn's second bad man, Tom Bell. A doctor by profession, Bell tried to make a living in the gold country as a miner and then as a gambler. Failing in these, he methodically decided on armed robbery as the more promising pursuit. Tom Bell was like that—calm, calculating, daring, a sort of intellectual bandit.

The brains he brought to the highwayman's profession were not enough to keep him out of jail after his first escapade in 1855. But he soon broke loose from the state prison and took the road again—this time at the head of a sizable band of desperadoes.

For more than a year Tom Bell terrorized the roads in and around Auburn. At least three highway taverns were his secret hideouts, with the proprietors tipping him off on the departures of well-heeled guests.

In August 1856, Tom Bell heard of a $100,000 gold shipment on the Camptonville stage, and resolved to make holdup history. This was a mistake. His gang got nothing for their pains but a running fight with the guard and passengers. And all the law in Northern California rallied to track him down.

The Placer County sheriff caught up with the gang at an inn near Auburn, but during the battle Bell got away. With a remnant of his band he left the mines and hid out near Firebaugh's Ferry, on the San Joaquin River. There he was surprised by a posse, taken without a fight and hanged without ceremony.

It looked as though life in quiet Auburn might be duller than ever.

Then in May 1858, six bandits halted the Auburn stage and seized over $21,000 from the Wells Fargo chest. Soon afterwards at Yankee Jim's, Auburn's nearest neighbor, robbers made off with another express box. Just beyond Yankee Jim's near Forest Hill, a squad of six or seven men pulled another holdup early in 1859.

The Auburn country was a mighty poor risk for Wells Fargo, but it was painfully quiet.

Meanwhile, the Iron Horse had invaded California and was heading Auburn's way. Theodore Judah, the man who later surveyed the Central Pacific crossing of the Sierra, had launched his original Sacramento Valley Railroad. Construction began in February 1855, and a year later trains began operating from Sacramento to Folsom.

When the line stalled at this point, the eager Auburn people were not to be denied their railroad. They founded another line and had trains running into Auburn by October 1862.

But this little Gold Rush railroad was left behind in the bigger race for a transcontinental connection. In 1863 the Central Pacific, owned by the Big Four firm of Stanford, Crocker, Huntington and Hopkins, started still a third line from Sacramento toward Auburn—and the challenging Sierra.

Four months later the original Sacramento Valley Railroad resumed construction beyond Folsom toward Auburn. California's first big railroad race was on.

Auburn itself came into the drama when Central Pacific rails reached the town in June 1864. This was a death blow to Auburn's own little railroad. But the Sacramento Valley line bought up the corpse and began ripping up the valuable rails for use on its own route.

At this, Auburn and the Central Pacific joined forces. First they got an injunction against destroying the track, but the Sacramento Valley officials were able to dodge the server. Then a Placer County deputy arrived at the disputed roadbed with a posse and a warrant for the superintendent's arrest. Where could that gentleman be found, he asked.

"He's up in the cabin car ahead," answered a foreman. "Better take all your boys with you—he's an ornery cuss!"

So the deputy and all his men walked into the designated car—and a neat trap. The foreman locked the door and signaled to the locomotive. The train steamed out of Placer County and out of the deputy's jurisdiction.

From then on the contest was a grim railroad war. Each side got reinforcements and guarded its work camps with armed sentries. Prisoners captured by the Central Pacific forces were thrown in the Auburn jail. But the next time a sheriff's posse tried to interfere with the Sacramento Valley crews, the railroad was ready with its own warrant—secured from a friendly justice of the peace. The deputies were packed off to another jail, charged with carrying concealed weapons and disturbing the peace!

When one of the victims escaped and rode into Auburn with this news, the town virtually exploded. Local militia, the intrepid Auburn Grays, marched over to the railroad and fell upon the work gang with fixed bayonets. After an almost bloodless skirmish, the railroaders surrendered. The Auburnites marched them triumphantly off to the town jail.

In the end it was not Auburn blades but the bankruptcy

courts that defeated the Sacramento Valley line and sealed a Central Pacific victory. The railroad of the Big Four went on over the mountains to span the continent with iron.

And Auburn went along her quiet, uneventful way.

Auburn is, of course, only a part of the Placer County tradition. This is the land of the ridiculous place names—most of them now unmarked sites and all of them monuments to the Forty-niner's sense of humor. Here were Shirt Tail Canyon, You Bet, Last Chance, Deadman's Bar, Rattlesnake Bar, Frytown, Ground Hog's Glory, Milk Punch Bar, Drunkard's Bar, Humbug Bar, Ladies' Canyon, Miller's Defeat, Devil's Basin and Hell's Delight.

Yes, the rugged spirit of '49 lies over the Auburn country. But it's powerfully quiet and law abiding—and always has been.

### POINTS OF INTEREST

AUBURN. The lower or "old" section remains one of the best-preserved and most picturesque of Mother Lode ghost towns, with its Spanish-type plaza, its firehouse surmounted by a quaint bell tower, and its row of false-front buildings marching staunchly up the hill. Some of the oldest buildings are: the Wells Fargo office (1852), east of the firehouse on the "island" facing Lincoln Way; the "oldest post office in continuous operation in the West", further along on the corner facing the plaza; several Chinese stores on the south side of Sacramento St.; the Mercantile Building (1855) on up Sacramento St.; and on Commercial St. near "Lawyer's Row", the Masonic Hall (1860) and Feldberg & Newman's clothing store (1850s).

YANKEE JIM'S. Once a large mining town, Yankee Jim's is marked today by a few old buildings in a delightfully shaded dell west of Forest Hill.

FOREST HILL. The spirit of the Gold Rush hangs over this remote town in the Sierra pines about 17 miles north of Auburn. Chief among the oldest buildings is the Langstaff general store (1859).

MICHIGAN BLUFF. Roughly eight miles beyond Forest Hill is Michigan Bluff, once the center of vast hydraulic mining operations, and marked today by a few old structures.

Paralleling the North Fork of the American River, U.S. Highway 80 runs north to other historic spots beyond Auburn:

COLFAX. Not a mining town, Colfax was founded and remained as a railroad shipping point. It was named for Schuyler Colfax, who was elected Vice President on the ticket with Gen. U. S. Grant in 1868. A long row of old brick, false-front buildings faces the railroad.

GOLD RUN. Principal relic of this once-prosperous hydraulic mining town is the Pioneer Union Church, built in 1855 by subscriptions from the miners.

DUTCH FLAT. Located a short way off Highway 80, Dutch Flat was originally named for two Germans who settled here in 1851. Like a treasured heirloom, the sloping town has been preserved against the ravages of fire, storm, and commercialism that have spoiled other Mother Lode gems. Its name became a household word in California during the 1860s, when Charles Crocker and his partners of the Central Pacific built their transcontinental railroad across the Sierra over the "Dutch Flat Route". Today it is a picturesque village of white Victorian homes and picket fences. Among the oldest buildings are the Odd Fellows Hall and Masonic Temple (1856), the Dutch Flat Hotel (1851-2), the Methodist Church (1861), and the Dutch Flat Trading Post and Store (1854).

# PART III. THE SOUTHERN MINES

REACHED MAINLY *through the San Joaquin River port of Stockton, the Southern Mines had a distinctive character of their own. They nestled along Sierra foothills dotted with oak and piñon—a pastoral setting so characteristic of California. On the first visit one may be disappointed not to find them farther up in the forested mountains, where mines ought to be.*

*But they retain other rewards not found in most American mining districts. The plazas, the overhanging balconies, the occasional iron grillwork show a strong cosmopolitan influence. Among the earliest arrivals were native Californians, Mexicans, Chileans, Frenchmen, Italians, and Chinese. The Southern Mines had their fandango halls, their bull-and-bear fights—and their grim racial clashes.*

*Partly because of this rich and varied heritage, the Southern Mines have had a penchant for legend that is reminiscent of the Old World. Combined with the American weakness for exaggeration, this has created a mature body of folklore that survives all the arrows of spoilsport historians.*

*Thus visitors in search of history must often dig through layers of fable. They will learn to discount the number of men executed from each of numerous Hangman's Trees. They will learn to downgrade the peak population figures claimed by towns now marked by a stone wall and a gas pump.*

*Yet the traveler through the Southern Mines is struck by the sheer number of communities. Now one of the least populated in California, this region once teemed with young men in a hurry. One realizes that big things happened here.*

*So it is not surprising that a mythology would spring up among people with an epic period behind them. To these inheritors of a Golden Age, the men of the Gold Rush have become giants.*

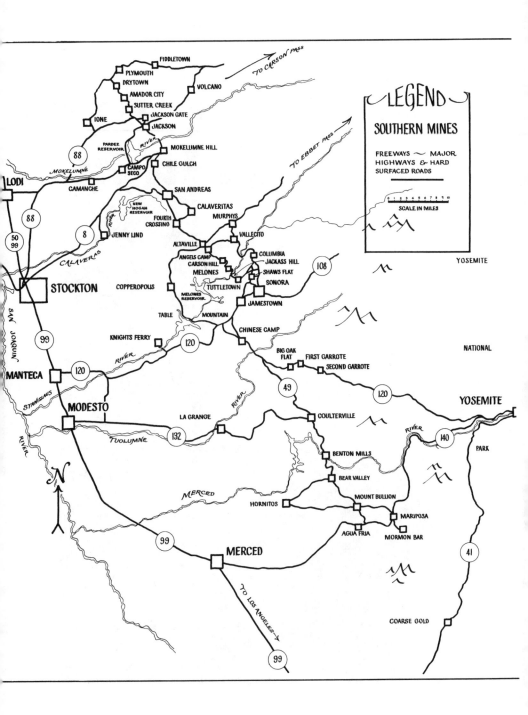

*Daguerreotype showing the narrow and crowded main street at Fiddletown, 1850's.*

*View of mines near Volcano showing extensive flume construction.*

*Group of miners at Sutter Creek (3rd man from right wears a Mexican War Army shako on his head), 1851.*

*Placer mining by Chinese using sluice boxes, about 1856.*

*Jenny Lind, example of board and shingle mining
community in the oak-dotted hills of Calaveras County.*

*Early miners cabin construction, using hand-felled
High Sierra timber.*

*Rare portrait, believed to be of George Angel,*
*founder of Angel's Camp.*

*Busy center of Jackson, one of the larger communities
among the Southern mines.*

*Iron shutters and false fronts characterize
legendary Angel's Camp.*

*Natty boulevardier, Charles E. Bolton, committed 28 stage holdups under the name of Black Bart.*

# Chapter 6. Volcano and the Amador Mines

THE BEST OF MOTHER LODE ghost towns lie off the beaten path, and near the top of the list is Volcano. From Jackson in Amador County, a good road takes you twelve miles to what is left of one of the rousing camps of the Gold Rush. And what is left breathes the flavor of the Fifties.

First of all, this was the land of contradictory names. Contrary to miners' belief, there were no volcanoes at Volcano. Fiddletown was supposedly named for the numbers of Missouri fiddlers who took turns playing a tune while their partners mined the stream; but a visitor of 1850 reported that "not a fiddler was to be had in Fiddletown." And Drytown had, in its heyday, twenty-six saloons. Of course, there were other local names that were only too true: Helltown, Hogtown, Loafer Flat, Bedbug, Whisky Slide, Murderer's Gulch.

Despite its remoteness, Volcano was the first real excitement of the Amador country. Troops who had come to California in the American conquest were the first Argonauts on the ground, giving the place its original name of Soldier Gulch. They found placers and clay beds so rich that the early comers averaged $100 per day. By 1849, gold-seekers were pouring into the new camp. Finding rocks and crags that resembled volcanic craters, they mistakenly gave it the name of Volcano.

But the wilderness camp was born to trouble. Sierra Indians, having discovered the value of white man's gold, were also mining in Volcano. Natives and intruders got along well enough until the summer of 1849. One day an American missed his pick, and claimed the Indians had stolen it. The chief, anxious to preserve peace, told a group of miners that if the pick was in the Indian camp, he would bring it back. When he ran off to fulfill the mission, an American rifle cracked and brought him down. Rod Stowell, a former Texas ranger, had mistaken the Indian's move and was too quick on the trigger.

Volcano's peace was broken, and the outraged Indians prepared for war. To cover their own blunder, the Americans who had precipitated the trouble announced to their comrades that the Indians had attacked them and murdered one. At this, the whites armed themselves and stormed the Indian stronghold. The natives were driven out, but not without leaving at least one American dead on the Volcano trail. This was the end of the Volcano War—except that when its citizens discovered that the Stowell group had lied about the cause of the trouble, they ran the rogues out of camp.

This finale was typical of Volcano's light respect for legalities. In the first state elections of 1849, territorial officials neglected to notify Volcano. But Bayard Taylor, news correspondent for Horace Greeley's *New York Tribune*, visited the town in the same month and carried with him some political messages from candidates in Mokelumne Hill. The Volcano boys concluded that he was an official who had come to call an election, and insisted on it even after Taylor pleaded that he was a reporter. So he consulted with the Alcalde (a combination mayor, sheriff and judge) and recommended an election procedure. They not only followed this out scrupulously, but finding a candidate on the ballot with the name of Taylor, mistook him for their visitor and gave him a unanimous vote.

"Had I known this fact sooner." noted Bayard Taylor, "I might have been tempted to run for Alcalde, at least."

The majesty of government was just as carelessly dismissed throughout the Amador country. Justice was less a matter of due process than of mob decision. When a stabbing occurred in Volcano, the boys lynched the supposed culprit within half an hour. At Sutter Creek a gambler stabbed a man, and was immediately tried by miners' court; he was given 75 lashes while the victim still lived, but was hanged next day when the man died—a double punishment that seemed perfectly reasonable to Sutter Creek.

In Fiddletown, $9,000 was taken from the Wells Fargo office, and five men were arrested for the crime for the good and sufficient reason that they had bad reputations. Lacking evidence, the boys sought to produce some by taking out three of the prisoners and hoisting them by the neck until they confessed. But with much hoisting the score stood: no confessions, no evidence, and after the sheriff arrived from Jackson, no prisoners.

Fiddletown, in fact, was quite at home outside the law. Before Amador County was established, it somehow managed to reside in a no-man's land between El Dorado and Calaveras counties. It was perfectly willing to vote with El Dorado, but at tax collecting time it stood squarely behind its geographic barriers. Fiddletown, too, produced a classic in courtroom procedure. When a witness exhausted the court with his outlandish story, the judge took care of the situation:

"I declare court adjourned. This man is a damned liar. Court is in session."

Things were much the same in Amador City. Justice of the Peace for 1854 was Henry Lark, a horse-trader who held court in the Magnolia Saloon. He was playing seven-up with the bartender one day when Sheriff Jim Wall hauled in a man accused of stealing meat from his neighbor. The sheriff knew better than to break up the game.

"Here judge, give me your hand while you settle this business."

"Git, and don't bother me!" answered the magistrate, who was evidently winning. But at the end of the hand he managed to change places with the sheriff. Throwing his leg over the table, he scrutinized the prisoner.

"Well, what you got to say for yourself?"

So while the judge examined the prisoner, the game went on with much shouting and commotion.

"Sheriff, keep silence in the court," shouted the judge. A

moment of quiet, as Justice Lark resumed his questioning.

"I was only borrowin' the meat, your Honor."

"No, you don't, Mr. Wall; put your little old jack on that ace."

And though the judge kept demanding silence in the court, he couldn't stop watching the game. At the next shout from the bar he jumped up, furious, but caught a glimpse of the barkeeper's hand.

"Wall," said the justice, "I'll bet you five dollars you're beaten."

"Done! Come down with the cash."

The prisoner, quietly remembering a previous appointment, vanished.

"Fraud and cheating!" screamed Justice Lark. "I fine you both ten dollars for contempt of court."

If Amador County played loose with the law, its isolation was partly to blame. For the first two years of the Gold Rush, traffic to Volcano moved along trails by foot or horseback. When a stage coach service finally reached the town in 1854, it had a dubious reception. Down-stages carrying out gold shipments were apt to encounter masked men who took professional interest in the Wells Fargo box. It was soon noticed that they were remarkably adept at guessing which coaches carried the loot, and the suspicion was raised that they just might be getting inside help. Unable to catch the robbers, Wells Fargo finally took the hint and pulled out of Volcano. That ungrateful camp could shift for itself.

Meanwhile, the rest of Amador had taken more permanent root with the discovery of rich quartz veins. The first strike was made at Amador City in February 1851 by a Baptist preacher. An indirect descendant of this and neighboring mines is the famous Keystone, one of the fabulous producers in California. Quartz leads were also discovered at Sutter Creek in 1851, and the next year in Fiddletown. Together with the mines of Jackson, these produced the real gold boom of Amador County.

Despite its provincial name, Fiddletown became an important point on the Mother Lode. As late as the 1860s it was a trading outpost for surrounding camps. Bret Harte publicized it with his *An Episode of Fiddletown*. But by 1878 its citizens could no longer see the joke in its priceless name, and changed it to the colorless title, Oleta. After half a century they came to their senses, and today its entrance sign announces, almost impudently, that this is Fiddletown.

As for Volcano, it lay largely outside the quartz belt. By 1855 it was resorting to hydraulic mining, and was showing signs of wear. But if Volcano died early, its remains have outlasted those of other camps down on the traveled highway. Volcano is still Volcano, though its erupting days are over.

### POINTS OF INTEREST

VOLCANO. Another gem off the beaten track, Volcano is well worth the 12-mile drive eastward from either Jackson or Sutter Creek. First among its historic buildings is the three-story St. George Hotel, which the newcomer faces upon entering town. Built in 1862 or '63, it is still in operation. Among the oldest buildings are, starting on the south side of Main Street, the ruins of the Kelley & Sigmond Building (1855) and the Clute Building (1855), with its iron-shuttered doors; on the north side, Meyers' cigar store (1856) next to the parking lot at Main and National, and the brick general store (1852). At the corner of Consolation Avenue and the Charleston Road is the Sing Kee Store (about 1854), and beyond in an adjacent building on Charleston Road, the Odd Fellows and Masonic Hall (1856). Across the street is the old jail, while the pioneer brewery is on the east side of Consolation Avenue. Across that street next to the Sing Kee Store is the ceremonial cannon, "Old Abe", brought to Volcano by the local militia, the "Volcano Blues", during the Civil War. On a side street is the schoolhouse (1855-6), now a private home. And on a hill overlooking Volcano is the Methodist Church, where Thomas Starr King preached as part of his tour to support the Union cause at the onset of the Civil War.

FIDDLETOWN. Another quaint community east of Highway 49, Fiddletown has a number of buildings dating from the 1850s, including the Chew Kee herb doctor's store, an adobe on the north side of the main street as you enter town; a brick-and-stone Chinese gambling house on the south side; a general store (1855) near the end of the block; the brick Wells Fargo office (1853) across the street and now part of the Community Hall; a blacksmith shop (1852) with brick front and iron doors; the Schallhorn blacksmith and wagon shop (1870), on the north side of Main Street; the restored school-house (1860), located on the American Flat Road; and the Farnham residence, probably the earliest home left in Fiddletown, located across Dry Creek on Jibboom Street.

SUTTER CREEK. One of the most picturesque towns located on Highway 49, Sutter Creek is decorated with old balconies over the sidewalks and has not been spoiled with an overabundance of modern signs. Among the oldest buildings are the Bartolo Brignole general store (1858) and the Bellotti Inn (1860s), both on the west side of Main St.; and across the street, the Levaggio Opera House, whose front part was built in 1860. Two bed-and-breakfast inns on the west side of Main Street date from the 1850s. On a side street is Knight's Foundry (1873), said to be the last water-powered foundry in the United States.

AMADOR CITY. Smaller but equally charming is Amador City, home of the famous Keystone Mine (1853), whose works still stand on the south side of town. While most of the buildings were constructed after the 1878 fire, a few older ones include the Fleehart store (1860s), Amador Hotel (the main front section built about 1855), and the Keystone Mine headquarters (1867), now an inn.

PLYMOUTH. While this mining locality began in the Gold Rush, the buildings are of later 19th Century vintage. The most historic structure is the Empire Mining Company's office and store (early 1870s), with its brick walls and iron shutters.

DRYTOWN. Founded in 1848, Drytown includes a few buildings dating from the 1850s, including a brick store believed to have been the mine office of George Hearst, the father of William Randolph Hearst; and the Le Moine House (1857), a brick and board home on a side street. In a shaded garden on Old Plymouth Road is a plastered adobe home said to be the oldest dwelling in Amador County.

---

# Chapter 7. Mok Hill & Its Feudin' Twin, Jackson

IF CALIFORNIANS ARE INCORRIGIBLE hometown boosters, they can lay the original blame on the exuberant citizens of the Gold Rush camps. And the finest examples of this local bombast were the neighboring (and feuding) towns of Mokelumne Hill and Jackson, in the heart of the Southern Mines.

From the beginning these two camps were headed for trouble out of conflict of character. Mok Hill, as it was called, was the northernmost of the camps with a cosmopolitan flavor. Here were large colonies of Frenchmen, native Californians, Mexicans and Chileans; here flourished the fandango hall and the bull-and-bear fight. Jackson had its mixed population, but it definitely bore the American stamp.

In lawlessness the camps were also rivals. In both places the man who was robbed looked to his own gun rather than to the law for justice; and if he shot one of the offenders there was no thought of a trial. Mokelumne had at least two lynchings and, according to one report, five killings in one week. Jackson hanged ten men from the same execution tree.

When the Gold Rush began, Mok Hill got a head start on its neighbor. Discovered in August 1848 by veterans of Stevenson's Regiment, it was a thriving, canvas-tented camp within a year. Jackson, in fact, was founded as a way station on the road from Sacramento to Mokelumne Hill; by the end of 1849 its population was only some sixty persons. But as rich diggings were uncovered along Jackson Creek, the camp flourished in its own right.

Then trouble began. Calaveras County (which then included Jackson) was formed in 1850, and the county seat was won by the nearby camp of Double Springs. Since it had only one building, Jackson and Mok Hill considered this a deliberate insult. So in July 1851 an election was held to relocate the county seat. Mokelumne, still having the larger population, naturally won—or at least that was the result reported by the county clerk, Colonel Collyer.

But the Jackson men were not through. Three of them rode down to Double Springs and invited everybody in the Courthouse (which also served as saloon) to drink to the new county seat, Mok Hill. This suggestion could hardly be ignored, even by Col. Collyer. And while everybody was toasting, one Jackson man grabbed the official records from a nearby table, threw them in a wagon and dashed off to the new seat of Calaveras County. By the time the county clerk arrived, one Judge Smith had recounted the ballots and declared Jackson the winner. This was county government, Gold Rush style.

Col. Collyer accepted the situation and set up office in Jackson. But when he was defeated at the next election, he adopted the Jackson system and locked up the ballots. Judge

Smith thereupon broke into his desk, counted the votes and declared Collyer the loser. The Colonel then made the mistake of promising to shoot Judge Smith on sight, and lost out a third time in a contest of bullets.

Meanwhile, Jackson's triumph as the county seat lasted only nine months. In April 1852 Mokelumne Hill won a second election, and possession of the crucial records. Jackson and neighboring camps then walked out of Calaveras and formed their own Amador County—with Jackson as the official seat. As for Mokelumne, it finally relinquished the seat of Calaveras County in 1866 to the more thriving community of San Andreas. This time Jackson had no objections.

The miners did not always take their elections seriously. When California applied for admission to the Union in 1849, a convention assembled at Monterey and framed a state constitution. With characteristic audacity, California held an election in November 1849 for ratifying the Constitution and choosing state officers—before Congress had fairly begun to debate the question of admission to the Union.

At Mok Hill, as elsewhere in California, election day was rainy and miserable. Despite the momentous occasion, few citizens stirred from their tents until noon. Finally the *Alcalde* appointed two inspectors and set up the polls in the camp's largest tent—a saloon. Observing the scene was the 19th century journalist and author, Bayard Taylor, who noted that the inspectors were seated "behind the counter, in close proximity to the glasses and bottles, the calls for which were quite as frequent as the votes."

Since most citizens knew neither Constitution nor candidates, their judgment was limited. A candidate named Fair received a number of votes on the strength of his auspicious name. Another lost about twenty votes for having previously appeared on the river wearing a stovepipe hat. Admitted one voter:

"When I left home I was determined to go it blind. I went it blind in coming to California, and I'm not going to stop now. I voted for the Constitution, and I've never seen the Constitution. I voted for all the candidates, and I don't know a damned one of them. I'm going it blind all through, I am."

Mokelumne's unanimous vote in favor of the Constitution was representative of the California balloting. As it happened, the 1849 Constitution has been recognized as one of the most admirable documents of its kind.

This gambler's spirit was characteristic of miners in the Mokelumne-Jackson region, if not in the whole Mother Lode. In Mok Hill, a black miner arrived and asked some of the boys where to dig. They pointed out, by way of a practical joke, a hill that had already been combed over and pronounced barren. A week later he was back on the street, loaded down with gold. And the boys promptly stampeded to their "barren" hill.

The same thing happened to three young Germans in Jackson. They were directed to some mine tailings—rock that had already been worked over. Within a few days they had earned $700, having dug down through the tailings to a rich vein beneath.

These chance strikes, according to an early Mok Hill citizen, were not the exceptions. The reason so many miners failed, he insisted, was that they were trying to go by some sensible geologic theory. Such men "would be baffled at every turn," for the irregular distribution of mineral in the Mother Lode defied geology. One miner named Clarke was famed for his rich discoveries. He once fell down a steep hill, got to poking around at the bottom with his knife, and made a million-dollar strike. The secret of Clarke's success, claimed the Mokelumne chronicler, "was that he had no theory. . ."

With such diggings under foot, most miners fell easy prey to the gambling tables of Mok Hill and Jackson. If they lost their pile on Saturday night, they could dig another next week. It also made them connoisseurs of the most expensive food and drink. "It was no unusual thing," reported Bayard Taylor, "to see a company of these men, who had never before had a thought of luxury beyond a good beefsteak and a glass of whiskey, drinking their champagne at ten dollars a bottle, and eating their tongue and sardines, or warming in the smoky campkettle their tin canisters of turtle soup and lobster salad."

Such epicurean tastes were especially costly in a land where prices were topsy-turvy. At the "Brandy and Sugar" Hotel in Jackson, a slice of bread was $1.00. Buttered, $2.00. In Mokelumne, board for mules was comparable: barley was $1.00 a quart and grass $1.00 a handful.

Prices like these are the chief reason why many, if not most, of the fortunes made in the Gold Rush came not from mining, but from trading. In 1849 a man named Fash so succeeded in cornering the commerce of Mokelumne Hill that the camp acquired the nickname, "Fashville." His operation of the only store in camp and the only mule team from the outside world was merely the beginning of his accomplishments. One of Fash's most lucrative assets was a big sheet-iron stove, on which a miner could cook any item at a $1.00 fee. Fash's specialty was apple pie, which sold fast at $2.00 each. One day he ran out of apples, but having a heavy stock of beans on hand, produced a bean pie and sold it as a "novel and delicate luxury." Poker games were the fashion at Fash's place, subject to the house rule that whenever somebody won a pot with four-of-a-kind, he had to order drinks for everybody. Fash's muleteers brought in Mok Hill mail as a free service, until he hung out a new sign: "Fash's Letter Express." After that, incoming letters were $2.00 apiece.

The Hillites, as they were called, might overlook such business tactics, but the mining profession had strict moral rules. One of these was that no man could mine his claim with slave labor. Near Mokelumne Hill a Chilean named Dr. Concha was working his mine with a force of peons; what was more, he staked a number of claims in their names. This did not please the American miners, who may also be suspected of opposing Chilean miners in general. When the report reached Mokelumne Hill that Dr. Concha's men had driven a party of Americans off some rich ground, the trouble exploded into the "ChileanWar".

The American miners met on "the Hill" and passed a resolution banishing Chileans from the diggings. Dr. Concha in turn went down to Stockton and secured a warrant for the arrest of the Americans. Some sixty of his men marched into Mok Hill in December 1849, killed two miners and made off with thirteen prisoners. At this, the Mokelumne miners rose in arms, and a company of Rangers was hurriedly sent from Stockton.

But before the night was over the prisoners had struggled free and captured the Chilean band. The new captives were brought into Mokelumne for trial; three were hanged and others given lesser punishment. The Chilean War was over, but the resentment it kindled reached from California to South America.

Nor was this the only battle between Yankees and foreigners at Mok Hill. On a nearby knoll, a group of Frenchmen were working an exceedingly rich claim. When some American miners tried to seize the property, the French dug in for a fight and planted a Tricolor banner in their midst. At this provocation, several hundred Yankee miners assembled and stormed the fort, carrying off a fortune in high-grade ore. The whole act of piracy went unpunished, and was soon dignified with the name, "French War"—another monument to the primitive side of Gold Rush California.

But Mok Hill had its refinements. Late in 1851 the Hillites established a theatre—complete with candles for footlights and genteel-looking miners for the female roles. One young actor, eager to show his talents at tragedy, was given the lead in Richard III. But the Mok Hill boys took the role less seriously. When Richard rushed to the front of the stage, sank to his knees and shouted, "My kingdom for a horse!"—a Mexican burro that had been smuggled under the stage answered with a fearful braying. In the confusion, a stagehand raised the footlights and a candle caught Richard in the nose. While the house roared, the outraged king rushed from the scene and his talents were lost forever to the tragic stage.

Such was the riotous spirit of Mok Hill and Jackson in the Golden Fifties. Mokelumne, a thriving camp when Jackson was still unborn, now remains a quaint but quiet town on Highway 49. But Jackson, spurred by the development of such famous mines as the Argonaut and the Kennedy, outpaced its rival and stands today as one of the busiest towns in the Mother Lode. And tempers have cooled since the days when county seats were won by the town with the fastest buckboard.

### POINTS OF INTEREST

MOKELUMNE HILL. Most historic buildings of Mokelumne Hill are located in a two-block area around the junction of Main and Center Streets. They include the Hotel Leger, rebuilt twice after its original construction in 1851; the adjoining theater, which served as Courthouse when Mok Hill was the county seat; the History Center building (1851); the "Italian Store" (1854); McFadden's Store (1854); the ruins of the L. Mayer & Son store (1854); the stone Wells Fargo office (1865); and the Odd Fellows Hall, whose lower two stories were built in 1854 and the third story in 1861. To the northwest are the Protestant and Jewish cemeteries, started in 1851, while the wooden Community Church (Congregational) on South Main Street dates from 1856 or '57. A hill overlooking town is known as French Hill, where the Americans stormed the fort of the beleaguered Frenchmen.

CHILI GULCH. South of Mok Hill along Highway 49 is the site of the "Chilean War". A few rock foundations remain.

JACKSON. A good place to start in this relatively large and lively town is the Amador County Museum at 225 Church

Street (building constructed in 1859). Most of the downtown buildings were erected after the 1862 fire. Among those predating that fire are the stuccoed Masonic Hall (1854) at 14 Water Street, the lower story of the red brick-and-plaster Wells Fargo building (1856) at 2 Main Street, the old Levy Brothers dry goods store (1854) at 38 Main, the lower two stories of the brick-and-stone building (1858) at 104 Main, the Levy & Co. building (1857) at 105 Main, and the structures at 111-115 Main (built in 1855 and '56).

JACKSON GATE. Principal landmark remaining at this outpost north of Jackson is the Chichizola Store at 1324 Jackson Gate Road. While the family started its business in 1850, the oldest part of the present building (on the south side) dates from about 1857. The huge wheels located off the road between Jackson Gate and Martell were installed in 1912 to convey tailings from the Kennedy Mine.

---

# Chapter 8. Calaveras: Jumping Frog Country

ONE SPOT IN THE HEART of the Southern Mines is general headquarters for California folklore—from Joaquin Murieta and Black Bart to Bret Harte and Mark Twain. Here lie the twin capitals of the Jumping Frog Country, Angel's Camp and San Andreas.

It was not from spotless virtue that the roaring camp of Angel's got its name. Its founder was George Angel, who had come to California as a soldier during the Mexican War. When news of the gold strike at Sutter's Mill reached Monterey, he was one of some ninety men who struck out for the Sierra. Reaching Calaveritas Creek in May 1848, Angel built a trading post on what came to be called Angel's Creek. Within a year the hills at Angel's Camp were "dotted with tents," in the words of one observer, "and the creeks filled with human beings to such a degree that it seemed as if a day's work of the mass would not leave a stone unturned in them." Four years later the population reached 4,500, and Angel's was one of the hubs of the Mother Lode.

Meanwhile, the rival camp of San Andreas had sprung up a few miles away. Founded in 1848 by Mexican prospectors, it was one of the earliest to suffer from the racial clashes that rocked the Mother Lode. When the richness of San Andreas became known, American miners poured in and drove many of the Mexicans out. At least one of the San Andreas victims, according to legend, struck back.

The story goes that Joaquin Murieta was living near town when a gang of Americans descended on his place. They hung his brother for a crime he didn't commit, ravished his sweetheart and horsewhipped Joaquin for good measure. Swearing vengeance, the proud youth took the outlaw trail and formed a band of cutthroats to prey on American settlements up and down the Mother Lode. All of the 21 murderers of his brother were brought to justice—19 by Joaquin's own hand. Between 1851 and '53 he was in and out of nearly every camp in the Southern Mines, robbing where he chose, laughing at the law, taking from the rich and giving to the poor—all in true Robin Hood tradition.

At least this is the version in the popular literature on Joaquin. Probably no American bandit—not even Jesse James—has been more widely chronicled. Joaquin is the subject of more than two dozen biographies, counting all the separate editions—eleven of them in Spanish; two novels; two epic poems; one play, one motion picture; and almost countless newspaper serials, magazine articles, and separate book chapters. Scarcely a town in the Southern Mines of the gold country fails to claim some landmark as a favorite haunt of Joaquin.

Beginning in the 1930s, Francis P. Farquhar and Joseph Henry Jackson applied literary scholarship to the Murieta biographies, tracing all of them in a direct line of descent back to an original story by John Rollin Ridge published in 1854. Most of the rest were piratings, or piratings of piratings, usually with added layers of fancy. As for the original version, Jackson called it "as preposterous a fiction as any the Dime Libraries ever invented. . . ."

Although alert scholarship had exposed the Murieta fiction, it hardly proved there were no facts to be had. Was there a Joaquin, and if so, what is his real story?

The public nature of Joaquin's exploits would suggest contemporary newspapers as the best hunting ground. From these sources—often providing two or three supporting reports of the same episodes—there emerges a Joaquin who terrorized Amador, Calaveras, and probably Mariposa Counties for just two months—January to early March, 1853. At first he was called simply, Joaquin. When the governor and the legislature offered rewards for his capture they attached a variety of last names, including Carrillo, Ocomorenia, Valenzuela, Boteller and Murieta, with the latter winning out as the accepted form, though in various spellings.

There had been, in fact, a horse thief operating in the Los Angeles area named Joaquin Murieta in 1851 and '52.

But the public record of Joaquin the bandit operating in the gold mines began on January 23, 1853, when a Mexican suspected of horse stealing was captured by two Americans at Bay State Ranch near San Andreas. He was rescued at gun point by three other Mexican riders. Reinforced from San Andreas, a party of five Americans pursued the outlaws to the vicinity of Calaveritas Creek; but when they overtook their quarry near the top of a hill south of San Andreas, they found the Mexicans had increased to twelve. The gang promptly rode down upon their pursuers, firing as they came. The Americans, exhausting their ammunition in a short battle, returned to San Andreas. The Mexicans proceeded to a place called Yackee Camp, two miles south of San Andreas, where they shot at any Americans they found. Killing one man, they pushed on to a nearby quartz mill and murdered two more Americans before going into hiding.

At this outrage—the first recorded appearance of Joaquin and his band—the whole Calaveras community was aroused. Mass meetings were held in San Andreas and Double Springs; resolutions were passed ordering the Mexican population to leave the county; parties were stationed at the ferries on the Stanislaus and the Calaveras; and the region in between was scoured for the outlaws. Three Mexicans supposed to have been part of Joaquin's gang were taken at various places and hanged without ceremony. Bands of Americans drove the Mexican population from San Andreas and the upper Calaveras River. Reported the Stockton newspaper, "If an American meets a Mexican, he takes his horse, his arms, and bids him leave."

For two weeks, while posses patrolled Calaveras County, Joaquin and his band remained hidden. By the first week in February the region was too hot for comfort; one of the gang, said to be Joaquin's brother, was captured and hanged at Angel's Camp. Joaquin and his men headed north. At Winter's Bar they forced the ferryman to carry them across the Mokelumne River; then they rode around Jackson, robbing as they went, through the present Amador County.

On February 8 they attacked a Chinese camp near Big Bar on the Cosumnes River, massacring six persons and making off with $6,000. Near Fiddletown three of the band were surprised by a posse on February 12 and were forced to decamp with a single horse—two men riding and the other running behind hanging to the animal's tail. When the last one was wounded, one of the riders changed places with him. Shortly afterward the horse was shot, but with their usual resourcefulness the bandits managed to escape in the brush. Doubling southward, they killed three Chinese and one American near Jackson.

With these atrocities, northern Calaveras County (later Amador County) rose in fury. Mass meetings at Jackson and Mokelumne Hill dispatched posses in pursuit. Wrote one correspondent, "Woe to the Mexicans if they are caught." One unfortunate was taken on the Mokelumne River and hanged at Jackson without trial. When Joaquin's band robbed a German traveler north of Jackson, a posse of twenty men rode out of town and encountered four of the bandits, including Joaquin himself, near a chaparral-covered hill. One outlaw was killed and Joaquin was said to have been wounded in the cheek—which could account for later descriptions of him specifying a scar on the right cheek. But the bandits scrambled into the chaparral, which as one witness wrote, was "so thick even a dog canot git through it."

Overnight the besiegers tried to surround the mountain and sent for reinforcements. By the morning of February 17 some fifty Americans and a hundred Indians had gathered, spurred on by a local reward of $1,000 offered for Joaquin's head. But once again the fugitives made their escape. Stealing horses and saddles, they rode south and crossed the Mokelumne River—on a stolen boat, according to one report. At a Chinese camp near Rich Bar on the Calaveras River they killed three persons, wounded five more, and corralled and robbed the rest (one report said the victims totalled 200 persons, and the haul $30,000).

Riding northward to Forman's Ranch, near the Mokelumne River, the bandits were surprised there by a posse early in the morning of February 22. But they escaped under a hail of bullets, with one of their number wounded in the hand. While their pursuers followed only ten minutes behind, they descended on another Chinese camp, killed three, mortally wounded five others, and rode off with several thousand dollars.

All next day they flew ahead of their pursuers, plundering Chinese camps along the way. Just before dark, as the posse later reported, "we saw them about three quarters of a mile distant, robbing some Chinamen. They turned and saw us advancing, but they stirred not an inch until we were within half a mile of them, when they mounted their horses and rode off at the speed of the wind. . . . We attempted pursuit, but our horses were worn out. . . ."

With this catalogue of butchery in four weeks' time, Joaquin made himself the terror of the Southern Mines and the sensation of California. More than ever the settlers were panicked; at least two posses were in the field, and citizens of the Cosumnes River collected $1,000 reward for Joaquin. The Chinese, who had suffered the brunt of Joaquin's ferocity, were leaving their isolated camps and congregating in the large settlements for protection. The *Calaveras Chronicle* reported: "It is to be regretted that, so insecure is life now considered in this county, in consequence of the recent outrages, that there is a perceptible falling off in the population."

A few days after his last daring escape on February 22, Joaquin was reported in the town of Hornitos, in Mariposa County—apparently having left Calaveras for good. With his usual bravado he was playing monte in a saloon and drinking freely until his comrades dragged him away for fear the authorities might take him. About March 4 all of the stock at the ranch of an American near Quartzburg, Mariposa County, were run off by a band of Mexicans. The determined owner, one Prescot, tracked them into Hornitos, found them in a tent, and collected seven or eight Americans to surround and capture them. Entering the tent with a light, Prescot and a companion had seized one man when they were met with a fusillade of bullets which wounded them both. While the rest of the Americans opened fire, the fugitives escaped unharmed in the dark. It was widely reported that this was Joaquin and his band.

On May 17 the Governor signed a bill authorizing Captain Harry Love, a former Mexican War express rider and California peace officer, to raise a company of 20 rangers and bring Joaquin to Justice. The rest of the story is comparatively well known. On July 25 Love's rangers came upon a band of Mexicans in the San Joaquin Valley near the mouth of Arroyo Cantua, north of the present town of Coalinga. In the fight that followed the rangers killed the leader (supposedly Joaquin) and also a man identified as Manuel "Three-Fingered Jack" Garcia, well known in California as a brigand and cutthroat.

To prove they had actually killed Joaquin, the rangers brought back the leader's head and Three-Fingered Jack's deformed hand preserved in a keg of brandy. In Mariposa County and other parts of the state, Love sought out 17 persons supposed to have known the bandit and secured affidavits that this was indeed the head of Joaquin. The grisly trophies were put on display at Stockton, then in San Francisco, where the curious paid $1.00 admission.

No sooner had the head been placed on exhibit than some persons claiming to have known the bandit said it was not Joaquin's. In fact, through the spring of 1853 a series of newspaper stories reported appearances of a band of Mexicans—sometimes said to be that of Joaquin—at succeeding places moving southward toward Mexico.

Whether he was killed by Love's rangers or whether he went into permanent hiding, the fact remains that there was a bandit named Joaquin. He was not very much like the bandit described by Ridge and subsequent biographers. Yet he was not, as scholar Joseph Henry Jackson believed, "manufactured, practically out of whole cloth. . ." For two months he and his band ravaged the Southern Mines and killed approximately 24 people—perhaps more. In that flash of time he was the biggest news in that part of California.

For the Mother Lode traveler, one lesson to be drawn is that particular landmarks pointed out as the haunts of Joaquin should be appreciated only as legend, as yet unsupported by historical evidence. But contemporary sources at least bear witness that he probably visited San Andreas, Campo Seco and Lancha Plana in Calaveras County; Drytown, Jackson Gate and Fiddletown in Amador County; and Quartzburg and Hornitos in Mariposa County.

A far more durable bandit was Black Bart, in whom San Andreas also takes a proprietary interest, since it was the scene of his trial and conviction. When it came to pure robbery, both in quantity and quality, Black Bart was assuredly the prince of California bandits. To be sure, he was somewhat late getting started; Bart robbed his first stage in 1875. But for the next eight years, armed only with a shotgun and a stern voice, this bold highwayman stopped no less than 28 stages.

Bart was no ordinary ruffian. He planned and executed his robberies with careful research and admirable finesse. He always worked alone, though he sometimes mounted a battery of broomsticks over a rock beside the road to impress stagedrivers with his imaginary confederates. He always left the passengers alone, and on one occasion is supposed to have returned to an excited lady her proffered purse.

Bart ranged as far north as the Oregon border, but it was the stage drivers of the gold country who most often heard his stentorian command, "Throw down that box." He left no clues, except in two early robberies when he placed a tantalizing bit of poetry in the empty Wells Fargo chest, signed by "Black Bart, the PO8." Two stanzas gave a hint of Bart's character, but not his identity:

> *"I've labored long and hard for bread*
> *for honor and for riches*
> *But on my corns too long yove tred*
> *You fine haired sons of bitches*
> *Let come what will I'll try it on*
> *My condition cant be worse*
> *and if thers money in that Box*
> *Tis munny in my purse."*

By the time this colorful scoundrel had perpetrated 27 successful holdups, he had California sheriffs, Wells Fargo detectives and the U. S. Postal authorities in a high lather. But every enterprise has its bad days. On November 3, 1883, the Sonora stage rolled westward toward the Calaveras town of Copperopolis. At the bottom of Funk Hill the lone passenger, a young boy with a rifle, got out to do some hunting; the driver agreed to pick him up on the other side of the hill. As the laboring team neared the top, out sprang Black Bart with leveled shotgun.

This time he ran into trouble. The Wells Fargo chest was bolted to the floor of the coach. To gain time in opening it, Bart ordered the driver to take the horses on over the hill out of sight. But there the driver came upon the boy and his gun. He came back over the hill just as Bart was making off with the loot, sent him a volley of three shots and hit him.

The wounded Bart escaped, but in the confusion he left behind a handkerchief—with its telltale laundry mark. Wells Fargo detectives traced it to the apartment of Charles Bolton, San Francisco. There they arrested a dapper little man who had been leading a double life as San Francisco boulevardier and Mother Lode stage robber. Those fine haired sons of bitches, whoever they were, had the last laugh, after all.

Black Bart was taken to San Andreas, seat of Calaveras County, and tried for his last holdup. It was the biggest excitement in the town since the Gold Rush. The trial was cut short when Bart pleaded guilty, but he tried to make up for that by delivering a long courtroom speech. The outlaw served a few years at San Quentin, and then faded from history. It was small punishment for 28 robberies, but then Bart had never fired a shot. Besides, he had been uncommonly polite.

It was in the area from Angel's Camp south to Table Mountain that Bret Harte spent two months on the Mother Lode in 1855. Here most of his identifiable story settings were laid, and here alone does he show real familiarity with gold country geography. In this Calaveras country that chivalrous old reprobate, Colonel Starbottle, held forth. And in Angel's itself were laid such stories as *Mrs. Skaggs' Husband* and *The Bell Ringer of Angel's.*

Still, Bret Harte arrived too late to capture the Gold Rush spirit in his Mother Lode stories. As one critic puts it, "The flavor of decay hangs about his mining towns; they are just the places which he might have seen in Calaveras in 1855."

Even later came Mark Twain, who described the Angel's of 1865 as a "decayed mining camp." True, he got a poor first impression from boarding a week at the local French restaurant, which served a straight fare of chili beans and "bad, weak coffee" for every meal. On the first day Twain's companion, Jim Gillis, called the waiter and told him he had made a mistake. They had ordered coffee. "This is day-before-yesterday's dishwater."

A few days later Mark Twain made a momentous entry in his notebook: "Coleman with his jumping frog—bet a stranger $50—Stranger had no frog and C. got him one:—In the meantime stranger filled C's frog full of shot and he couldn't jump. The stranger's frog won." Coleman later became Jim Smiley, and this fragmentary anecdote—probably related by the bartender at the Angel's Hotel—became Mark Twain's first famous story, *The Celebrated Jumping Frog of Calaveras County.*

First published in *Clapp's Saturday Press*, it was reprinted across the country and even translated into French. This latter effort dealt such a horrifying blow to the picturesque Western dialect of the *Jumping Frog* that Mark Twain later retaliated by translating it literally back into English. Such phrases as, Well, I don't see no p'ints about that frog that's any better'n any other frog," became, "Eh bien! I no saw not that that frog had nothing of better than each frog." This, said Twain, was sheer martyrdom.

In any case, the *Jumping Frog* made Mark Twain famous, and immortalized Angel's Camp. In return, the town each spring honors Mark Twain, his story and the Gold Rush days in general with a three-day festival climaxed by a Jumping Frog contest—one of the biggest community celebrations in California.

SAN ANDREAS. Though some old buildings were sacrificed in widening the highway through town, other winding streets in the hillside business district are redolent with antiquity. As in other large Mother Lode towns, a good starting point for an historical tour is the local museum, located here in three adjacent buildings in the historic block sloping from Highway 49 to Court Street. These are the Odd Fellows and Masonic Hall (1856), the Calaveras County Hall of Records (1893), and behind it, the Courthouse (1867), where Black Bart was confined, tried and convicted. Some Gold Rush buildings in this same block are, starting at the top, Gooney's saloon (1858) at 6 N. Main Street, an old tin shop and hardware store (1857) of brick stuccoed over at 10 N. Main, another brick store camouflaged with stucco (1858) at 14 N. Main, and the oldest building in town (1855), a stone structure housing the library and Chamber of Commerce at 46 N. Main. Across the street two buildings at 35 and 41 N. Main (lower stories, 1856 and 1859) are now part of an inn. On side streets both north and south of Highway 49 are numerous homes from the last half of the 19th Century.

CAMPO SECO. The old Adams Express building, a number of rock walls, and a few adobe houses are the main features of this once-lively town, located on a dirt road west of San Andreas.

JENNY LIND. Named in a burst of enthusiasm for the Swedish Nightingale, this ghost camp is marked by the remains of Sinclair's adobe store and the Rosenberg building,

101

made of sandstone.

All along the lower reaches of the Mokelumne, as on most other rivers flowing out of the Mother Lode, the visitor sees mile upon mile of rock piles—the residue of dredge mining that occurred over many decades.

CALAVERITAS. On a road southeast of San Andreas are the remains of Calaveritas, once populated largely by Mexican placer miners. Once the home of 42 businesses, Calaveritas now displays one store building founded in 1854 by an Italian merchant, Luigi Costa, located in the bend of the road where descendants still live in an adjacent home. Elsewhere in Calaveritas a few rock walls remain.

ALTAVILLE. Prominent among the landmarks of Altaville are the Prince and Garibaldi store (1857) and a red brick grammar school serving Altaville children from 1858 to 1950, located on the west side of the street north of town.

ANGEL'S CAMP. Information on the historic buildings is provided at the Visitor Center, corner of Main and Bird's Way at the south end of town, and the Angel's Camp Museum, north of town on the east side of Main Street. The chief point of interest is the Angels Hotel at Main Street and Bird's Way, where bartender Ben Coon is supposed to have related the Jumping Frog story to Mark Twain. Others of Gold Rush vintage are the E. & G. Stickle general store (1856) further up Main Street from the Angels Hotel, the Peirano Building (1854) by the northeast corner of Main and Church Streets, and the Love House (built in 1850 and the oldest building in town) on the west side of Main Street near the north end of Angel's Camp. Most other early buildings fell victim to the fires that destroyed many mining towns. The existing structures, while picturesque enough, date from the town's hard rock mining days later in the century.

COPPEROPOLIS. Founded as a staging center, Copper-opolis boomed as a focal point of the copper craze that seized California in the 1860s. Dating from that period, a few old buildings remain, constructed of used brick brought from the then-fading town of Columbia.

VALLECITO. Among the landmarks in this quaint settlement are the ruins of the Wells Fargo office (1854) and the stone Dinkelspiel store (1851) with its iron-shuttered doors. On another street is the stone Cuneo Building, also erected in '51.

DOUGLAS FLAT. Two miles south of Murphy's is a short side road paralleling Highway 4. Here the main remnant of the old town of Douglas Flat is the Gillead Building (1851), with its two tall iron-shuttered doors.

MURPHY'S. The lore of the Gold Rush runs strong in Murphy's, easily one of the best-preserved towns on the Lode. Named for the founding brothers, Daniel and John Murphy, this out-of-the-way camp thrived first as a placer mining center and later as gateway to the Calaveras Grove of Sequoia Giant trees. In the Murphy's (or Mitchler) Hotel, built in 1856 as the Sperry and Perry Hotel, one may still see in copies of old register books the signatures of Mark Twain, Henry Ward Beecher, Ulysses S. Grant, Black Bart and one "Old Dan the Guide" from "God Knows Where". When I first visited Murphy's as a college student an old-timer in the hotel bar pointed to two bullet holes in the door casing and confided, "That's where Joaquin Murieta shot it out with the sheriff." I dutifully examined the holes with appropriate awe, knowing that Joaquin's days had ended three years before the hotel was built.

On the north side of Main Street, other historic buildings include the Thompson building (late 1850s), the Thorpe bakery (1859), the Peter L. Traver building (1856) now housing the Old Timers Museum, and Victorene Compere's store (about 1860), all with the characteristic iron shutters. On the south side of Main Street near the Murphy Hotel is the Segale building, constructed as a store and bakery in 1856. The Putney-Sperry house (about 1857) at 518 Church Street is a fine example of an early Victorian residence. North of town on Sheep Ranch Road is St. Patrick's Catholic Church (1861), financed and built by the miners. The Murphy's grammar school (1860) served children for more than a century on the hill near Main and Jones Streets.

# Chapter 9. Columbia: Gem of the Southern Mines

EVEN IN THE GOLD RUSH, Columbia held a special place in California's heart. With her red brick face, wrought iron trimmings and myriad shade trees, she was the gaudy show-place of the Mother Lode. To the boys she was like a beautiful, if slightly tarnished, woman—the toast of the mines.

The years have not dimmed Columbia's reputation. Though the throbbing life which once surged through her streets is gone, she is today the ghost town supreme to Californians. In 1945 the state park system took over the crumbled camp and restored her faded charm as a monument to California's golden era.

Columbia was not quite a Forty-niner camp. Nearby Sonora was born in the summer of 1848, but two winters passed before prospectors struck the Columbia treasure. In March 1850 a party headed by Dr. Thaddeus Hildreth found gold in a dry gulch; in the next two days they took out thirty pounds of gold (worth some $4680) and started one of the biggest stampedes of the Gold Rush. Since the discovery spot lay in the heart of the teeming Southern Mines, it mush-roomed overnight. Within a month, according to reports, population jumped from zero to 5,000—one of the most tumultuous rushes on record.

Out of this explosive beginning sprang a town that astounded California with its headlong growth. By 1852 she still wore a board-and-canvas look, but she had no less than four banks, three express offices, eight hotels, a daguerreo-type parlor, 17 general stores, two fire companies, 40 saloons, numerous fandango houses, 43 faro tables with a combined capital approaching $2 million—and withal such badly-needed institutions as three churches, a Sunday school, two book-stores, a temperance group and a choral society.

Outside communication was provided by pony riders of the "Chain Lightning Express", covering the thirty miles from Knight's Ferry in the less-than-lightning time of three hours. Eight stages brought passengers from the nearest connection at Sonora. And in the height of the boom, the four miles between the twin cities was solidly lined with miners' shanties.

For all her roughness, Columbia believed in culture. She had three theatres, including a Chinese version with 40 Oriental actors. Most elaborate was the Exchange, where Edwin Booth played Richard III. In this festooned emporium, its stage decorated by a pine sapling growing up through the boards, William and Caroline Chapman delighted Columbia audiences night after night. The whooping miners flung gold purses to the players on opening night until the stage was literally covered; threw so much silver coinage on succeeding nights that they created a shortage in town for several months; and finally escorted the Chapmans in triumph to their next engagement in Sonora.

Irrepressible Columbia never did things halfway. When word reached camp that the first woman was arriving, the boys dropped their shovels, decorated Main Street with arches, took the brass band and marched down to Sonora several thousand strong to provide an escort.

Like other Sierra camps, Columbia put decent women on a marble pedestal. Word got around that Big Annie, a notorious madame, had pushed the town schoolmarm into the street. The outraged fire boys dragged their machine to Annie's place and washed the old girl out of the building. Columbia chivalry could do no more.

The town's first chance for a big celebration came on Independence Day, 1851. Sonora, still the metropolis of the Southern Mines, had just been laid waste by fire, and all of Tuolumne County gathered at Columbia for the Fourth. The town seized the opportunity with fervor. From every roof waved the stars and stripes, with others hung across Main Street. There was, according to one eye-witness, "a continual discharge of revolvers, and a vast expenditure of powder and squids and crackers, together with an unlimited consumption of brandy."

But this was merely the informal phase of celebration. The official event was launched with a grand parade consisting of: the Columbia brass band; the teachers and pupils of the town school, who sang hymns whenever the musicians "had blown themselves out of breath"; 100 or more Masons in full regalia; a long cavalcade of horsemen, including "whoever could get a four-legged animal to carry him," with "horses, mules and jackasses" thrown in together; a hook-and-ladder brigade; several hundred miners walking in pairs, each dragging a wheelbarrow containing pick, shovel, frying pan, coffee-pot and tin cup—symbols of mining life; and finally another gang pulling a long tom on wheels, while several pretended to be operating it with much flourish of shovels. All of this was greeted with cheering and catcalling from the sidelines.

The whole procession wound up at the town arena, which usually served for bull-and-bear fights. Here, while the band appropriately played *Hail, Columbia!* the celebrants took their seats for the solemn program, consisting of the reading of the Declaration of Independence and the Fourth of July oration. This was delivered in rousing fashion by what an observer described as "a pale-faced, chubby-cheeked young gentleman, with very white and extensive shirt-collars." The fledgeling spellbinder covered everything from Plymouth Rock to George III, until his restless audience raised some unceremonious shouts, "—Gaas, gaas!" Then, after a chorus of dinner bells had called the boys to a meal, the festivities were capped by the Latin touch—a bull fight.

The orator may well have been James Wood Coffroth, a man of unbounded optimism, good cheer and personal ambition. Known as "Columbia's favorite son," he was described as the "jolliest, freest, readiest man that ever faced a California audience. . . the typical politician of early-day California."

Arriving in the mines the previous year at the age of 21, Coffroth had applied for work at the *Sonora Herald* office with the modest acknowledgement that he was a "Philadelphia editor". They had him busy writing poetry and editorials, both of which he finished off with fantastic rhetoric.

Finally several irate gamblers invaded the *Herald* office on a question of editorial policy, and one of the bullets barely missed the editorial writer. Coffroth took up law.

By the end of '51 young Coffroth had settled in the booming Columbia camp, a promising attorney with an impromptu legal education. He quickly got himself elected to the state Assembly, then to the Senate. His rise was not hindered by a fine flair for publicity. In 1855 he challenged a man to a duel for slandering his character to a lady and "interference in my private affairs"; the other refused, but Coffroth got his satisfaction in the liberal amounts of free newspaper space. Yet it was said of him that he "never had a personal enemy, " and his easy-going humor was famous. When he was boomed for governor, Coffroth said that his reason for running was that he wanted to pardon his many friends in the state prison.

Coffroth had no intention of letting all this personal talent go to waste. He threw it into the stream of Columbia history whenever occasion offered. His first opportunity to sway events came when a knifing scrape stirred Columbia in November 1853. Pete Nicholas, an Austrian miner, had drunk himself into a fighting mood when he encountered John Parote, a citizen of nearby Pine Log, in a Main Street store. Pete grabbed Parote, who tried to struggle free; he struck his assailant and fell back over a sugar sack, pulling Nicholas with him. Pete produced a knife and stabbed his victim, who fell back unconscious. Pete was arrested and held prisoner to await trial.

This episode was a familiar story in rough-and-tumble Columbia, but now her citizens decided it was too familiar. Besides, the men of Pine Log marched into town ready to wreak justice in the name of their friend, Parote. Next morning Columbia calmly ate breakfast and then proceeded to drag Pete from the care of the town constable and down the street to a waiting tree. Just as the victim was about to be swung off his feet, the constable and his deputy climbed into the tree to cut the rope. Under their weight the limb broke, dropping everything to the ground. The crowd was equally determined, and brushing aside the officer, took the helpless prisoner to another tree.

At this timely moment appeared James Coffroth. Nicholas was his friend, and he hoped to stall the mob till the sheriff arrived. Gaining attention, he launched his speech. He was, said Coffroth, also anxious that justice be done. The murderer ought to be hanged—at this the boys nodded agreement.

"But for the everlasting honor of our glorious republic," added the speaker, "let all things be done decently and in order. . . . As a matter of course Nicholas will be hanged. . . . But for the credit of Columbia give the man a trial."

Coffroth's strategy worked. Before he had finished the sheriff arrived from Sonora, moved through the crowd organizing his deputies, and finally addressed the boys.

"Gentlemen, you will excuse me, but this man is going to the Sonora jail, there to await his trial by law. I am going to take him there."

The gentlemen thought different, and swarmed forward to grab the prisoner. But the sheriff's deputies held firm, and the mob was stopped at last. While the angry men cursed Coffroth and the sheriff, Nicholas was hauled off to Sonora. The following February he was tried and sentenced to hang. It looked as though Coffroth's promise would be fulfilled.

But by this time Pete had another lawyer who was as cunning as Coffroth. He knew that the entire state was then absorbed in the problem of choosing a permanent state capital. The legislature at Benicia was flooded with petitions from San Jose, Sacramento and other towns scrambling for the honor. Not to be outdone, the boys of Pine Log got up a petition to make their camp the state capital and circulated it throughout the county. After it had gained 10,000 signatures, Pete's lawyer saw it on a store counter in Columbia one day and quietly stuffed it in his pocket. Back in his office, he tore off the original heading and substituted a plea for commutation of Pete's death sentence. Then he sent it off by pony rider to Governor John Bigler at Benicia.

Mr. Bigler had never heard of Pete Nicholas, but he did recognize 10,000 votes when he saw them. He didn't know that some of the very names on the petition were those of the men who had helped fix the noose around Pete's neck. Any man who had the confidence of 10,000 neighbors, he decided, couldn't be all bad. The governor commuted Pete's sentence to ten years' imprisonment—a term that was later reduced to four.

Columbia was cheated of justice, but she went along with the joke. In fact, she embellished it into an even more fantastic legend that still persists in California. Columbia, it is claimed, missed becoming the state capital by two votes.

As the decade of the '50s faded, so did Columbia's golden treasure. Shouldering pick and blankets, the boys answered the call of richer stakes. By 1867 an observer reported "almost total desertion" of the once fabulous town.

COLUMBIA. As one of the earliest to become a ghost town, Columbia is a wonderful outdoor museum of the Gold Rush. First visiting point is the museum of the California Department of Parks and Recreation. Here you can obtain guide literature and directions from a park ranger before exploring this charming town of red bricks, iron shutters and fancy grillwork. Some of the key buildings are the City Hotel (1856), the Wells Fargo building (1858), the Odd Fellows Hall (1855), the Fallon hotel and theater (about 1860), a replica of the *Columbia Gazette* newspaper office (1855), the restored school house (1860) north of town, St. Anne's Catholic Church (1857) south of town, two saloons, two firehouses, a blacksmith shop and a tiny wooden jail house. A number of old buildings are operated as stores, restaurants and inns.

---

# Chapter 10. Sonora: Queen of the Southern Mines

"SONORA IS A FAST PLACE and no mistake." wrote a citizen of 1851. "We have more gamblers, more drunkards, more ugly, bad women, and larger lumps of gold, and more of them, than any other place of similar dimensions within Uncle Sam's dominions."

In her Gold Rush heydey, Sonora was a city of superlatives. With a permanent population of 5,000, she was the biggest in the Southern Mines. With an all-time yield well into the nine figures from Tuolumne County mines, she was possibly the richest. And with an average of around one unpunished murder a week, she was certainly the wildest.

Though more than 60 miles south of the discovery site at Coloma, Sonora was one of the first Mother Lode camps. Among the original Forty-eighters were Mexicans from the state of Sonora. As early as August they found rich placers on the Stanislaus and Tuolumne Rivers, and settled what came to be called the Sonorian Camp.

It proved a fabulous treasure. The gold was coarse and nuggets were frequent. In the first months, men were taking out several ounces apiece daily.

This kind of news traveled fast. By early 1849, Sonora was no longer a Mexican camp. American miners jammed the decks of river steamers to Stockton, then raised a continuous cloud of dust on the trail to the new diggings. At night, campfires lighted the road all the way from Stockton to Sonora. By the end of '49 there were over 10,000 Mexicans and 4,000 Americans and Europeans in the Sonora district.

From then on, the town was the most cosmopolitan center in the mines. Its streets were lined with a conglomeration of Spanish-type adobes, with their overhanging balconies, and American frame buildings of high false fronts. Its saloons and gambling dens were lavishly decorated with crystal chandeliers and sexy paintings. Entertainment varied from brass bands to strolling guitarists to a lady piano player "in black velvet who sings in Italian." On Sunday, a day reserved for merrymaking, the visitor could take in anything from a bullfight to a circus.

From the moment the Forty-niners arrived, Sonora's day of peace and plenty was over. The lusty Americans, convinced of a divine right to dominate the continent, had just had their belief confirmed by the Mexican War. California was theirs, and they had no intention of letting the best mines fall to Mexicans, whether from Sonora or California. There followed a shameful campaign of abuse against the "foreigners."

111

At first the Mexicans gave up their claims without a fight, but in July 1849, 1,500 more of them reached the Tuolumne diggings. In the clash that followed, Sonora was the storm center. Many of the persecuted Mexicans took to outlawry and preyed on their tormentors. Within one month twelve murders were committed in and around Sonora.

This explosive situation was capped in June 1850, when the state Legislature passed a law requiring a $30 tax from all foreign miners—an open jab at the Mexican population.

When the collector arrived in Sonora to levy his iniquitous tax, the fireworks began. Thousands of Mexicans in the district held meetings, denounced the tax, and swore to defy the authorities. At this, the Americans armed themselves and marched into Sonora, where they organized a rifle company and set up a night patrol in the streets. Mexican guerrillas stepped up their raids; miners slept with their gold dust under their pillows, but even then thieves dared to rob them. The men camping on the hillside above town took turns standing watch through the night.

"No man dreams of travelling without the pistol and the knife," reported the *Sonora Herald*.

On July 10, in the midst of this tension, miners at a nearby camp discovered three Indians and a Mexican burning the bodies of two Americans. Concluding that the four were the murderers, the enraged men marched them into Sonora and turned the town into a frenzy.

While the prisoners were given a preliminary hearing, hundreds of angry citizens gathered at the courthouse. The accused were abruptly snatched away and borne to a tree on a nearby hill. Here the mob selected a jury, help a rump court, and found the four guilty. Ropes were looped around their necks and the Mexican was already swinging in the air when four county officials broke through the crowd and halted the lynching. In a moment Sheriff George Work and a deputy were backing them up with leveled revolvers. The miners grudgingly parted ranks and let the four go to jail.

Four days later, while Sonora still seethed, a rumor ran through town that a number of Mexican guerrillas—allies of the prisoners—were camped several miles away. The sheriff then struck out with 20 armed riders and came back with no less than 110 Mexican prisoners—all murder suspects. They were herded into a corral to await examination. Next day, when the four original captives were to be tried, a thousand more miners marched into town from the hills to make the confusion complete.

That afternoon the courthouse was packed with armed citizens for the opening of the trial. In that anxious moment a pistol went off accidentally. Pandemonium took over. A hundred guns were out and the shooting was general. The courthouse instantly disgorged its contents by every door and window. Out of the buildings in Sonora's streets men came running with revolver and rifle, some of them shooting at several Mexican bystanders.

Amid the dust and smoke, the district attorney mounted a stump in the street and pleaded for order. When the crisis had passed, the only blood was found to be on the wrist of the original shooter.

Somewhat sheepishly, the Sonora crowd settled down to wait out the trial. Finally it was determined that the four prisoners had found the two bodies several days after the murder, and had been cremating them according to their religious custom—as an act of charity. As for the 110 Mexicans in the corral, they were each examined, exonerated, and in the words of the presiding judge, sent "joyfully homeward." Most of them, having arrived at the mines only a few days before, gained a rather negative first impression.

But Sonora's temper still raged. With rumors reaching town of more murders, a mass meeting was held July 20—attended by several thousand armed miners. Lacking any murder suspects, they vented their anger on Mexicans in general. Resolutions were passed ordering all foreigners to get out of Tuolumne County in 15 days, and furthermore, to give up their firearms. They might avoid either penalty by getting a permit from a committee of three Americans in each camp, who would decide which aliens were "persons engaged in permanent business and of respectable characters."

For several days after this fanatical outburst, Sonora was an armed camp. At night guards stood watch at the edges of town to meet a surprise attack. The banishment order was actually enforced in a few outlying camps, but most harassed Mexicans needed no invitation to leave. Two hundred of them, all with pack burros and some with families, passed through Sonora on their way back to Mexico—a sorrowful and disillusioned company.

By September, with three-fourths of the Mexicans gone, Sonora was a dead town. With its population shrunk from five thousand to three thousand, it lapsed into hard times. The *Sonora Herald* suspended for lack of patronage, and one citizen noted with relief that in six weeks "there have been only two men shot in our streets."

In 1851 the foreign miners tax was repealed, and Mexicans felt a measure of safety in Tuolumne County. But Sonora's big boom had been killed by mobocracy at its worst.

Still, the Queen of the Southern Mines was not downed this easily. Center of a galaxy of lesser mining camps, she was soon gaining a degree of refinement that set her apart from her rougher neighbors. In Sonora the traveler could get decent lodging in several clean hotels, could even enjoy that almost forgotten luxury, ice cream. With snow regularly packed in on mules from the higher mountains, even the drinks were iced.

On Sundays the population, miners and all, turned out in its best attire. The most striking item of dress was a bright silk neckerchief—usually red—tied loosely over the chest and hung over one shoulder. Some local dandies had their broad-brimmed hats decked with feathers, flowers, or squirrels' tails. Many tried to outdo each other with fancy whisker styles; some beards were braided and coiled up "like a twist of tobacco," while others were separated into three tails that reached to the belt. One extremist divided his long beard in two and tied it in a big bow under his chin, where it served as a necktie.

The reason for all this foppery in the midst of the Gold Rush was obvious enough. In yard after yard on Sonora's residential streets, clotheslines were now hung with dresses and petticoats.

"Time was," observed the *Sonora Herald* in July 1852, "when the presence of virtuous women in the mines was a thing wished for, not enjoyed."

Even this was not the most striking evidence of Sonora's orderliness, according to one visitor who had traveled the length of the Mother Lode. When he saw a policeman collar a disorderly drunk and march him sternly off to jail, he knew he had reached civilization.

The magistrate of old Sonora was a priceless character, Major Richard C. Barry—a veteran of the Texas war of independence and the Mexican War. A stocky, red-faced frontiersman, Barry became Justice of the Peace in 1850 and brought Sonora a certain amount of order—but no law. Ignorant, prejudiced, bullheaded, and inordinately proud, Barry was the legal dictator of Tuolumne County. His surviving docket, kept on scraps of paper, records the most amazing justice court ever operating under the United States Constitution. Take the case of Jesus Ramirez, who was charged with no less an offense than stealing a mule from the sheriff, George Work. Reported Justice Barry:

"George swares the Mule in question is hisn and I believe so to on heering the caze I found Jesus Ramirez guilty of feloaniusly and against the law made and provided and the dignity of the people of Sonora steeling the aforesade mare Mule sentesed him to pay the costs of Coort 10 dolars, and fined him a 100 dolars more as a terrour to all evel dooers. Jesus Ramirez not having any munney to pay with I rooled that George Work shuld pay the costs of Court, as well as the fine. . . ."

For some reason, this admirable arrangement brought protest:

"H. P. Barber, the lawyer for George Work in solently told me there were no law fur me to rool so I told him that I didn't care a damn for his book law, that I was the Law myself. He jawed back so I told him to shetup but he wouldn't so I fined him 50 dolars, and comited to gaol for 5 days for contempt of Coort in bringing my rooling and dississions into disreputableness and as a warning to unrooly citizens not to contredict this Coort."

Sonora's days of frontier justice are gone, but unlike most gold camps of the Southern Mines, she is still a thriving city—the center of a mining, lumbering and orchard country.

### POINTS OF INTEREST

SONORA. With its many old buildings and its narrow streets that wind among its hills, Sonora is one of the most picturesque of Mother Lode towns. Many of the historic buildings are on Washington Street (Jackson Street divides south and north Washington). Some of those dating from the Gold Rush are the Gunn House (lower floor, 1850) at 286 S. Washington, where Sonora's first newspaper, the *Herald*, was published; the Linoberg building (1856) at 87 S. Washington, an early home of Wells Fargo; Servente's building (1856) at 64 S. Washington, with its unique cast-iron front; the Odd Fellows Hall (1853) at the north end of Washington Street; and St. James Episcopal Church (1860) at the junction of Washington and Snell streets. Others are St. Patrick's Catholic Church (1863) at 127 Jackson; the Cady home (1850s) at 72 N. Norlin St.; and the Sugg-McDonald House (1857) at 37 Theall Street; its lower story was made from adobe bricks by William Sugg, a black pioneer whose descendants occupied the house for more than 120 years. Information on the many other historic structures from the

1850s and later can be obtained at the Visitors Center, 94 N. Washington, and the Tuolumne County Museum (built 1857 and rebuilt 1866) at 198 W. Bradford, which was the county jail for more than a century. The visitor is well rewarded by a walk along the residential streets, where one is charmed both by the well-kept Victorian homes and by the unhurried, neighborly ways of their inhabitants.

JAMESTOWN. The covered balcony architecture typical of the best-preserved Mother Lode towns is never more boldly displayed than in Jamestown, which still carries the look of the California mining frontier. Though most of the prominent frame buildings are of a later vintage, a few brick, stone, and adobe structures date from the days of gold. Among these are the National Hotel (1859) and A. B. Preston's meat market (late 1860s).

KNIGHT'S FERRY. On Highway 120 southwest of Jamestown is Knight's Ferry, where William Knight started the first ferry over the Stanislaus River on the road from Stockton to Sonora. The present covered bridge, one of the few remaining in California, dates from 1862. Other points of interest are the remains of the flour mill, saw mill, and woolen mill located west of the bridge. Another is the old Dent House, where Ulysses S. Grant visited his brother-in-law in 1854. Knight's Ferry was also the center of placer mining along the lower river, and was the seat of Stanislaus County from 1862 to '72.

CHINESE CAMP The thick growth of "Trees of Heaven" planted by its Oriental pioneers tends to obscure at first glance several old buildings in Chinese Camp. They include ruins of the Wells Fargo building, the stone-and-brick U.S. Post Office (1854), St. Francis Xavier Catholic Church (first built 1855), and Rosenbloom's Store. Despite its name, Chinese Camp was equally well populated by Americans and Europeans at its heyday in the 1850s.

TABLE MOUNTAIN. The plain at the foot of this mesa, located north of Chinese Camp, is supposed to be the field where some 2,000 Chinese staged a battle with spears, knives, tridents, and a few muskets on the morning of September 16, 1856. After several hours of combat the casualties were four killed and four wounded.

BIG OAK FLAT.   The northernmost approach from the Mother Lode to Yosemite National Park takes its name from this town. Among several historic rock structures still standing are the Odd Fellows Hall (lower story, 1852 and '54); the Gamble Block (early 1850s), which housed the Wells Fargo office in one of its three rooms; the Gamble-Harper home (oldest part built in the 1850s) near the corner of Highway 120 and Scofield Street; and the Catholic Church (first built in 1861 and later reconstructed) on the east side of town. As for the Big Oak Flat Road to Yosemite, it's an interesting drive, but don't take it if you're in a hurry.

GROVELAND.   First called Garrote because of a hanging that occurred here (garrote is Spanish for "strangle").   Today Groveland presents many 19th Century buildings.   Some dating from the Gold Rush are, on the north side of Main Street, Reboul's Trading Post and restaurant (adobe built between 1849 and '52); and on the south side, the Watts & Tannahill two-story adobe building and stone mercantile store (both about 1851), and the adobe Groveland Inn (between 1849 and '52).

SECOND GARROTE. Here are two examples of how the many Mother Lode myths are born.
   In a two-story house located here lived two men whose careers paralleled those in Bret Harte's famous tale, *Tennessee's Partner*; speculation that they were the actual source of the story has been embellished to the point where the house

has been claimed as the one-time home of Bret Harte.

At the edge of this tiny hamlet is a Hangman's Tree where, it is solemnly reported, 60 men were executed.

No firsthand historical evidence has been advanced to support either of these notions.

---

# Chapter 11. Mariposa: Mother Lode Outpost

THERE IS NOTHING ghostly about the Mother Lode town of Mariposa. American tourists passing through it on the road to Yosemite are unaware that this was a flourishing camp before white men entered the famous valley. For Mariposa today is a community of commercial signs and automobiles and busy stores. Ghost towns, perhaps, at nearby Hornitos, Mt. Bullion and Bear Valley—but not Mariposa.

From the beginning this locality has dared to be different. Situated at the extreme southern end of the Mother Lode, it was one of the few camps founded on a Spanish rancho. And it was here that miners first abandoned placer mining in the stream beds and struck pick in the actual Mother Lode.

The big man of old Mariposa was that California immortal, Col. John C. Frémont. After playing his part in the conquest of the territory during the Mexican War, Frémont decided to settle down near San Francisco Bay. In 1847 he sent $3,000 to the American consul and asked that he buy a certain ranch near San Jose. What he got was Rancho Las Mariposas, known as the Mariposa or Butterfly. It was a mammoth tract of 45,000 acres in what was then a wild and worthless region. Frémont angrily demanded either the San Jose ranch or his $3,000. He got neither.

Two years later, Frémont's cast-off rancho turned out to be

the richest one in California. The tumultuous wave of fortune-seekers that descended on the Mother Lode in the spring of 1849 spread as far south as Mariposa—and found placer gold. In August prospectors uncovered the fabulous Mariposa vein—a section of the vast Mother Lode—and began hard rock mining.

Frémont complained no more. Next month he was in San Francisco waving rock samples and boasting of Mariposa's treasure.

This was exciting news for gold-mad Californians. The unknown quartz ledge which they knew had yielded the rich gravel of Sierra streams had now been discovered! A bigger quartz strike was soon to be made at Grass Valley in the Northern Mines, but this was Mariposa's hour.

Down to this southernmost outpost came the gold hunters—afoot, horseback, or by wagon and team. From San Francisco they took steamer for Stockton on the San Joaquin, then pushed on by trail for Mariposa. From the mines they passed through Angel's Camp and Sonora, crossed the Tuolumne and Merced Rivers to reach the diggings.

It made no difference that this was Frémont's land. The new Mariposans founded their town on that frontier institution, "squatter's rights." But Frémont was less worried about the townsite than the mining claims. Since his rancho was one of those "floating grants" without definite boundaries, gold seekers were freely staking out ground and claiming that it was outside Frémont's territory. They charged instead that Frémont arbitrarily extended his borders to cover every new strike. It was the one big point at which Spanish titles clashed with the Gold Rush.

Mariposa's ore was so rich that claim-jumping had been a favorite pastime from the start. Around March 1850, a party of Missourians drove ox teams into Mariposa flat, took up claims on the creek, and seized the property of the nearest neighbors. The victims then went upstream and secured the services of the newly-elected peace officer—a tall and robust

Kentuckian. He first went down and tried to reason with the claim-jumpers, who defied him in appropriate language.

Next morning the Kentuckian was back—this time with 90 armed miners anxious for excitement. Before he could restrain them, they jumped into the holes and threw the Missourians' tools across the flat. Then, while the officer tried to calm them, they told the interlopers to get out of camp or see all their equipment wrecked. With mighty oaths the Missourians yoked up their animals and drove off. Justice in the California mines was sometimes crude, but usually effective.

Meanwhile, Mariposa was stricken with worse troubles than claim-jumping. Rumors reached the settlement that Indians of the Sierra foothills were planning to drive out the American intruders. One of the leaders at Mariposa was James D. Savage, who operated trading posts on Mariposa Creek and the Fresno River. On a trip to San Francisco he took with him an Indian chief, in order to impress him with the strength of the whites and the folly of attacking them.

When they returned, Savage found the Indians already on the warpath. A party of whites had been murdered near Mariposa. Other Argonauts were forced to pay tribute in order to pass through unmolested. Savage hurriedly called a conference of Indians in front of his store and warned them of the dreadful consequences of a war on the Americans.

"A chief who has returned with me," he concluded, "from the place where the white men are so numerous can tell you that what I have said is true."

But the chief's part was unrehearsed. He stepped up and astonished Savage by telling his tribesmen that if they would unite in a war, "all the gold diggers could be driven from the country." At this the Indians gathered around in ready approval while one chief solemnly pronounced, "My people are now ready to begin a war against the white gold diggers."

Savage could hardly take time to kick himself for his blunder. He pulled out of Mariposa with a warning to the miners of imminent attack. In quick succession the Indians

121

pillaged his Fresno River store and two other Mariposa County trading posts.

Hurriedly the Americans formed a company and retaliated by surprising a large Indian village near the North Fork of the San Joaquin. While the victims ran out of their burning wigwams, the Americans shot 24 of them, including the chief. With this merciless blow, the shooting phase of the Mariposa Indian War was ended.

But meanwhile the whole state feared a general Indian uprising. The governor called for a volunteer militia to take the field, and most of the men in Mariposa County joined up. Electing James Savage as their major, they formed the famous Mariposa Battalion. Early in 1851 Savage led his men through winter snows to track down the remaining tribes and make an enforced peace. They rounded up the Indians, but they also penetrated far enough into the Sierra to find a breath-taking valley of towering cliffs and magnificent waterfalls. And so the Mariposa Battalion's historic fame lies not so much in its Indian fighting, but in the effective discovery of Yosemite.

Beginning in the mid-'50s, the Mariposa country was torn by new strife over Frémont's rancho. Since the exact boundaries of his grant were undetermined, Frémont had them surveyed to include Mariposa, Bear Valley, and much of the richest mining property. Men who had worked this ground for years while the ownership was unsettled were now outraged. In 1857 one group, the Merced Mining Company, "jumped" Frémont's Black Drift and Josephine Mines. Shunning violence, he counterattacked with a lawsuit.

Irresistibly, The Butterfly was leading him further into the financial woods. And while the lawyers fought in court, the Merced outfit cast covetous eyes on Frémont's third and last mine, the Pine Tree.

Into this tense situation the explorer brought his wife and family in the summer of 1858. Settling in a cottage behind Bear Valley, the group consisted of Jessie, her three children and several young friends. While Frémont busied himself with his mine, Jessie and the others made up a gay and carefree company, riding horseback by day, holding sprightly conversation in the evenings. For the cultivated Jessie it was an adventurous contrast to the drawing rooms of Washington and Paris.

Within a few weeks this idyllic life was rudely shattered by the hard realities of the Gold Rush. In the small hours of July 9, more than 50 Merced Company men rode grimly through Bear Valley and pressed on for the Pine Tree Mine.

This time Frémont was ready for them. Working deep within the blackness were six well-armed men. When the Merced party swooped down upon the entrance, these defenders held the advantage of position. With boulders and mining equipment they threw up breastworks inside the tunnel mouth. Barrels of gunpowder were rolled into place. Before they would give up the mine, hollered the Frémonters, they would blow up the entrance!

Balked by this stubborn handful, the Merced army turned to new strategy. The main force camped on the level ground before the tunnel entrance. Guards were posted higher up the mountainside at the Black Drift, which connected with the Pine Tree workings deep inside the earth. Others were stationed at every trail to cut off outside communication. They would lay siege to Frémont's mine.

Before dawn word of the attack reached Frémont at his ranch house. Outraged, he still kept his soldier's cool head. While Jessie and the family slept, he held a council of war with his lieutenants. The veteran warrior was almost enjoying the challenge.

"They'll find," he snapped with a satisfied smile, "they have jumped the wrong man."

Mustering some 27 men, Frémont promptly besieged the besiegers. His force was soon guarding the Pine Tree road behind the Merced men, cutting off their line of supply. Though outnumbered two to one, Frémont's men announced they were "prepared to die sooner than yield a single hair."

And so the silent war began—each side overawing the other. Sheriff Crippin of Mariposa County arrived and ordered the Merced men to disperse. Openly ignored, he rode off to Mariposa and returned later with a handful of warrants. Only four men surrendered. When the sheriff rode back into town with this pitiful haul, the *Mariposa Gazette* demanded that he raise a citizen's posse.

"Unless it be done." cried the editor, "all law-loving people might as well leave the county at once."

The realistic Frémont had already abandoned hope of local help. He was sending messengers to the governor in Sacramento, calling for the state militia. But the Merceders guarded every ford and pass. As Frémont's riders galloped out, they were as quickly intercepted.

In this situation, the young people of Frémont's cottage were eager to act. One of them, a young Englishman named Douglas Fox, rode into the brush and managed to elude the enemy sentries. At Coulterville he roused help; other riders pounded across San Joaquin Valley to Stockton, where telegraph lines hummed with Frémont's message to the governor.

But until a reply could arrive, the desperate siege continued. After four days the Merceders tried another tactic. To Frémont's ranch they sent a letter, offering to pull out if he would remove his own men from the mine and leave it in charge of a neutral committee until the lawsuit was settled, Next day Frémont's defiant refusal was read aloud to the sullen Merced crowd.

"The demand you make upon me." he declared," is contrary to all my sense of justice and what is due to my own honor."

Warned also that the governor had been notified, the Mercedera now stirred themselves to action, Since the Pine Tree opening was well guarded by Frémont's men, it was resolved to take them from behind through the connecting chambers of the Black Drift. But on the night of the assault the colonel's outside force overheard the plan. A towering, broad-shouldered Frémonter, weighted down with fighting equipment, appeared out of the brush and deliberately walked past the Merceders to the mouth of the Pine Tree.

"Sandy." he shouted, "look out for the Black Drift."

With a chorus of clicks, a battery of Merced rifles cocked for action. The man's bold move had caught the enemy off guard. But slowly he moved back across the clearing and disappeared in the underbrush. The Merceders still could not fire the first shot.

Desperate, they now switched to a final strategem. Frémont's wife and family were sheltered a few miles away. Threaten the ranch house, and the colonel would surely divert his forces to the rescue. Then the Pine Tree would fall into Merced hands.

Next day a messenger came to Jessie Frémont's door, giving her and the family 24 hours to flee before the ranch would be burned. But far from alarming the colonel, brave Jessie sent back a note, stalling for time. A few hours later, before the plotters could carry out their threat, a messenger from Sacramento was pounding up the trail to the Pine Tree. To the Merced men in the clearing, the governor's command was terse and pointed: Disperse, or he would send in the militia.

Their attack already foiled by the courage of the Frémonters, the Merced men were ready to quit. For five days they had held a bear by the tail. The governor's order now gave them a graceful means of letting go. Back over the Pine Tree trail rode the Merced army. They had, indeed, jumped the wrong man.

The ordeal was too much for Jessie. Frémont did his best to make Bear Valley a gracious home. Among the distinguished visitors they entertained in the following months were Horace Greeley and Richard Henry Dana. But the charm of the place had been broken. In the spring of 1859 Frémont bought Jessie a home in San Francisco. And although he won his lawsuit against the Merced Company, the colonel himself was soon to leave Mariposa forever. No businessman, he found himself in financial troubles that cost him control of the rancho in 1861. Before he turned his back on The Butterfly, it had cost him the best years of his life.

## POINTS OF INTEREST

MARIPOSA. At this gateway to Yosemite stands one of the prize landmarks of the Mother Lode, the Mariposa County Courthouse. Built in 1854, it is the oldest continuously used county courthouse in California, and one of the few made of wood. This New England-style edifice, looking more like a country church than a courthouse, was the scene of the litigation over Frémont's Pine Tree Mine.

Other reminders of Mariposa's early days remain. In the center of town on the south side of Charles Street is the two-story Schlageter Hotel (1859), whose guest roster includes U.S. Grant and James Garfield. Next door is the John Trabucco building of early vintage, while the red brick Trabucco warehouse, dating from the gold era, stands across the road at the corner of Fifth Street. The Odd Fellows Hall (1867) is located at Charles and Sixth streets. On Bullion Street between Fourth and Fifth is the jail (1858), made of granite blocks from the intrusion which halts the Mother Lode vein two miles south of town. Farther south is St. Joseph's Catholic Church (1862), while at the County Fair Grounds off Highway 49 south of town is the California State Mining and Mineral Museum, with its dazzling display of gold rock samples and nuggets. On the north side of town on Jessie and 12th streets is the Mariposa Museum and History Center, offering a view of life in the gold days.

MORMON BAR. Two miles southeast of Mariposa is Mormon Bar, technically the lowermost camp on the Mother Lode. Founded by Mormons in 1849, it is marked today only by some crumbling adobe walls hidden among the trees and boulders on the east bank of Mariposa Creek.

COARSEGOLD. Proving that some spurs of the Mother Lode extended below Mariposa County is the settlement of Coarsegold, founded by Texans in 1849. First and largest among a number of Madera County placer camps, Coarsegold later became a center of hard rock mining.

HORNITOS. The tough reputation for the Mariposa district goes to Hornitos, which was founded by outcasts who were run out of the neighboring town of Quartzburg for the crime of being Mexicans. They formed their own community at Hornitos, which soon outgrew Quartzburg. Today Hornitos lives on as one of the best preserved ghost towns in the Mother Lode. In its heyday Hornitos was a wide-open camp whose streets were lined with fandango halls, bars, and gambling dens. One visitor of 1857 was walking past the sidewalk gaming tables when two players flashed knives at each other. The dealer then covered them with his pistol and suggested with evident logic that they could go somewhere else and finish the dispute without interrupting his game. Followed by a crowd, the pair adjourned to a nearby lot and fell upon each other with their knives.

Soon one of them staggered back covered with vicious wounds, tossed down a glass of brandy, and retook his seat at the card table. Despite this show of bravado, he was soon buried with his opponent in what the visitor called "Dead Man's Gulch".

This was Hornitos in the roaring Fifties. Today its turbulent spirit still lingers in the ruins of the old Wells Fargo office, the stone Masonic Hall (1856), the jailhouse, the store where the firm of D. Ghirardelli got its start in the 1850s, and other buildings of stone and adobe—most with the iron-shuttered doors and windows characteristic of Mother Lode towns.

LA GRANGE. Founded as a mining camp in 1852, La

Grange lived on as a commercial center and was for several years the seat of Stanislaus County. A few old structures still stand in this quaint village. For a time Bret Harte taught school at La Grange, and it is the probable setting for several of his short stories.

THE FRÉMONT COUNTRY. Driving north from Mariposa on Highway 49, one comes immediately into what might be called California's Frémont Country.

First locality is Mt. Bullion, named for Jesse Benton Frémont's father, Senator Thomas Hart Benton, who was nicknamed "Old Bullion" for his campaign to maintain hard currency.

Most important of the Frémont communities is Bear Valley, founded by the explorer as a company town for operation of his mines. Here are several old buildings and ruins of the 1850s, including the Bear Valley General Store (1850), the Simpson and Trabucco store (1857) and the Odd Fellows Hall (1852).

North of Bear Valley, a dirt road turns off to the left and doubles back to the mouth of Frémont's Pine Tree Mine, scene of siege and counter-siege. Finally, near where the highway crosses the deep gorge of the Merced River are the remains of Benton Mills, where Frémont dammed the river and milled his ore. These, too, he named for Thomas Hart Benton.

COULTERVILLE. Among the oak-dotted hills so typical of the Southern Mines, and roughly halfway from Jamestown to Mariposa on Highway 49, lies the picturesque town of Coulterville. Like some other ghost towns along the Mother Lode, Coulterville is returning to life with some businesses in its old buildings. A number of landmarks survive: the three-story Jeffery Hotel (oldest portion built of stone and adobe in 1851); the Barrett blacksmith shop (early 1850s); the Canova store (early 1860s) and warehouse (1870); the adobe Bruschi store (1853); and the Odd Fellows and Knights of Pythias halls. At the upper end of Main Street in what was then Chinatown is the adobe Sun Sun Wo store (1851). At the lower end of town across Highway 49 is the old Wells Fargo building (1856), now containing the Northern Mariposa County History Museum. In front of it is another so-called "Hanging Tree" and the "Whistling Billy" steam engine that pulled ore from the Mary Harrison Mine over four miles of track called "the crookedest railroad in the world."

# PART IV. THE NORTHERN MINES

*CALIFORNIA'S NORTHERN MINES were served by stagecoaches from the Feather River port of Marysville, as well as from Sacramento City itself. Often the Central Mines, located on the forks of the American River, were included by popular usage with the Northern Diggings. In any case, the latter extended northward to the Feather River, and they took in some of the finest scenery in California.*

*Here the gold towns, whether living or deserted, nestle in the most charming and often astounding spots—on the slopes of mountains, in the bottoms of steep canyons, alongside turbulent rivers. They are like the gold and silver camps of Colorado, and from a distance some of them with their gleaming church spires resemble forest-bound hamlets of middle Europe.*

*Also occasionally included among the Northern Mines is a whole empire of camps in the upper end of California's Coast Range. Founded between 1849 and '51, they represent a second rush within the bigger stampede to California from 1848 to '53.*

*If California ever had any frontier, it was this untamed country north and west of Sacramento Valley. For a time, to paraphrase an old Texas saying, there was no law north of the Pit River, no God north of the Trinity.*

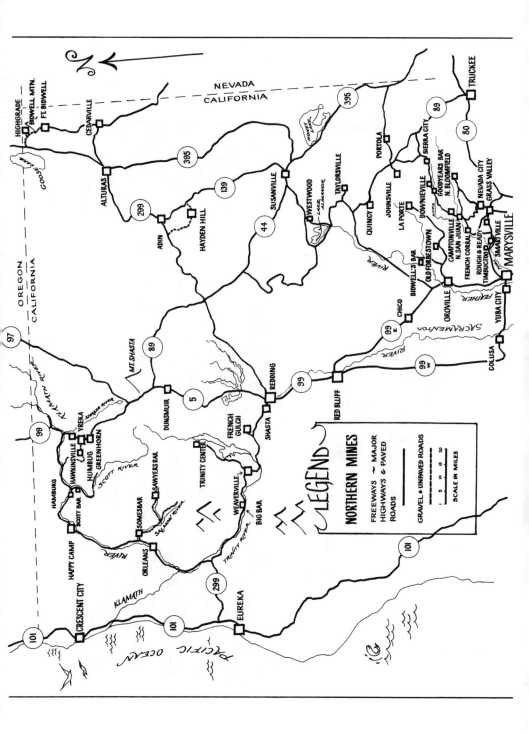

*Home office of the Coyote and Deer Creek Water Co., Nevada City, 1852.*

*Elbow room was rare in the mines when a rich pocket was found, 1851.*

*The backbreaking hand labor of moving tons of rock is temporarily suspended for the pleasure of the visiting daguerreotypists, 1851.*

*Elaborate flumes were constructed to turn river and expose rich sand bars, 1852.*

Courtesy of George Eastman House

*Grass Valley's first celebrity—internationally famous entertainer Lola Montez.*

*Gold is where you find it—best at your doorstep, Sugar Loaf Hill, Nevada City, 1852.*

*No gold-bearing stream could escape the swift appearing sluice boxes, Nevada City, 1852.*

*Johnsville, a latter-day gold town of the 1870's, remains a gem of the Northern mines.*

# Chapter 12. Grass Valley:
# Miner's Mining Town

LEAST GHOSTLY OF ANY TOWN on the Mother Lode is
Grass Valley, which for most of its life was called the greatest
mining city in the Far West. A place named Butte, Montana,
may dispute this. But Grass Valley was at least the biggest
mining town in California. In mid-19th Century it was the
eighth largest city in the state—bigger than Los Angeles, San
Diego and Oakland.

Unlike most mining camps, Grass Valley never really had a
decline and fall. Even in the depression, its streets and hotel
lobbies were bustling with mining men. One traveler of 1933
pronounced Grass Valley the one city in the United States
where you had to wire ahead for hotel reservations. Since the
Gold Rush the place has turned out upwards of $100 million
in gold. For many years  its Empire and Idaho-Maryland
mines were the second and third deepest gold mines (after the
Homestake of South Dakota) in the world.

Grass Valley is, moreover, the point which sparked the big
shift from placer to quartz mining in California. Situated a
scant 33 miles north of the discovery site at Coloma, the
Grass Valley streams were virtually ignored in the first two
Gold Rush years. A handful of men had worked the creeks
since 1848, but neither placer mining nor obscurity was to be
Grass Valley's lot.

Half the camps in the West were, according to tradition,
discovered while a prospector was chasing after his straying
burro. But Grass Valley rose before the day of jackass
prospectors, and in her case the animal was a cow. One day in
October 1850, a miner named George Knight followed his
wayward bossy as far as the pine-covered slope of Gold Hill.
There he stubbed his toe on a piece of quartz. In the custom
of all true miners, he scrutinized his providential find—and
promptly forgot about his cow. Back at his cabin he pounded

the rock into dust and panned out a bright showing of gold.

Immediately the original Grass Valley miners hurried up the hillsides. One of them found a small boulder worth $500. That was enough. The big rush to Grass Valley, and to the new business of shaft mining, was on.

Knight's discovery was not the first quartz mine in California. Lode mining, as contrasted to placer mining in the stream beds, had begun a year earlier at Mariposa, in the Southern Mines. But the Grass Valley strike can be called the effective discovery. It started the boom in shaft mining which eventually supplanted the placer workings.

Scarcely four miles away Nevada City, a flourishing placer town, suddenly went quartz mad. From all over the Mother Lode, miners hurried to Grass Valley by the hundreds. Demand for ore-crushing tools was so great that within a week all the hammers and anvils for 20 miles around were lugged into camp. Every pharmacy from Sacramento to San Francisco was relieved of its mortar and pestle. They all went to Grass Valley.

Soon came more elaborate machinery. Mexican miners, who knew about quartz mining, built arrastres—by which the ore was ground by millstones turned with one-mule power. Then came the stamp mills, which were simply gigantic, multi-barreled mortars and pestles operated by steam engine. They were not invented in Grass Valley, but were developed here to a fine point. By 1853, with its placer beds faltering, California was turning wholeheartedly to the job of tapping the underground source of gold.

It was at Grass Valley, too, that mining stock promotion was first perfected. The town was equally at home digging gold with shovels or stock certificates. The stock frenzy grew so uproarious that one newspaper burlesqued the whole business by advertising the "Munchausen Quartz Rock Mining and Crushing Company." with a board of directors including P. T. Barnum and Robinson Crusoe. Grass Valley was the original spot where one could apply Mark Twain's definition of a mine: "a hole in the ground owned by a liar."

But Grass Valley was never a phoney. In seven years' time Knight's original Gold Hill mine produced $4,000,000. Through the 1850s dozens of other mines were opened, yielding millions more. By 1853 Grass Valley was a city of 3,000, the bustling center of several daily stage lines, a hospitable town with a reputation for good hotels in a region where these were an oddity.

Hardrock mines—requiring capital, machinery and steady payrolls—had given Grass Valley a permanent air in contrast to the boom-and-bust placer towns. It was one of the first cities on the Mother Lode to temper its rough male population with an influx of wives and families. The civilizing effect was remarkable. Numerous churches—several of them still in use—were built in the 1850s. And it was one of the first mining camps to have a legitimate theater, even though it was fitted up in the Alta Saloon. Complete with footlights and orchestra, the "Grass Valley Theater" company played every night to a packed, exuberant house.

Though Grass Valley might have been partly refined, it was never quiet. In the early 1850s, one visitor strolled down the street on a Sunday morning and heard in close succession a streetside Church sermon, a mule auction, a street vendor selling tea, a drunken sailor singing *Auld Lang Syne* and a sidewalk dance by two Swiss girls to the tune of hand organ and tambourine. All this was in addition to the clank and clatter of the stamp mills which rang in the ears of Grass Valley night and day.

In September 1855 the thriving city was struck flat. An incendiarist kindled her wooden walls, and in two hours her entire 300 buildings were devoured in a furious blaze. With roofs crashing about them, the people rushed into the streets and made for the hillsides. It was known as the "million dollar fire"—probably the worst in the Mother Lode. But with their belongings and property wiped out, the Grass Valley people started anew before the ashes cooled. Next morning the Wells

Fargo agent rolled a portable shack up against his only surviving asset—a brick vault. With the ground still hot under him, he tacked up a sign and opened for business. Spurred by this example, the town turned to the job of rebuilding; soon a city of brick walls and iron shutters rose from the ruins. Modernized versions of these buildings, dating from 1855, are seen along Grass Valley's streets today.

The spirited town could hardly let this disaster pass without trying to catch its author. An innocent but disreputable citizen was seized and accused of the crime. An angry crowd gathered, and one bloodthirsty character demanded an immediate lynching. After all, he argued seriously, Grass Valley couldn't afford to let neighboring Nevada City, which had already had a hanging, run off with all the honors. This precious reasoning, which probably appealed to a certain element, was argued down. The man was set free after a trial.

But while there is no record of a lynching in Grass Valley, the town was far from dull. There's a story, for example, of a late poker game in the bar of the Peckham Hotel. A crowd gathered as the stakes mounted, and one of the onlookers was a rough-looking pioneer known as Old Mississippi. All at once an argument began. The players grabbed for the pot. A free-for-all fight followed, in which Old Mississippi was knocked to the floor. When things quieted down he propped himself on his elbow, exhibited a bloody face, and asked:

"I reckon there's been a row here, boys—hain't there?—is anybody hurt?"

With its dander up, Grass Valley was ready for anything. In the wet winter of 1852-53, roads from Sacramento were choked with mud and Grass Valley was almost isolated. Supplies were scarce, and what food there was sold at fantastic prices. So the embittered townsmen acted; they held a Hunger Convention at Beatty's Hotel. Awful maledictions were hurled at the "soulless speculators" in San Francisco who were cornering the food market. "We will," they resolved, "go to San Francisco and obtain the necessary supplies—peaceably if we can, forcibly if we must."

In this ugly mood, 100 men made ready to descend on the Bay City—until the question of financing the expedition came up. With this sobering thought the meeting adjourned, and the boys cooled their wrath until the weather cleared and new supplies arrived. Grass Valley would let San Francisco off, this time.

Rough and refined, primitive and civilized, Grass Valley was a city of violent contrasts that could only have been born of the California Gold Rush. But while it thought it had seen everything, Grass Valley was hardly prepared for the coming of Lola Montez.

The incomparable Lola, Countess of Landsfeldt, would have disrupted things anywhere. Dancer, actress, adventuress—she was the mistress of a king and the toast of mid-Century Europe. Born in Ireland, she had crashed the London stage as an exotic Spanish dancer with the assumed name, Lola Montez. From then on her life was a whirl of sensations, pretense and trouble. Ludwig I of Bavaria became infatuated with her, and bestowing the title of Countess of Landsfeldt, made her his mistress. For a time the fiery Lola was the power behind the throne—and not a particularly evil power, at that.

Then came the revolution of 1848, and while a student mob stormed the palace, Lola appeared in the window drinking champagne. Leaving Bavaria, she settled for a time in Paris. Here she is supposed to have given soirees that included such names as George Sand, Alexander Dumas and Victor Hugo.

In 1851 she came to America—probably for several reasons. For one, she had picked up two husbands in her travels, and faced a bigamy rap in London. Second, she was now past thirty and her charms were not increasing. Perhaps enthusiastic American audiences would be more appreciative.

New York, Philadelphia and Boston greeted her effusively, but the excitement soon wore thin. Her celebrated Spider

Dance, in which she released a skirtful of cork-and-rubber spiders at the climactic moment, naturally aroused interest. But while Lola was vivacious, she was not a brilliant dancer, and her acting was less than inspired. Her attraction lay in her striking beauty—particularly the flowing black hair and flashing eyes.

Still, Lola had been disappointed by her American reception. She craved above all things to be the center of attraction, even if this meant notoriety. She resolved next to go to California, where the rousing miners would surely do her justice. She invaded San Francisco with much fanfare in May 1853.

But the Bay City was already taking on a sophisticated air. While the audiences went wild, the critics sniffed at Lola's performances. By way of a dramatic exit, she took another husband and went to Sacramento. Here she was charivareed one night by a raucous mob, which she faced from the balcony with fierce epithets: "Cowards, low blackguards, cringing dogs and lazy fellows." A few days later a local editor slurred her dancing ability, and she challenged him to a duel—either with pistols or with the choice of two pills in a box (one of them deadly poison). But even this did not greatly impress Sacramento.

All of which explains why Lola, seeking an appreciative audience somewhere, wound up next in Grass Valley. With her husband and her reputation, she descended on Grass Valley in the fall of 1853 and scandalized the good ladies of the town. Settling in a house whose replica is still the most prided landmark of the city, she kept Grass Valley in a state of confusion for nearly two years. Her idiosyncrasies were the talk of the town—and of all California. She frequently strolled the streets, dressed in low-cut gowns and smoking a cigar. And she raised two grizzly bear cubs, which were kept chained in the front yard.

Grass Valley had a large European, and particularly French, population. So Lola also revived her Parisian hobby, the salon. Every evening her parlor was crowded with young blades of the town—holding sprightly conversation, drinking champagne and flirting with Lola. Her husband was obviously in the way, and she got rid of him. Besides, he had killed one of her pet grizzlies for biting him in the leg.

But Lola had her tender side. Among her neighbors was the Crabtree family, and little Lotta Crabtree was permitted to spend time with Lola, learning to sing and dance. It was the beginning of a stage career that was to win the acclaim of California and the nation. Lotta, the opposite of Lola in girlish innocence, was to outshine her teacher.

Lola might have got along with Grass Valley, but she could not keep out of the limelight. When a preacher condemned her spider dance, she went around to his house, knocked on the door, and went through the whole dance before his astonished eyes. Later the local newspaper offended her, so she horsewhipped the editor.

By 1855 Lola's antics were wearing hard in Grass Valley, and she was off for a new gold rush in Australia. Six years later she died in poverty in New York—an event which sentimental California noted with more generosity than it did her personal appearance.

### POINTS OF INTEREST

GRASS VALLEY. Rebuilt of brick after the fire of 1855, the center of modern Grass Valley contains many buildings dating from the gold days. Among these are the Union Square Building (early 1860s) at 151 Mill Street; the Empire Livery Stable (1855) at 115 Mill Street; the Holbrooke Hotel (1855 and 1862) at 212 W. Main Street; and a few doors east, the Loutzenheiser Pharmacy (1855), where two merchants settled their differences in a duel in 1867. The side and back streets hold some interesting residences, including a replica of the home of Lola Montez (original built in 1852) at 248 Mill

Street, now a history museum and the chamber of commerce; and the home of Lotta Crabtree (early 1850s) at 238 Mill Street, now a private residence. The Emmanuel Episcopal Church at 245 S. Church Street has served its parishioners steadily since 1858.

On lower Mill Street just past the entrance to Allison Ranch Road is the Nevada County Historical Mining Museum, housed in the old power station of the North Star Mine. In the hills across the Highway 49 freeway from Grass Valley is the Empire Mine State Park at 10791 E. Empire Street. Here you can visit one of the oldest and certainly the richest of the hard-rock mines in California, as well as the spacious Bourne mansion or "Empire Cottage", occupied as a summer home for decades by the owners of the mine.

ROUGH AND READY. West of Grass Valley on Highway 20, this once-thriving gold town bears the nickname of General Zachary Taylor. The founding group that arrived in 1849 was headed by an officer who had served under Taylor in the Mexican War. Since "Old Rough and Ready" had recently been inaugurated President of the United States, it was natural to christen the new town after him.

To protest the Miners Tax being considered by the Legislature, the citizens of Rough and Ready voted to secede from the Union in April 1850. The rebels couldn't resist the forthcoming Independence Day celebration, however, and forgot their cause on the Fourth of July. Among the oldest buildings are William H. Fippin's blacksmith shop (1850s), the Odd Fellows Hall (1854) that now serves as the Grange Hall and community center, and to the east of town, the Old Toll House, which exacted such fees as 25 cents for a horse and rider and $3.00 for a flock of geese.

TIMBUCTOO. Another flourishing town of the 1850s was Timbuctoo, which is marked only by the shell of the Wells Fargo office, now fenced off to prevent further vandalism.

FRENCH CORRAL. Better preserved is French Corral, on a road winding from Highway 20 north to Highway 49. Enjoying both a placer boom and a hydraulic mining boom, this town was lively from 1849 to the 1880s. Chief among the oldest buildings are the schoolhouse, the Odd Fellows Hall and the Wells Fargo office.

---

# Chapter 13. Nevada City: Gold Metropolis

CALIFORNIANS have always delighted in labeling towns, regardless of size, with the dignified title of "city". Granddaddy of these honored places—and incidentally one of the most deserving—is Nevada City, in the heart of the Northern Mines. With true California modesty her citizens acknowledge:

That she was the biggest mining camp in California.

That she was named long before the state of Nevada.

That the four miles separating her from the sister city of Grass Valley were once the most heavily traveled in the state.

These claims are amply justified. In her heyday during the middle 1850s, Nevada City was for a time even bigger than Grass Valley. With a population of 10,000 she was outdistanced only by San Francisco and Sacramento.

First prospected by James Marshall in 1848, the place was named Nevada City two years later in honor of the Sierra Nevada. In 1861 when the territory of Nevada was organized, the people of Nevada City sharply objected on the ground that they had first claim to the name. Congress was unimpressed, and Nevada City has been strenuously explaining her origin ever since.

As to the third claim, in Gold Rush days this route bore more traffic than any other four miles in the state. And considering the procession of ox and mule teams, stage coaches, burro trains and cattle herds that raised dust on this road, it was probably as dangerous as any modern highway.

From the first, Nevada City was never quite like her neighbors. Her miners were not absorbed in the usual placer mining, but found richer rewards in the ancient river deposits nearby. These were mined with small shafts known as coyote holes, which became so famous that a main thoroughfare in Nevada City is called Coyote Street. With early-comers reaping as much as $6,000 per day, Argonauts flocked in by the thousands. Mining laws were non-existent and claim disputes were rife, but one old-timer had his own solution. A newcomer found him at work one day and opened conversation. The pioneer was noncommittal until he was asked the boundaries of his claim. Straightening up, he pointed to his gun leaning against a tree.

"D'ye see that rifle there, stranger?"

"Yes."

"Well, jist as fur as that rifle carries, up and down this ravine, I claim—and no further."

This was not the only case of gunpoint mining law in Nevada City. Eager treasure-hunters were driving a shaft in the main street when a storekeeper called a halt. The men went ahead, answering that there was no law against it.

"Then I'll make a law," concluded the merchant, leveling a revolver. The pertinence of this statute was quickly acknowledged.

In the city's first two years, hardrock mining was a curiosity. One early arrival reported that the men of his camp had a good laugh over the busy efforts of nearby miners, who were actually "digging up the rock for a foot or more down." But after the big quartz discovery at Grass Valley in October 1850, Nevada City's hardrock ledges took on sudden luster. The frenzy that marked this new rush is shown in one miner's tale of Nevada City's first mining suit. Charles Ferguson and a partner returned from a trip to find two men had jumped their claim. When the interlopers ordered them off, they stood ground and began sinking a shaft. At this the jumpers brought suit and somehow won their case. A sheriff's posse was called in to eject Ferguson and his partner, who were busy washing the ore through their long tom. Ferguson tried to stall by arguing but the possemen shut off the water and picked up the long tom.

"As the water ran off," Ferguson later recalled, "I saw the yellow gold glittering in the box. I seized hold of it and carried it off bodily about fifty yards farther, although at any ordinary time it would have taken two men to do it, but the sight that I had seen gave me for the moment superhuman strength—the gold was so thick in the wet mass in the box that it looked like yellow pudding."

Scooping up the richest of it in a tin dish, he sunk it out of sight in a pool of water. He was panning out the rest when one of the jumpers came up and saw what was left. Disappointed, the man soon sold the claim for $100 to a buyer who turned it back to Ferguson.

Although claim jumping was a major sport, Nevada City was fairly civilized for a mining camp. Beginning in 1851 whole families arrived in town, and henceforth the presence of decent women had a sobering effect. Though miners might be used to the company of saloon girls, they treated a virtuous woman with near-reverence. Recalled one Nevada City pioneer:

"Every miner seemed to consider himself her sworn guardian, policeman and protector, and the slightest dishonorable word, action or look of any miner or other person would have been met with a rebuke he would remember so long as he lived. If, perchance, he survived the chastisement."

By 1850 Nevada City consisted of some 250 buildings ("frame houses, dingy old canvas booths and log cabins") extending along the bottom of a ravine. She was hardly a metropolis, but she did have one cultural jewel—a theater. This barn-like building, situated on Main Street, was the first playhouse in the Sierra, and one of the most famous on the Lode. Here Edwin Booth trod the boards in the hectic '50s, and here *Richard III* was performed for spectators who delighted in "hooting, yelling, whistling and stamping their feet."

Isolated as she was, Nevada City early became a great staging center for the Yuba River camps, the Sierra summit and points northeast. By 1851 Nevada City stages ran out of Sacramento several times a day—carrying express at the rate of $2.50 a letter. A traveler of that year describes the confused scene at stage departure time in Sacramento. The entire street was jammed with coaches and horses, prospective passengers and their baggage, and frantic "runners" who were drumming up business for their respective lines.

"All aboard for Nevada City," shouts one. "Who's agoin'? Only three seats—the last chance today for Nevada City—take you there in five hours. Who's there for Nevada City?"

Sighting a man who reveals some indecision, the runner descends on him without mercy.

"Nevada City, sir? This way—just in time."

Grabbing the man's arm, he hustles him through the crowd and is boosting him into the Nevada City stage when the victim manages to declare that he wants to go to Coloma. Unmoved, the runner holds tight and shouts for one of his fellows.

"Oh, Bill! Oh, Bill! Where the devil are you?"

"Hullo." answers Bill.

"Here's a man for Coloma."

And runner No. 1 clutches his quarry by the arm until runner No. 2 arrives to claim him. The whole thing, concludes the observer, was ridiculous. "Apparently, if a hundred men wanted to go anywhere, it required a hundred more to dispatch them. There was certainly no danger of anyone being

151

left behind." In fact, the chances were that an innocent passerby would suddenly find himself bound for Nevada City and points north.

This was scarcely the only hazard on roads in the Northern Mines. Nevada City highways, especially that four-mile route between the town and Grass Valley, were the especial haunt of road agents. In May 1858, the Auburn stage was just outside Nevada City when five bandits stepped into the road. The passengers prepared for a thorough fleecing—all except a Nevada City bank messenger, carrying a sizable load of gold dust. He drew his pistol, with no other effect than to bring a remonstrance from one of the robbers to "be careful." At this, the unruffled bank man agreed that there was really nothing to fight about, that all the treasure was in a Wells Fargo chest on the next stage. After a cursory search, the outlaws let the first stage go, and robbed stage No. 2 of $21,000. The clever bank agent felt bad about getting off at Wells Fargo's expense, but after all, business was business.

The arch-bandit of Nevada City did not appear until the mid-'60s, when a character bearing the alias of Jack Williams invaded the highroads. At first he concentrated on lone travelers. One night he stood on the road from You Bet to Nevada City and stopped no less than six men in a row. Another time he and his gang chased a recalcitrant victim all the way into Grass Valley, where they sent two shots at his disappearing heels.

In May 1866 they opened business with the express lines. First, the stage from North San Juan was stopped three miles above Nevada City, and its two Chinese passengers robbed despite furious protest. But when they came to the Wells Fargo box, the robbers found the treasure stored safely in an inner chest made of chilled iron. The stubborn object could not be broken. The stage clattered on with Wells Fargo triumphant.

But Jack Williams had a one-track mind. A few mornings later his men were on the road again, stopping the northbound stage at the summit north of Nevada City. This time they had two sledges, a crowbar, a portable blacksmith's kit and a can of giant powder. They would get that gold, they said, or blast the coach into the Yuba River.

While passengers watched, they went grimly to work and on the second explosion, blew open the box. Jack Williams heaved the gold sack over his shoulder, passed a flask of brandy among the passengers as an act of courtesy, and made off with his two companions.

Nevada City was broadminded, but this effrontery almost at her gates was unforgivable. A six-man posse headed by the sheriff of Nevada County swung out of town and pushed into the brush in pursuit. Unaccountably, five of them left the trail while a sixth man pressed on alone. This was Steve Venard, packing a formidable 15-shot Henry rifle.

Crossing the South Yuba, he suddenly came face to face with his quarry. Two of them were already aiming at Steve when he opened fire. His first shot found Jack Williams' heart, the second pierced the head of another, and a few moments later a fourth shot brought down the last bandit. It was a busy day's work for deputy Venard and his Henry rifle. By early afternoon the chest had been returned to Wells Fargo and Nevada City's face had been saved.

Graced as she was with fine women, a theater, and other marks of culture, Nevada City was not a particularly rough town. "There were but very few cases tried before Judge Lynch," recalled an early resident; "only three cases of shooting, and those poor shots." She did indulge, however, in the more genteel method of slaughter—dueling.

Late in 1851 a sailing man named George Dibble got into an argument with one E. B. Lundy, a Canadian known chiefly as a son of the owner of Lundy's Lane, where a War of 1812 battle was fought. Dibble called Lundy a liar and then challenged him. Lundy was a sure shot—the survivor of several previous duels. He tried to avoid the encounter, and on the day before the meeting he shot the wick off a candle in an attempt to dissuade his challenger. But Dibble was intent on getting "satisfaction". For the duel he adopted the dubious strategy of drawing Lundy's fire and then shooting him at leisure. This was a mistake. Lundy's first shot struck home. Dibble walked off the field and died.

There were other duels less tragic. Two rival doctors quarreling in a saloon resorted to arms, fired five shots each while the roomful of men scrambled for cover, satisfied their honor without inflicting a scratch, and celebrated with another drink. A third duel looked completely tragic when one contestant fell covered with blood—until the blood proved to be currant jelly loaded in the two pistols by local pranksters.

Nevada City, dubbed a "laughing camp" by one chronicler, has never taken things too seriously. Unless, of course, you ask whether she was named for the state of Nevada.

## POINTS OF INTEREST

NEVADA CITY. At least as well preserved as Grass Valley, Nevada City has been called "the most charming of all the major Gold Rush cities". For a sightseeing tour the place to start is the Nevada County Historical Museum housed in the quaint Firehouse No. 1, located on Main Street above Commercial Street. Some of the oldest historic buildings are, as you enter town on Broad Street, the National Hotel (building completed 1856), the oldest continuously operated hotel in California; the Citizens Bank (late 1850s) at 221 Broad Street; the Flagg Building (1858) and the Kidd-Knox Building (1856) on opposite corners of Broad and Pine; the newspaper/printshop building (1854) at 301 Broad; the Nevada Theater (1865); Firehouse No. 2 (1861); the United Methodist Church (1864); and further up at 449 Broad, the home of Senator Aaron Sargent (1856). Another Victorian home is that of Senator William M. Stewart (at 416 Zion Street on Piety Hill south of town), who joined the rush to the Comstock Lode and became the "Father of Nevada" (his law office was in the Kidd-Knox Building).

Also among the oldest buildings in the business district are, starting at Main and Coyote streets, James J. Ott's assay office and the South Yuba Canal Building, now housing the chamber of commerce (both 1855); the First Baptist Church (1857) on Church Street and St. Canice Catholic Church (1864) on Washington Street. A few brick buildings mark the old Chinatown on Commercial Street. But beyond individual landmarks, the winding, tree-shaded streets themselves, with their Victorian trimmings of another age, make Nevada City what another chronicler has called "a story-book town."

NORTH SAN JUAN. Once called San Juan, this delightful old town had the "North" added to its name in 1857, when the U.S. Postal Service wanted to remove the confusion with the San Juan in San Benito County. The town center includes eight brick buildings, some with iron shutters, said to date from the mid-1850s. The crumbling brick building on the south side of Highway 49 was once a general store, while the two-story ruin on Cherokee Road was the office of the superintendent of the North San Juan Mining Company. The white frame United Methodist Church (1856) has been one of the oldest continuously operated churches in California.

NORTH BLOOMFIELD. Nineteen miles northeast of Nevada City is North Bloomfield, like North San Juan a center of hydraulic mining. The town is part of the Malakoff Diggings State Park. Among the historic buildings are St. Columncille's Catholic Church (1860), Knotwell's drug store, King's saloon, the Ostrom livery stable with its wagon collection, and the McKillican and Mobley general store, which also houses the post office.

WASHINGTON. On another long road 19 miles eastnortheast of Nevada City is the relic of Washington, settled in 1849 and now comprising a few old buildings.

155

# Chapter 14. Downieville and the Yuba River Camps

THE BRAWLING, tempestuous Yuba River, with its equally unruly tributaries, hurtles out of the Sierra Nevada and then glides easily into the Feather River at Marysville. Into this remote country, containing some of the most splendid mountain scenery in California, came a horde of miners in mid-19th Century. But they scarcely saw the native beauty; they simply saw the Yuba streams as sources of gold, the mountains as obstacles in the quest.

Gold was first discovered on the Yuba in June 1848 at Rose's Bar, 18 miles east of Marysville. As eager prospectors worked up the river and its branches, they founded new camps—Bullard's Bar, Foster's Bar, Goodyear's Bar and Downieville. All of these were located at spots where the streams had changed their course enough to reveal sand bars rich with gold.

By the early '50s, miners were so thick along the North Fork that, according to the story, a piece of news could be carried by word of mouth the whole 70 miles from Downieville to Marysville in 15 minutes. The accuracy of the dispatch, by the time it reached its destination, was not guaranteed.

Metropolis of the Yuba mines was, and still is, Downieville. In the fall of 1849, William Downie, a Scotsman with a flair for leadership, headed up the North Fork with a party consisting of an Irishman, an Indian, a Hawaiian and ten blacks. At the present site of Downieville they struck rich gold, built a log cabin and settled down to wait out the winter.

Things went well in this far-off outpost until the holiday season. A serious question then arose over whether the party should drink its only bottle of brandy on Christmas or on New

Year's. For several days the boys argued heatedly and earnestly on this point of etiquette, finally settling on Christmas. On the appointed day they made a punch of brandy, nutmeg and hot water, and then launched the celebration with toasts to sweethearts, wives and country. At the height of the festivities, Downie, who was by then going under the title of Major, decided that the occasion required a formal observance. He climbed to the roof of the cabin with an American flag in one hand and a pistol in the other.

"I made a short speech." the Major recalled, "waved the flag and fired a few shots and finished up by giving three cheers for the American Constitution."

This somewhat unorthodox celebration of the first Christmas on the North Yuba set the tone for the roaring Gold Rush town of Downieville. It specialized in festivities of any kind, particularly the Fourth of July. And in its heyday, it was hardly a rewarding field for temperance workers. Major Downie records that in this cold and rugged country, any miner who abstained was considered either "a crank or a suspicious character." Bottles were opened not by drawing the cork but by the quicker method of breaking off the neck. In earliest days when Downieville had only one saloon, any celebrant who stood a round of drinks for the house paid the flat price of one ounce of gold ($16). If there weren't enough men in the bar to fill out an ounce's worth, someone went out and rounded up neighbors and passers-by.

One of Downieville's first justices of the peace was a saloonkeeper. In 1850, a man was brought before him for stealing a pair of boots. Finding him guilty, the justice ruled that he return the property and, as a fine, stand the drinks for the crowd. The hilarious court then adjourned to the bar and proceeded to make the most of the opportunity. So, after several rounds, did the prisoner. In the midst of the orgy he disappeared, leaving the saloonkeeper-justice to stand the fine.

Downieville could appreciate this kind of joke. One day a

157

greenhorn approached the claim of miner Jack Smith, who immediately dropped his work and began poking in the trunk of a pine tree. Palming a gold nugget, he pretended to pull it out of the bark. The astonished newcomer then began working the bark himself.

"No, you don't," put in Jack. "This is my tree." The stranger tackled another pine nearby, but without success.

"Maybe you are too near the ground," advised the miner, authoritatively. "Some of them are 'top-reefers' as we call them here; try about 20 feet higher up."

So the greenhorn shinnied up the tree. At Jack's urging, he kept climbing higher. Finally when the man was well out on a high limb busily searching for gold, Jack could hold himself no longer. Howling with glee, he ran off to tell the boys, while the greenhorn wondered what demon had suddenly seized his newfound friend.

Downieville's greatest hoax was pulled by a store clerk named William Slater, a fast-talking character who had somehow earned the trust of the miners. In 1850, Downieville had neither roads nor express service, and its chief problem was to market its golden treasure. Slater had once remarked that a man who knew where to go in San Francisco could sell gold for $22 an ounce. So when it came time for someone to "go below" with the camp's collective savings, the boys chose William Slater. They were so grateful for this service that when he left with $25,000 in gold dust and nuggets, they generously told him to keep for himself $2 for each ounce.

That was the last Downieville ever saw of William Slater. He passed through San Francisco and was seen at the Isthmus of Panama by a traveler who later turned up in Downieville. Slater, the new arrival reported, had strongly recommended that he come to the North Yuba camp and meet its jolly citizens. They were in no mood to return the compliment.

In that same year Downieville began to lose its isolation. Sam Langton, who was to become one of the stagecoach kings of the Mother Lode, started a pony express from

Marysville to Downieville. Pack trains began operating over the route, bringing in scarce goods that sold for outrageous prices in the mountain-bound camp.

But the jagged country still made the Downieville trail a distinct adventure. One traveler wrote thus of a particularly rough section: "At last, after a great deal of scrambling and climbing, my shins barked, my clothes nearly torn off my back, and my eyes half scratched out by the bushes. . .I considered that I had got over the worst of it." In another spot the precipitous trail was too narrow for man or beast to pass one another. Down-traffic had to cling to the upper bank while the up-traffic passed by.

'The mules," reported the observer, "understood their own rights perfectly well. Those loaded with cargo kept sturdily to the trail, while the empty mules scrambled up the bank, where they stood still till the others had passed. It not infrequently happened, however, that a loaded mule got crowded off the trail. . . This was always the last journey the poor mule ever performed."

Above Downieville, the trail was worse. Along one narrow section there was a sheer 80-foot drop to the rocky stream below. Hikers could only pass at certain places, and then only by holding on to one another. At one spot even this path was broken by a gap of several yards, which the miners had bridged with a thin pine log. As you teetered on this support, with one foot stepping on the cliff itself, you could look down between your legs and see sharp rocks, "strongly suggestive of sudden death."

Despite its alpine location, Downieville had a population of several thousand by 1851. Completely surrounded by mountains, its single street barely found room between the hillside and the river. It boasted a newspaper, a theater, several hotels. Though everything had to be packed in by muleback, the saloons were as elegantly decorated as any on the Mother Lode. There was a notable absence, however, of plate glass mirrors.

Quaint and peaceful-looking, like a "toy village" when seen from afar, the Downieville of the '50s bore a veneer of refinement. In its restaurants, as one visitor observed, "men in red flannel shirts, with bare arms, spread a napkin over their muddy knees, and studied the bill of fare for half an hour before they could make up their minds what to order for dinner." But its exuberant, rougher side made itself apparent at every opportunity.

Downieville's first Independence Day, 1850, was celebrated with a rousing spree that including a knifing and a public horsewhipping. The event of 1851 was marked by another carnival that ended in the worst tragedy of Downieville's history. Late that night, one Joe Cannon reeled his way homeward with several companions, and accidentally fell through the doorway of a house. In this dwelling lived a Spanish-American and his paramour, Juanita, a beautiful woman who was favorably known among the miners. Before the two were aroused, Cannon's companions pulled him outside and the group continued its unsteady way. Next morning Cannon passed by and stopped to apologize. Apparently the more he said the more infuriated the Spanish couple became. Finally Juanita grabbed a knife and plunged it into his side, killing him instantly.

When the news of this act spread up and down the river, the angered miners assembled in Downieville, seized the hapless pair, chose a popular court and held a trial. The man was acquitted but Juanita was found guilty and sentenced to be hanged. The mob improvised a gallows by the river and performed the deed—only a few hours after the knifing episode.

The news that Downieville had hanged a woman immediately spread throughout California. Her citizens were shocked that lynch law had come to this shameful extremity. Popular tribunals had been accepted as a stern necessity in a lawless region; vigilantism was, in fact, the order of the day in 1851. Blame for this final crime was not Downieville's alone, but also that of a California citizenry that had embraced mob justice. The state recoiled at the Juanita incident, and for the next five years, at least, Californians relied more on established legal processes than on Judge Lynch.

By 1855, Downieville resolved to have a quiet Fourth of July. Miss Sarah Pellet, a noted temperance lecturer, was on her way up the Yuba River, and was engaged for the principal oration. In anticipation of this splendid diversion, the boys launched a veritable reform crusade and joined the Sons of Temperance Society by the hundreds. Downieville saloons were all but deserted.

The festive day arrived, and thousands of miners assembled in town. The boys were so anxious to hear Miss Pellet that when another speaker waxed exceedingly long, they fired a volley of pistol shots in the air to shut him up. This in turn led to a duel between the orator and one of his tormentors, with double-barreled shotguns as weapons. The erstwhile speaker was killed, Miss Pellet left town, and Downieville's saloons reaped the result of a fallen crusade.

### POINTS OF INTEREST

DOWNIEVILLE. Probably the most charming of the Gold Rush towns in the Northern Mines, Downieville and its sister towns of the Yuba River are fully worth the drive up the last lap of Highway 49. For the beginning of your Downieville tour, start at the Pioneer Museum, once a Chinese store and gambling house (1852) located on the south side of Main Street. Also on Main Street: the stone Hirschfelder Building (1852), the Mackerman & Co. Building (about 1852), and the brewery (1854). The brick-and-stone Craycroft Building (1852), on the southeast corner of Main and Bridge Street, housed a saloon, a courtroom, jail, newspaper office, restaurant and the Masonic Lodge. Juanita took refuge here after the stabbing incident. The number of buildings constructed as early as 1852 make Downieville a unique display from the actual Gold Rush.

Across the Downie River, just above its confluence with the North Yuba, are the Masonic Hall and the Odd Fellows Hall (both 1864) and the Methodist Church (1865), claimed to be the oldest continuously used Protestant church in California. The quaint neighborhood streets that wind along the steep hillsides add to the luster of this Sierra jewel.

CAMPTONVILLE. While this lower Yuba town was once a thriving gold camp, repeated fires destroyed its old buildings. Today's houses are mostly of relatively late construction. Among the points of interest are a small old wooden jail and a red schoolhouse still in operation.

GOODYEAR'S BAR. Below Downieville a short way off Highway 49 lies what is left of Goodyear's Bar, named for two Goodyear brothers who were among the founders in the summer of 1849. What the village lacks (it has only wooden structures) in historic interest, it makes up in exhilarating mountain scenery. A notable building is the charming old wooden schoolhouse.

SIERRA CITY. Founded in 1850, Sierra City is the last gold town of consequence at the north end of Highway 49. Among its remaining structures are the three-story Zerloff Hotel (1860s), the Masonic Hall (1863), and the large Busch Building (1871) with its brick walls and iron shutters.

ALLEGHANY. A long drive on unsurfaced roads brings the incorrigible ghost towner to Alleghany, which sports a mine and one or two wooden buildings.

JOHNSVILLE. North of Sierra City and a few miles west of Highway Alternate 40 is Johnsville, whose few wooden buildings give it a capsule appearance of the frontier town popularized in Western movies. Though Johnsville retains some earmarks characteristic of the Gold Rush towns—overhanging balconies and a quaint belltower—it was actually founded in the 1870s. Also known as Jamison, it is preserved by the California Department of Parks and Recreation, whose headquarters and museum are housed in an old miners' boarding house.

---

# Chapter 15. Feather River: Canyon Country

NOWHERE is the proverb, "Gold is where you find it." better applied than in the Feather River country. There is no other explanation why thousands of men invaded this remote and rugged region in mid-19th Century. To reach their goal they braved raging torrents, precipitous trails, merciless weather. When they arrived they carved precarious townsites between river and canyon walls, and proceeded to lead a life as wild and untamed as their surroundings.

The Feather River discoveries were not completely accidental. Though fully 90 miles north of the original discovery site at Sutter's Mill, the lower Feather mines were opened as early as July 1848. John Bidwell, the frontiersman who had led one of the first two emigrant trains into California in 1841, had a ranch on Chico Creek; a few weeks after Marshall's strike, Bidwell visited the Sutter mill and found the sand bar reminiscent of his Feather River country.

Back he went to the Feather, panning its shores as he traveled. Only a few miles above the present Marysville he found light gold. By the time he reached the region of the river's three main forks, the gold was so rich that he went no farther. At this spot on the Middle Fork rose Bidwell's Bar, first of the rough and wealthy Feather River mining camps.

Then in the winter of 1849-'50, one Thomas Stoddard came into the young camp of Downieville with tales of a fabulous Gold Lake, which he had discovered in the Sierra fastnesses. When he had leaned over to drink from its water, he had seen at its bottom nothing less than boulders of pure gold!

That was enough for the boys of Downieville, and of the whole Northern Mines, for that matter. Could the estimable Stoddard find this Gold Lake again? He thought he could, but everything would have to wait until the spring thaws. By May 1850, when Stoddard led a stealthy, 25-man party out of Downieville on the momentous quest, it was followed by a thousand Argonauts.

For days they scrambled over the unbroken country of the upper Feather watershed. When the Gold Lake remained unfound, Stoddard grew hesitant. They had, he said, taken the wrong "divide." His followers were furious.

"If you've deceived us," growled one, "we'll blow the top of your damn'd head off."

At this point the miners held a meeting, and reported to Stoddard that if he did not produce his Gold Lake within 24 hours, he would be strung up to the handiest pine tree. At this sobering promise, Stoddard forgot about Gold Lake and took the first opportunity to decamp. Back to Downieville trudged an angered, sheepish crew. Never again did Stoddard dare show himself in the California mines.

But his Gold Lake proved the first of the breed of lost mine legends that produced real strikes as a by-product. Three Germans straggling back from the Gold Lake stampede cut across into the North Fork of the Feather River. On the east branch of this stream they found shining gold particles lodged in rock crevices. Within four days they are said to have taken out $36,000 worth of pure gold.

When this news reached the camps around Bidwell's Bar, a second rush set in for the upper Feather country. A party of 100 reached the discovery site, found a big gold nugget, washed $285 from a single panful, and decided this was the right spot. By the end of July 1850, several hundred men had arrived to found the well-named camp of Rich Bar. Soon after were discovered the equally-fabulous localities of Smith Bar, Indian Bar and Missouri Bar. This rugged treasure-house, teeming with thousands of gold-hunters, became the northern outpost of the Mother Lode.

Meanwhile, the lower Feather diggings had been booming since Bidwell's first discovery. A few miles west of Bidwell's Bar, Ophir City sprang up in 1850. Later its name was changed to Oroville, the one Feather River camp still thriving today. North of Oroville the Feather enters its craggy, steep-walled canyon, and for this reason the town became as much a transportation center as a mining camp. From Marysville, head of steam navigation on the Feather, stages and mule teams brought passengers and cargo as far as Oroville and Bidwell's Bar. From there, pack trains carried freight 53 miles along the tempestuous North Fork to the Rich Bar diggings.

Just getting to the end of wagon navigation at Bidwell's Bar, however, was a real adventure. As far as Marysville, at the junction of the Feather and Yuba Rivers, travel was civilized enough on board the gilded steamboats. Unless, of course, rival captains took to racing and sent the pressure gauges above the safety limit—at which time crews, boat and passengers were liable to be exploded sky high.

Above Marysville, an eyewitness account of travel hazards is provided by a New England lady named "Dame Shirley" Clappe, who journeyed to Rich Bar with her husband in 1851. The northbound stagecoach, as she described it, was "the most excruciatingly springless wagon that it has ever been my lot to be victimized in. . ." The first 30 miles were smooth and scenic, but 10 miles below Bidwell's the road took to the mountains and ran along a harrowing precipice. Shirley was too petrified to scream.

"It seemed to me," she wrote later, "should the horses

deviate a hairbreadth from their usual track, we must be dashed into eternity."

"Wall," said the driver when that stretch had been safely passed, "I guess yer the furst woman that ever rode over that ere hill without hollerin."

North of Bidwell's, Dame Shirley and her husband proceeded on muleback, twice losing their way before looking down upon the rude camp of Rich Bar. The last five miles into town were so steep and precarious that riders dismounted and led their animals; but despite warnings, the plucky Shirley rode her mule all the way and arrived safely after falling off only once.

The early Feather River camps were as primitive as the trail. In '51 Oroville was so insignificant that Dame Shirley failed to mention it. At Bidwell's Bar "there was nothing to sleep in but a tent, and nothing to sleep on but the ground, and the air was black with the fleas hopping about in every direction.. . ." But by the mid-'50s the rich diggings of the lower Feather had made Bidwell's a city of 2,000—complete with a newspaper, three daily stages and the first suspension bridge in California.

By '56 Oroville had surpassed its neighbor; wrote one citizen: "Coaches are rattling through our street at all hours of the day and night." Early next year the *Gazelle*, a bantam-sized stern-wheeler, pushed up the Feather all the way to Oroville. For three months in that high-water year other steamboats arrived, making Oroville one of the few California mining towns ever reached by water.

But on the upper river, Rich Bar and its neighbors never got beyond the shanty stage. Dame Shirley described the camp as a single street with about 40 nondescript structure—tents, "plank hovels," log cabins and one unique edifice "formed of pine boughs and covered with old calico shirts." Only two-story building in town was the imposing Empire Hotel, a picturesque union of wood and canvas which Shirley called "just such a piece of carpentering as a child of two years old, gifted with the strength of a man, would produce." But since materials had to be freighted from Marysville at 40 cents a pound, "this impertinent apology for a house" cost $8,000 to build.

Social life on the upper Feather was even less attractive to a cultured New England woman of the 1850s. As she put it, "there are no newspapers, no churches, lectures, concerts or theaters; no fresh books; no shopping, calling, nor gossipy little tea-drinking; no parties, no balls, no picnics, no tableaux, no daily mail (we have an express once a month), no promenades, no rides or drives; no vegetables but potatoes and onions, no milk, no eggs, no *nothing.* "

As in other Mother Lode camps, the boys accepted this stern existence with exemplary fortitude—at first. In fact, when the first gamblers imported two painted ladies as a proper ornament to the camp (building for them what later became the Empire Hotel), the boys were shocked. Within a few weeks the tainted pair were forced to leave town by public opinion—and this at a time when they were the only females on the upper Feather. Crushed at this ingratitude, the gamblers sold their $8,000 investment to a hotelkeeper for a few hundred dollars.

But Rich Bar's honor was not long preserved. The gamblers soon recouped their losses many times over, and their numbers multiplied. Despite seemingly prohibitive freight rates, whisky was packed into the North Fork camps in enormous quantities. Though the miners treated Dame Shirley with near-reverence, she could not help being horrified to witness constant gambling, carousing, swearing and fighting. The Feather River mines had outgrown their age of innocence.

If anything, Rich Bar was more strenuously intemperate than other Gold Rush camps. A newcomer pulling in at three in the morning found the revelry in full swing at the hotel bar.

"It strikes me," he confessed to the proprietor, "your customers are rather late tonight."

"It's a little late this morning perhaps for night before last," admitted the host, "but for last night, why bless you, it's only just in the shank of the evening."

Dame Shirley herself describes a three-week "saturnalia" in nearby Indian Bar, where she and her husband moved in the fall of '51. In the following winter, life on the far-off Feather began to pall on the restless miners. As the holidays approached they made extensive preparations consisting chiefly of hauling in frightful quantities of brandy and champagne. They started out on Christmas Eve with an oyster-and-champagne supper and an all-night dance. For the next three weeks Indian Bar was on the warpath. Almost every day a boatload of celebrants capsized in the river; being too numb to get panicky, none of the victims drowned. Any citizen who withheld from the bacchanal was arrested by a kangaroo court and sentenced to "treat the crowd." Finally the marathon ended from sheer exhaustion—not of the revelers, but of the brandy.

Such excess living on the Feather usually led to violence, and July 1852 was particularly explosive. On Independence Day the ladies (four in number) and gentlemen of the upper Feather were enjoying an elegant dinner at the hotel when a fight erupted in the barroom below and two men rushed into the dining room with "blood-bespattered shirt bosoms." One lady fainted, and the festivities faltered.

A week later Dame Shirley and several friends went for a quiet walk in the forest and were returning laden with wildflowers when "a perfectly deafening volley of shouts and yells" rose from the camp. It marked the beginning of a battle between Americans and Mexicans which ended in the banishment of six of the latter.

Then a few days afterward Shirley was chatting amiably with two ladies at the door of her cabin when three or four hundred men suddenly rushed by with much shouting to the scene of the latest attempted killing. In all, three weeks in July produced what Shirley detailed as "murders, fearful accidents, bloody deaths, a mob, whippings, a hanging, an attempt at suicide, and a fatal duel." The North Feather in the early '50s was not noted for charm and serenity.

The Feather River camps lived hard and died early. Late in 1852 the fluming companies which had turned the river to work its gravel bed failed to find paying deposits. Almost overnight, Rich Bar and its neighbors were abandoned. Downstream, Bidwell's Bar was pronounced "another deserted village" by 1856. Except for the city of Oroville, little is left to mark the once-flourishing Feather River mines. In the North Fork of the Feather, even the scenery itself is marred by man-made dams, powerlines, a highway and a railroad. And though Rich Bar alone is said to have produced $3,000,000, no one has found the lake with boulders of gold.

## POINTS OF INTEREST

OROVILLE. Starting point for visitors to Oroville is the Pioneer Memorial Museum at 2332 Montgomery Street, operated by the Native Sons and Daughters of the Golden West. The Butte County Historical Society is housed in the Ehmann Home at 1480 Lincoln Street. The real flavor of old-time Oroville is found in Miners Alley, flanked by the backs of early buildings that face the town's two main streets. Another point of interest is the Judge Charles Lott home (1856) in Sank Park at 1067 Montgomery Street. There are also Chinese temples dating from the 1860s at 1500 Broderick Street.

East of town is the historic Bidwell's Bar suspension bridge (1855), which was moved from its original site at the old town of Bidwell's Bar, now under 600 feet of water behind Oroville Dam. The dam itself, filled with tailings from early-day dredging operations, is the highest earth-fill dam in the world. The state visitors center at the dam offers a superb panorama and a historic guide of the region.

CHEROKEE. Atop Table Mountain thirteen miles north of Oroville on state Highway 70 is the ghost town of Cherokee, dating from 1853. Among its interesting sights are a museum in an old hotel (1850s), the schoolhouse (1868), and a well-kept cemetery. Cherokee is the site of what was once the largest hydraulic mine in the world.

FORBESTOWN. On a dirt road off of Highway 162 east of Oroville lies the abandoned camp of Forbestown, started by B. F. Forbes in 1850. For many years a thriving gold town, Forbestown is marked today by crumbling rock foundations, wooden and stone walls, and a few old buildings—one claimed as the oldest Masonic Hall in California (1850s). The Forbestown Museum has many interesting exhibits.

OREGON CITY. Another old ghost town is Oregon City, founded in 1848 by a party of Oregonians headed by Peter Burnett, who later became California's first elected governor. There are today a few 19th Century buildings, including a one-room schoolhouse that now contains a small museum.

PARADISE. The earliest of several camps in the Paradise Ridge area was Dogtown, where mining began in 1850. Others included such names as Whiskey Flat, Toadtown, Helltown and Boneyard Flats. In 1859 a 54-pound nugget of almost pure gold was discovered in the Willard hydraulic mine. Today Paradise Ridge is a thriving settlement whose history is preserved in the Gold Nugget Museum at 502 Pearson Road, Paradise.

LA PORTE. Known as Rabbit Creek in the 1850s, La Porte was the scene of hydraulic mining and also of some of the earliest ski sports in the world; as early as the 1860s miners raced each other down the slopes on homemade skis. Almost depopulated except for a few inhabitants, La Porte has some early buildings, including the old hotel and restaurant.

SUSANVILLE. In 1855 a prospecting party led by the celebrated mountain man, Peter Lassen, discovered gold in Honey Lake Valley. On the site of Susanville a trading post had already been established in 1854 on one of the Sierra emigrant routes by Isaac Roop, who named the town after his daughter. Beginning in 1856 Roop, Lassen, and a number of other early settlers established the Territory of Nataqua, which included parts of both California and what was later Nevada. Afterward, when the Territory of Nevada was created in 1861, the Honey Lakers tried to maintain to California tax collectors that they were situated within the new territorial boundaries. Roop's cabin was requisitioned for a determined stand and called Fort Defiance. On February 15, 1863, a posse headed by the sheriff of Plumas County held a pitched battle with the secessionists entrenched in the fort. But when the boundary line was surveyed, Susanville was discovered to be in California for sure. The Honey Lakers consoled themselves by seceding from Plumas County and establishing their own Lassen County.

Today Susanville is a busy center of agriculture, stock raising, lumbering and vacationing. Still standing on Weatherlow Street is Isaac Roop's cabin, an interesting museum of California's "Little Confederacy". Another early-day building is the Pioneer Saloon (1862), said to be the oldest continuous business in Northern California.

# Chapter 16. Old Shasta: Gateway to Gold

"THE LONGEST ROW of brick buildings in California"—that was the boast of Old Shasta, whose ghost now nestles in the quiet hills six miles west of Redding. Such superlatives are typical of a town whose turbulent history and violent contrasts fire the imagination. Once the biggest settlement between Sacramento and the Oregon border, Shasta now has only a handful of faithful residents.

Shasta was, first of all, a gold town. Near here the first California gold discovery outside the Mother Lode was made by Major Pierson B. Reading, the state's earliest permanent white settler north of Red Bluff. Just where he found it is in dispute—both Shasta and Trinity Counties claiming the honor. But around July 1848 at a place called Reading's Bar, he and a crew of Indians began taking out gold at the rate of $832 per day.

Shasta's own gold discovery came in the spring of 1849, sparking California's second gold rush. Through the summer of '49, Argonauts from Oregon and the Mother Lode poured into this mushrooming camp. Known first as Reading's Springs, it was a tent city of more than 500 persons by October.

Rich as it was, Shasta was the most isolated town in California during 1849. An old mule trail blazed by the Hudson's Bay Company was all that connected it with Sacramento, 188 miles to the south. Pack trains and a few hardy teamsters carried supplies over this route at the stiff charge of $800 to $1000 a ton. At this rate, it looked like a cold and hungry winter for Shasta's pioneers.

Their fears were confirmed when the rains came. This was the wet winter that flooded Northern California and made the

172

streets of Sacramento a thoroughfare for ferries and at least one steamboat. Shasta, dreading both flood and isolation, was seized with panic. Many people sold their goods at sacrifice prices (20 cents a pound for flour) and struck out for the settlements. Soon Shasta was cut off when the swollen Sacramento River halted all traffic at the Colusa crossing.

Now the wily merchants who had bought up Shasta's meager supplies at panic prices made the most of the situation. Flour soared to $2.25 per pound, tacks to $1.50 per dozen. Shasta had been caught in the dizzy economics of California's Gold Rush.

After this experience, Shasta became transportation-conscious. By 1851 a new road was built up the Sacramento Valley, and the first stagecoach rolled into the bustling camp. At the same time, new gold discoveries in the Trinity and Siskiyou mountains had increased the northward traffic. Shasta stood at the gateway to this golden empire, the point where the road ended and the trail began.

For Californians traveling from the Mother Lode to the new diggings, Shasta became a link in a unique and colorful transportation hookup. From Sacramento you took a sternwheeler up the river to the head of steam navigation at Colusa—or in high water, as far as Red Bluff. Then you took a stage for Shasta, known as the head of "Whoa navigation". From there you rode saddleback over the rocky trail to Weaverville and points northwest. It was a route unhampered by luxury in any form.

Henceforth, Shasta flourished more as a transshipping center than a gold camp. By 1857, four stages from the south and three mule trains from the north raised dust into Shasta every day. The fastest mode of communication was the stagecoach, carrying passengers, mail and express packages. It was a highly specialized vehicle, distinguished from others by the leather thoroughbraces that supported the carriage and took up the shocks of the road for both horses and passengers. The favorite model was the elegant Concord coach, shipped all the way from New Hampshire around Cape Horn to California. Considered the last word in horse transportation, it carried nine passengers inside and from six to eight on top. Rival stages from Colusa to Shasta carried travelers through in just over 12 hours at the alarming rate of thirteen miles per hour.

While the six-horse stage was built for speed, the eight-and ten-mule freight teams specialized in tonnage. Plodding along at three miles an hour, they would cover the Colusa-Shasta route in around eight days. In mountain country the lead pair usually wore a bow of team bells over the collars, as a warning to head-on traffic coming around a blind bend. In contrast to the stage driver's box seat and six reins, the muleskinner rode astride the near wheeler and controlled the team by a single jerkline running through harness rings to the leaders. In her palmiest days, Shasta's streets were jammed with a hundred such teams every day.

At local wholesale houses, goods were unloaded and placed in saddle boxes for the most primitive transportation of all—pack mules. In trains of around 120 mules each, supplies moved on over bumpy, precipitous trails to Weaverville, Scott's Bar, Yreka and the Oregon settlements. As this means of transport had been employed in Mexico for some 300 years, operations were in the hands of hardened Mexican muleteers. Though each animal was limited to around 300 pounds, no cargo was impossible for the mule trains. Crates of squawking chickens, stamp mill machinery, dismantled pianos, printing presses—all swayed and jostled over Trinity trails to the tramp of hoofs and the Spanish oaths of the muleteers.

Accidents were common by this crude conveyance. Whisky Creek, located just beyond Shasta, got its name when a barrel of whisky fell from a mule pack and spilled into the stream—causing a rush of thirsty miners to the water's edge.

Over this same route beyond the head of "Whoa navigation", express was carried by pony rider. Competition was so furious between the rival lines of Wells Fargo and Adams &

Company that Shasta witnessed many a pony express race.

The most celebrated race began December 28, 1853, when a steamer brought an important message into San Francisco Bay. Since there was no telegraph connection with Portland, Oregon, the two lines sent pony riders hurrying northward with the news. Wells Fargo was leading when the scurrying hoofs passed through Marysville. Below Tehama the Adams messenger flew ahead.

At the Sacramento River crossing, rider Bill Lowden took the saddle for Adams over the last sixty miles to Shasta. He had just finished fording the river when the Wells Fargo man reached the opposite bank. Lowden hurried on, alerting each station with a whistle as he approached. Then the keeper would ride down the road leading a fresh mount at a gallop. Lowden, carrying his 54-lb. saddlebags, would switch horses without touching the ground and spur onward.

Some 35 miles below Shasta, Lowden struck a snag. He whirled up to Prairie House to find the Adams agent in a fist fight with the Wells Fargo keeper, and his relief mount running loose. This didn't slow down Bill Lowden. He caught up with the fresh horse, jumped to the ground, grabbed him by the tail and sprang into the saddle with one leap. Then he pulled the express bags from his old horse and pressed on.

"I lost about one minute here," Lowden later apologized. But the Adams man flew into Shasta so far ahead of his rival that Wells Fargo conceded the rest of the race to Portland. Lowden had changed horses 19 times and touched the ground only once, bringing the express to Shasta at an average speed of 23 miles an hour. Adams agreed to overlook the delay at Prairie House, and paid Bill Lowden $2,000 for his epic ride.

Through this reckless, roaring era, Shasta rode the crest of prosperity. Between 1852 and '57 she numbered several thousand citizens—one of the fifteen biggest cities in California. In the surrounding placer bars—bearing such picturesque names as Mad Mule Canyon, Salt Pork Ridge, Gambler's Gulch, Piety Hill, Grizzly Gulch, and Jackass

Flat—gold nuggets were numerous and miners were earning from $16 to $200 a day. From the Trinity and Siskiyou mines, pack trains were bringing in as much as $100,000 worth of gold every week.

In the earliest days, Shasta was a town of frame buildings, made of yellow pine lumber lined with cotton cloth. Fire struck this veritable tinder box on June 14, 1853, and in thirty-three minutes the whole business section went up in cinders.

But Shasta in her prime was too tough to burn out. In the next four years a fireproof Shasta rose from the ashes. With 28 new structures, she was claiming the longest row of brick buildings in California. Prosperity returned in force, and it was Shasta that sent the first shipment of gold received at the San Francisco Mint.

The golden treasure flowing through this thriving camp was not overlooked by California's knights of the road. Among the first of such gentry to arrive were five members of Rattlesnake Dick's gang, who were fascinated by a shipment of $80,000 worth of gold being packed over Trinity Mountain in the summer of '56. Since pack mules over the route were plainly branded and easily identified if stolen, Dick himself was to meet the gang with fresh animals for carrying the loot.

At an abrupt bend in the trail, the robbers descended on the pack train and quickly overpowered the muleteers, whom they tied to trees. Then they unloaded the gold and hurried off to a secret hiding place.

But Rattlesnake Dick failed to show up with the new mules, and was, in fact, resting in the Auburn jail on a charge of mule stealing. After several days' wait, one of the outlaws grew restless and was killed in a fracas with the leader. The remaining four buried half the gold and lugged the rest across Sacramento Valley to the Mother Lode country. But on the road near Auburn a Wells Fargo posse was waiting for them. In the fight that followed, the leader was killed and the other three captured. Half the loot was recovered, but the other

$40,000 hidden on Trinity Mountain stands high in the lore of California's buried treasure.

The failure of this robbery, one of the biggest in the Gold Rush, couldn't scare out other Shasta outlaws. In the late 1860s, a Shasta County barber named John Allen branched out into the horsetrading business—using other people's horses. When a posse caught up with him long enough to deliver a hail of buckshot, one of the men claimed a hit; he said it sounded like shooting a bird on a sheet-iron roof. John Allen got away, but his barbering days were over.

"Sheet-Iron Jack" finally carried his boldness too far when he rode openly into Shasta for an evening's entertainment. In a drunken brawl he shot an opponent and was promptly packed off to jail. Sentenced to two years in San Quentin, he was hustled out of Shasta on the next downstage. But at the outskirts of town, two robbers opened fire on the coach and then retreated into the brush. Infuriated at this competition, Jack leaned out the window and filled the air with epithets.

Jack soon escaped, and in November 1876, he and two companions robbed two Shasta stages and one Yreka stage. This triple blow was Jack's last important escapade. He was caught by the sheriff and sent back to San Quentin.

But long before this final flicker of excitement, Old Shasta's light had dimmed. In 1857 her citizens, anxious to prevent coastal ports from gaining the Weaverville trade, had extended the wagon road into the interior. By 1859, wheeled traffic was rolling to Weaverville in one direction and the Oregon border in another. Shasta kept her trade, but she was no longer the bustling head of "Whoa navigation."

Then in 1872, Shasta was shunted off the route of travel when the California & Oregon Railroad reached the new town of Redding. Six years later Shasta's gold placers were worked out, and by 1888, the fading city of brick relinquished the county seat to Redding. After that it was a ghost—one of the proudest and stateliest in California.

SHASTA. One of the truly romantic ruins among California ghost towns, Shasta has been improved as a State Historical Monument. On the northeast side of Main Street is the old Shasta County Courthouse, built originally for stores in 1855. From 1861 to '88 it was the courthouse and county jail. Today it houses a museum and art gallery operated by the State Parks. Also on the northeast side are the Visitor Center and the Masonic Hall (1854).

On the southwest side of Main Street are the ruins of the famous long row of brick buildings erected in the years 1853-'55. After the devastating fire of June 1853, the first to be rebuilt was the Jacobson clothing and dry goods store. Three others were built that year, including Bull, Baker & Co.'s general store and Tomlinson & Wood's supply store, which was built and opened within 13 days to win $600 in bets. Still others were finished within the next two years to round out the ten-building block. Further south on the same side of Main Street is the Litsch Store (1855).

FRENCH GULCH. Much of interest remains, including an industrious population, in this gold town of the 1850s, which still exhibits several brick buildings dating from wilder times. These include, on the east side of Main Street, the St. Rose Catholic Church and the E. Frank & Co. Building; on the west side, the Feeney or French Gulch Hotel and the Odd Fellows Hall.

# Chapter 17. Weaverville: Northwest Outpost

CALIFORNIA has mining camps that are more active or more ghostly, but none more quaint than Weaverville. Mountainbound in the crown of the Trinity Alps, this remote gold town is quiet, ageless, almost drowsy. But its tree-shaded streets and mid-19th Century buildings carry the unmistakable flavor of the roaring '50s.

The first strike at this remote spot below Trinity River was made in 1849 by William Weaver, a Mississippi-born frontiersman. Next year the town sprang up bearing his name; by 1852 it was the riotous capital of the Coast Range diggings, with 40 wooden buildings and a population of 1200.

But to mine gold was one thing; to get it marketed and haul in the trappings of civilization was another. By 1851, connection with the outside world was improved with construction of a wagon road up the Sacramento Valley as far as Shasta, and the development of ports at Humboldt Bay. But all goods still had to be packed by mule train 40 miles from the valley or 100 miles from the coast. With freight rates at forbidding levels, prices were outrageous and luxuries rare at Weaverville.

Life was rugged enough in summer months, but in the hard winter of 1852-3, Weaverville was completely marooned. Snow was so deep that it crushed the roofs of houses. For a week there was nothing to eat in town but barley. Many escaped on snowshoes and the rest were thinking about it when the first thaws came.

There was a more formidable danger in the Trinity Alps. Resentful at the white man's invasion of their mountain domain, the Digger Indians raided pack trains and isolated camps, killing horses and sometimes the miners as well. One early resident tells how a stranger stopped at his camp one night, and next morning found nothing left of his mule but the

179

carcass. Soon another newcomer came along, and they warned him about his mule. So he slept with the animal's tether rope tied to his wrist and his pistol within reach. In the morning the rope was undisturbed, but the Indians had gotten the man's mule, his pistol and his blanket.

This running war between whites and Indians came to a climax in May 1852, when a band of warriors killed the butcher of Weaverville while he was driving a herd of cattle. With the whole Trinity country aroused, a sheriff's posse trailed the Indians to their village and massacred over a hundred—all but two or three children. This barbarous act was enough to cow the rest of the Trinity Indians. In the fall of '52 the chief came into Weaverville and, in ceremonies attended by at least a thousand miners, signed a peace treaty.

But the backwoods camp was not freed of troubles. Being wealthy, isolated, and short on such civilizing influences as women and churches, Weaverville in the early '50s was one of the wildest towns in the mines. One citizen of 1852 wrote home that society "is decidedly bad—gambling, drinking and fighting being the amusements of the miners in their leisure hours. Saturday night is usually celebrated by such hideous yells and occasionally a volley from their revolvers, which makes it rather dangerous to be standing around." A few months later he added: "Nothing fatal has taken place since my last letter but there have been some awfully close shaves. One man has been shot through the cravat, one through the hat and one in the arm. The Weaverville Hotel has been sacked and fist fights without number have come off, but as nobody has been killed nothing has been done."

Law counted for so little that one saloonkeeper openly defied the Trinity County sheriff. On July 4, 1852, the officer came to take possession of the establishment on a creditor's attachment. The proprietor and his mistress drove him out at gunpoint. Soon the sheriff was back with a small posse, and while all Weaverville crowded about, went inside. The defending pair raised their revolvers.

"If you shoot you are a dead man," warned the officer.

Next moment a volley shook the building, and the sheriff was struck in the groin. The crowd pushed outside, while the combatants fought it out. After 15 or 20 shots the side of the law won a unanimous victory. One citizen drew a stern conclusion on the state of Weaverville society: "Sunday these two persons were killed; yesterday buried; and today almost forgotten."

Weaverville meant to uphold the majesty of the law, even if it took a lynching to do it. In the fall of 1852 an accused murderer was brought into town. The local judge admitted that the prisoner could not be tried until the next court session three months off. Everybody knew the camp had no jail.

The answer to this problem came quickly. The man was tried and found guilty by an impromptu miner's court. A second question arose over the time of execution. The majority of the crowd attending voted to wait ten days, but one group held out for a hanging next morning. An argument grew hot and pistols were drawn. Said one witness: "I thought for some time that half a dozen more lives would be lost in discussing this point." But at last the guns were put away and the ten-day period accepted peacefully. After all, Weaverville had to stand for law and order.

A few months later Weaverville got its jail, and after disastrous fires had made wood give way to brick, the place gained a more permanent look. By June 1853 Weaverville had over 2000 people, 14 stores, four hotels, four gambling houses, and 14 barrooms. It was in the mid-'50s, too, that Weaverville was struck with the spiral staircase craze. Main Street buildings were graced at one time with no less than seven outside spiral stairs, all of them made of iron in local blacksmith shops. Only three remain, but they give Weaverville a picturesque distinction among California mining towns.

High society came to Weaverville as early as 1852. With some 32 "respectable ladies" in the district, the citizens decided to hold a New Year's Eve Ball. The dance drew a crowd of miners who insisted on appearing in "store clothes"—dress coat, white vest, boiled shirt and polished boots. Since there weren't enough formal outfits in Weaverville to go around, they were passed among the miners, who would wear them for an hour or so and then retire from the dance floor and lend them to another. "It went off first-rate," reported one celebrant. "I was afraid there would be a row of some kind but everyone behaved themselves with propriety. . ."

After that beginning, Weaverville was a social-minded camp. The following Fourth of July it held not one ball, but two. Such events were so rare in the California mines that four ladies of Shasta rode 40 miles on muleback over rough mountain trails to attend.

By 1856 Weaverville was becoming positively refined. It had a theater, a schoolhouse, church, Sunday school, and naturally enough, a dancing class. Trained for such intricate steps as the waltz and the schottische, the miners were ready for even greater social triumphs. The next Fourth they held a magnificent ball at Chauncey's Hotel two miles out of town, danced till sunrise and horseraced back to Weaverville. Social notes from an eyewitness:

"Miss Burbank's horse fell going about 2.40, through an old bed of a stream. She went about 15 feet over his head and landed in a soft muddy place, with all her ball fixin's on. Some gents along with her washed off the thickest of the mud and got her in a buggy. Mrs. Todd broke down the seat in a wagon and created considerable confusion as she weighs about 200. . . .Taking it all together it was the greatest affair of its kind that has ever come off here. . . ."

But Weaverville could still have its stormy moments. Most famous of these was provided by its large population of Chinese, who were a familiar part of the California Gold Rush scene. With their patient methods they could make a living at gold mining in ground abandoned or worked over by

Americans. In its heyday Weaverville contained several hundred Chinese, who generally kept to themselves and settled their own quarrels. According to some accounts they were divided into two "companies"—one from Canton and the other from Hong Kong.

In the summer of 1854 they fell into an argument and made ready for war. The town blacksmiths were rushed with orders for spears, pikes and tridents. One munitions maker, obviously an opportunist, agreed to make 100 spears for the Canton Party at $1.50 each; within an hour the Hong Kongs won him over with an order for 200 spears; then the Cantons secured his services with a bid of 300 spears at $2.50 each.

But no matter; all the blacksmiths and merchants in town were busy. For the next few days both sides were marching, drilling and parading the streets with tin helmets, iron shields, home-made bombs, pikes, and squirt guns containing some foul liquid. With morbid anticipation the miners made no attempt to prevent a clash, but awaited it as a choice diversion.

Everything seemed to happen in Weaverville on July 4, and the Chinese war was no exception. On the appointed day the belligerents took up their positions in a field one mile from town. The sheriff arrived to stop the battle, but 2,000 American spectators interfered. The Chinese, they said, had gone to a lot of trouble for this event, and many Americans had come a long way to see it. Wouldn't it be a shame for the law to stop it all now? So the sheriff stepped aside.

Meanwhile, the two parties had been running through maneuvers with much beating of gongs and tooting of horns. Said one observer, "Now they would halt, with their poles upright looking like a forest of trees. Then lowering the points of their spears, with awful yells, they would run two or three hundred yards. Then stop, the front rank dropping on one knee, forming a perfect rampart of spears and shields."

Finally, the leader of the Hong Kongs rolled up his pantlegs, struck his sword on his shield and shouted a signal.

The army, some 150 strong, charged across a gully and into the blades of the enemy. The Cantons fell back. Then their reserves came up on the left flank. But by a prearranged plot with the Hong Kongs, some of the Americans drove them back. The Canton army then fled, leaving the Hong Kongs in possession of the field.

By this time the festive spirit of the occasion had turned sour. Eight Chinese and one American lay dead, with six to eight wounded. Most Americans were disgusted that some of their own people had taken sides in the battle.

Thus ended Weaverville's Chinese war, one of the curiosa of the Gold Rush. "We thought that the whole thing would be a farce," summarized one American, "but their coolness and courage surprised us and the play turned into a tragedy at the close."

Until the late '50s, Weaverville wavered between recklessness and refinement. Even its respectable ladies and its fancy balls could not dull the rough edge of the mining camp. When the sheet music for the latest song hit was sent to one young man from his sister in New England, he wrote back: "I received the music all right but there is only one piano in town and that is unfortunately in a house of ill fame."

By 1858 Weaverville shed its isolation when a wagon road was built from Shasta to replace the rugged mule trail. For several decades it continued to thrive as a gold camp. Today, with its iron-shuttered buildings and spiral stairs, Weaverville has lost its rough edge but not its atmosphere.

### POINTS OF INTEREST

WEAVERVILLE. A living museum of California's golden days, Weaverville is one of the most delightful mountain towns in the state. A number of brick buildings date from the late 1850s. On State Street at the south entrance to town are the Hafley House (1850s), said to be the oldest house in Weaverville, and the Hocker-Bartlett House (1859). At the north end of town are the Weinheimer House (1859), the Colbert House (1856), the Isaac Woodbury House (1850s or '60s) and the Karl Junkans House (late 1850s). In the center of town are the Trinity County Courthouse (1856-7 and since remodeled twice), first housing a store, hotel and offices, and serving as courthouse since 1865; the Hocker mercantile store (1854-5); Clifford Hall (1855), where various fraternal orders met; the Weaverville Drug Store (1855); Edgecomb Building (1856); Carr Building (1856), for decades a saloon and now the Trinity County Library; the Pacific Brewery (brick part, 1854-5); F. W. Blake Bank and Wells Fargo Building (1856); A. Solomon Building (1854), occupied largely by banks since construction; R. A. Fagg Building (1854); Buck & Cole Building (1856), operated for decades as a general store, with the Odd Fellows using the second floor; the W. J. Tinnin hardware store (1856); and the Eder Building (1854), used for many years as a men's clothing store.

Of special interest is the Chinese Joss House on Oregon Street west of the business district; built in 1874, it has been preserved by the state park system since 1956. The 1854 battle between two Chinese companies took place about a mile east of the center of town, south of Trinity Lakes Blvd.

BIG BAR. One of many camps by this name in the gold diggings, Big Bar is on the road from Weaverville to Eureka, through some of the thrilling scenery of the Trinity Alps.

HELENA. Near that highway roughly 16 miles west of Weaverville is Helena, known as North Fork in the gold days. A few brick and frame buildings remain.

# Chapter 18. Yreka and the Klamath Camps

TODAY, California's scenic Klamath country is a picture of peace and serenity. But then, things have changed in a hundred years. When the land was new in the gold-struck 1850s, life was as raw and rugged as the Klamath Mountains—and a lot less permanent. Indian attacks, stage robberies, shootings—these were the hazards of travel and residence in old-time Siskiyou County.

This far-north region got a slow start—for mining country. Argonaut wagon trains came over the Siskiyous and along the base of towering Mount Shasta as early as June 1849—but found no gold. By 1850 gold-hunters trudging overland from Oregon were testing the Klamath River bars. They made the big discovery in March 1851. After camping on what later became Yreka Flats, some Oregonians pulled stakes one morning and moved on. Abraham Thompson let his mules graze by the trail, and as one of them pulled up a tuft of grass, noticed yellow flecks in the roots. Quickly he panned out some of the dirt—and at sight of the coarse gold he ran after his friends.

"Come back! I've struck it."

That was the beginning of the big rush to the north border. Within six weeks 2,000 men had left the Mother Lode and flocked into Thompson's Dry Diggings. By late spring the new town of log cabins and brush wickiups got a second name. If you walked a short distance out of camp you could see far to the south the magnificent peak that dominates the Siskiyou country—Mount Shasta, or, as the miners called it, Shasta Butte. The town became Shasta Butte City.

But this sounded too much like that of the earlier camp, Shasta City, 100 miles southward. One day some of the boys were sitting about trying to think of a new name. The county clerk had an inspiration, and approached a nearby group of

Indians.

"What do you call the mountain," he inquired, pointing to Shasta.

"I-e-ka—'the white'," they answered.

By the time a citizen rode south to record the new name at the state capital, it had been corrupted to Yreka. So the boys succeeded in keeping a name for Shasta, or so they thought, and they would pounce on anyone who dared suggest that Yreka sounded too much like Eureka, the port city on the northern coast.

Yreka soon became the metropolis of the far north country. By 1852 it had an estimated 5.000 population, some fifty store buildings and a bursting energy. Its citizens wore guns as a matter of course. First building in town was a saloon, with a bar duly sandbagged and bullet-proofed for protection of the bartender. Behind another bar, a newcomer noticed a revolver "cocked and capped" for instant action.

Legal process in such a country was less than formal. One of the remarkable judges of California's gold days was Yreka's George C. Vail, whose decisions were wholly unencumbered by legal training. What he lacked in law, he made up in audacity and common sense.

A young Oregonian came into his court and charged that an employer was skipping town without paying him for an entire winter's work. Vail promptly left the bench and took two constables in pursuit. On the road from Yreka they overtook the accused and hauled him back to court. He acknowledged the debt, but said he had no money. This did not disturb Judge Vail.

"Constable," he ordered, "take that man and stand him on his head; then shake him well, and listen if you can hear anything drop."

Next moment the defendant was tried and found guilty. From his pockets fell a bag of gold dust in the amount of $2,000. Out of this came the plaintiff's pay and an ounce of gold each for the two constables and judge—as "court costs."

Then the culprit, having been placed right side up, was freed.

By 1854 Yreka's lawlessness was wearing hard on a small core of civilized residents. The few ladies in town decided to build a church—feeling, as one of them put it, "an imperative need of some influence other than the saloon and gaming table." Such a cause, pushed by persuasive femininity, captured the enthusiasm of the boys. Gallantly they contributed a fortune in gold dust, and prepared for quieter days. A Union Church, joined by Protestant and Catholic alike, was raised on the Plaza.

When it was almost finished, the ladies held a dedication supper inside. Just as the sheriff, in the place of honor, stood ready to slice the viands, the good assemblage was startled by a volley of shots. A man flung open the door.

"Sheriff, come quick! The Greenhorns are storming the jail."

Now the Greenhorns were miners of nearby Greenhorn Creek, who had clashed with the Yreka Flats Ditch Association over water rights. One of them had been jailed for cutting the Yreka ditch, and they were now in the process of liberating him—forcibly. The sheriff and every man in the church dashed outside and joined battle.

"Many ladies ran out in excitement and curiosity," recorded one churchwoman, "but hearing a fusillade of shooting, mingled with the uproar of angry voices, speedily retreated."

Some minutes later the churchmen trudged back to the supper table. The Greenhorns had succeeded in rescuing their man. Casualties included one dead and several wounded. Apologies to the ladies were made and accepted. There was a general feeling that the Gospel was arriving none too soon.

Early-day Yreka might be crude, but it was not all bad. Up and down the nearby creeks, the honest miner plied his trade with rocker and long tom, living a simple, outdoor life. The poet, Joaquin Miller, on an early morning stroll in the Yreka diggings, leaves this impression:

"Now the smoke from the low chimneys of the log cabins

began to rise and curl through the cool, clear air on every hand, and the miners to come out at the low doors; great hairy, bearded, six-foot giants, hatless and half-dressed. They stretched themselves in the sweet, frosty air, shouting to each other in a sort of savage banter, washed their hands and faces in the gold pans that stood by the door, and then entered their cabins, to partake of the eternal beans and bacon and coffee, and coffee and bacon and beans."

If the Yreka country was primitive, its transportation was still worse. For the first few years, travel to Yreka was by horseback and mule train from Shasta, 100 miles southward, although Oregonians managed to get a few wagons over the Siskiyou Mountains. The trail was rough and precipitous, with such other inconveniences as bandits and hostile Indians.

In fact, Shasta Valley holds distinction as the scene of the first organized road agentry in California. By October 1851, one Charlie Smith was leading an outlaw gang numbering as high as 30 men. On the 23rd four robbers disguised as Indians surprised two miners a few miles south of Yreka. But the intended victims opened fire, and were reinforced by another party of travelers who drove the bandits off.

Then in 1856 a stage road was pushed through to Yreka by the roundabout Pit River route. The *Sacramento Union* called the route "a terrible rough one," and one traveler complained of miserable lodging houses where arrivals waded "through mud and slush to find a dirty wash basin, dirtier towels and 'yaller' soap, or no soap at all." And for meals the tired passengers got "half-cooked beans, heavy bread, stale butter, and bread pudding."

Meanwhile,, the Pit River Indians were not agreeable to the white man's invasion. Travel along the route was repeatedly interrupted by their depredations. By late August 1856 they ventured to make the first Indian attack on a California stagecoach. Driver Jared Robbins, alone on the downstage south of Yreka, was a few miles below the Pit River ferry when a war party jumped his stage. He was hit in the first volley of arrows, but whipping up the team, he flew onward for the next station—17 miles away.

Down that rutted and winding road careened stage and team, with Indian riders swarming around like enraged hornets. Arrows struck both Robbins and his horses, but it was the bumpy road which brought down the first casualty. Jolted unmercifully, the coach broke down and overturned in the middle of an open meadow. By the time the Indians reached the wreck, Robbins was on his way again—riding one horse and leading the rest. More pounding pursuit and more savage arrows, but at the end of that 17-mile race Robbins flew into the safety of the stage station—wounded but very much alive.

After that the Pit River route was left to daredevils and the Indians. In 1857 work was begun on a new stage road north from Shasta City in the Coast Range. By 1860 the road was completed through Scott River to Yreka. Travelers could board stage for the Siskiyou country with a fair expectation of arriving with their scalps.

But the new route was not neglected by California's masked gentry. By the mid-1870s, with the Iron Horse supplanting the stagecoach on the state's main arteries, highwaymen turned to the long, rugged and rewarding road between Shasta City and Jacksonville, Oregon. On this route in 1876 robbers stopped no less than five stages, one of them carrying the Western transportation king and owner of the line, Ben Holladay. Of his 28 robberies, arch-bandit Black Bart honored the Yreka stages seven times. When President Rutherford B. Hayes and General William T. Sherman passed through Yreka in 1880, they received a proper welcome, but the crowd was meager. Most of the male population was off in the Siskiyous chasing stage robbers.

Still it was the unrelenting Indian who was the main danger for early-day Siskiyou settlers. The discoverers of Scott's Bar were driven out by Klamath Indians in 1850. By 1852 the Shastas, Modocs and Pit River Indians were all on the warpath. When the Modocs massacred an emigrant train, the whites organized a volunteer company and combed the north country. Failing to flush the quarry, they resorted to treachery. The Indians were invited to peace talks, and deliberately murdered.

This foul deed crippled Modoc strength, though Indian raids continued throughout the '50s. In 1873 the final chapter of the pathetic story was written when U.S. troops were called upon to put the remnant of the Modocs back on their reservation in southern Oregon. Led by the audacious Captain Jack, the Indians entrenched themselves in California's impregnable Lava Beds and held off as many as a thousand soldiers for three months. Then they played the white man's game and slew the opposing general in a truce conference. In the end Captain Jack was finally caught through the perfidy of some of his own warriors, and hanged according to white man's law.

Peace had come to the Siskiyou country, but the era of the gold placers had already seen its halcyon days. Shasta Valley people turned to farming and ranching. When the railroad invaded Siskiyou in 1887 it shunned Yreka by eight miles, but her citizens countered by spanning the gap with their own line, the Yreka Western Railroad. The modern Highway 99 passes through the city to assure its commercial position; today Yreka is one of the few California mining towns to survive on something else than gold. As for lofty I-e-ka, she still looks down from the clouds with the same benign tolerance that she showed to the Forty-niners.

## POINTS OF INTEREST

YREKA. Except for the matter of size, one might say of Yreka today what a 19th Century visitor called it: "a rather pretty little place." Seat of Siskiyou County, Yreka is today as appealing and as busy as it was in the 1850s. Heart of the old district is Miner Street, with many buildings dating from the

Gold Rush. On the south side of Miner, starting at Main Street, are: the Dewitt-Greathouse Building (lower story, 1859; second story, 1861), and the Odd Fellows Hall (1859). Further west, at the head of Third Street, is the Smith and Callahan Building (lower story, 1856). Then, starting at 225-9 W. Miner: Colton's Block (about 1856), the King & White Building (1854), the Livingston & Bro. Building (1854 or '55), the buildings at Nos. 315 and 317 (1850s), the City Meat Market (1854), Thomas Bros. Store (1853), the Bella Union Saloon (1854), Turner Hall (1856) and the Witherill Building (1859).

On the north side of Miner Street, starting just west of Oregon Street and going east, are: the Stimmel Building (mid-1850s), C. Peter's Yreka Brewery at No. 328 (about 1856), the Ruehle Building (1856), Brown & Nickell-Autenrieth Building (about 1856), and the Franco-American Building at Nos. 306-12 (constructed from the 1850s to 1868).

Among the many Victorian residences on Third Street are the Dr. J. Lytle Cammins House at No. 122 (1850s) and the Van Choate-Rosborough House at No. 301 (1858).

The center part of the Siskiyou County Courthouse at 311 Fourth Street was built in 1856 and '57. An interesting exhibit of gold samples is on display at the Hall of Records. The Siskiyou County Museum is at 910 S. Main Street.

Remains of the water ditch that Yreka miners dug for some 90 miles from Shasta River may still be seen paralleling Highway 99 to the west.

GREENHORN. Two miles below Yreka is the location of Greenhorn, where only a few frame buildings remain.

HAWKINSVILLE. Located north of Yreka, Hawkinsville dates from the early 1850s. Principal historic structure is the Catholic church, whose original brick portion dates from 1858.

HUMBUG CITY. Founded in 1851, Humbug is situated some ten miles northwest of Yreka. Little remains of the town, but the evidence of intensive mining operations still abounds in the vicinity.

FORT JONES. Southwest of Yreka is the mining town of Fort Jones, founded in 1851 and named for the nearby army fort that was operating from 1852 to '58.

SAWYER'S BAR. In the middle of the Salmon Mountains to the west of Yreka is Sawyer's Bar, once the biggest of several camps on the Salmon River and its forks. The principal old landmark is the wooden Catholic church, built in 1855.

SOMES BAR. Near the mouth of the Salmon is Somes Bar, founded as a mining camp in the Gold Rush and now a center for fishing and camping.

Like the Salmon, the Upper Klamath and its tributaries were more populated in the hectic '50s than they are today. Most of the camps lived hard and died young. In 1863 a traveler found them either deserted or in rapid decay, with most of the buildings abandoned.

SCOTT'S BAR. Traveling along the Klamath west of Highway 99, one may turn south at the mouth of Scott River to the deserted camp of Scott's Bar, located in a deep and awesome gorge. Founded by John Scott in 1850, the place contains a number of tumbledown structures and foundations to show the activity that once livened this remote canyon.

HAMBURG. Further west on the Klamath is Hamburg, today "a wide place in the road", in the gold days a flourishing town.

HAPPY CAMP. Another sizable settlement in the 1850s

was Happy Camp, which lives on as an outfitting point for fishermen and packers going into the remote Marble and Salmon mountains. With some stone structures and their characteristic iron shutters, it retains its mining town atmosphere.

ORLEANS BAR. From 1855 to 1875, Orleans Bar on the Klamath River was the seat of Klamath County, and relinquished the honor only when the county was broken up and redivided with other counties.

HAYDEN HILL. In northern Lassen County, 16 miles south of Adin, lies the old mining town of Hayden Hill. Its mines, producing mostly gold and some silver, had a very long production record in both the 19th and 20th centuries.

HIGH GRADE. In 1905 gold was discovered by a sheepherder in the rugged Warner Mountains, at the extreme northeast corner of California. The town of High Grade boomed first in the summer of 1905 and became the object of a still bigger stampede in the fall of 1909 and the spring of 1910. Its remains are located three miles northwest of Mount Bidwell near the dirt road from New Pine Creek to Fort Bidwell.

# PART V.  SAGEBRUSH CAMPS OF EASTERN CALIFORNIA

THE LINK *between California's Gold Rush towns and her desert mining camps was the stampede back over the Sierra to the Washoe mines in 1859 and the early '60s. At the very moment when the Mother Lode was declining, the Comstock Lode was discovered in the Washoe country—what would soon become the state of Nevada. The grand army of veteran miners trooped back over the old route of a decade earlier—perhaps feeling foolish that they had hurried past such a bonanza in the rush of '49.*

*Once in the sagebrush they remained to follow new strikes in Nevada and California throughout the 1860s and '70s. The lessons learned in placering the Sierra streambeds were useless now. The boys had to learn something about ores, both gold and silver, and where to look for them. Instead of earning a living standing knee-deep in icy water shoveling sand into a sluice box, the typical miner now spent his time trudging over the hot desert trying to find a rich claim that he could sell to a mine developer. Then he would live high in the nearest mining town until his money ran out. Undaunted, he would pile pick, shovel, and provisions on his burro and head back into the sagebrush.*

*So the men who coped with too much water in the Sierra now had to learn how to get along with too little. The log-cabin miner became the jackass prospector, and he made the transition because hardihood was his stock in trade. When he and his fellows first crossed back over the Sierra to the desert in the Washoe rush, one early Comstocker welcomed them with a salute that became a prophecy: "Let no man speak disparagingly of these men. Let no one sneer at the ragged miners. They are the pioneers in a great era."*

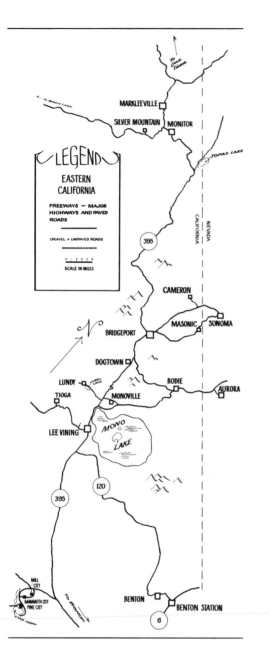

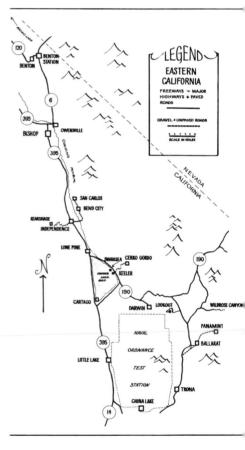

196

Down-canyon view of Cerro Gordo, leading silver producer of the 1870's.

*Sitting on a mountain top, the silver mining town*
*of Lookout flourished in the late 1870's.*

*Rich ore was packed by mule-back to these Modoc furnaces*
*at Lookout owned by Senator George Hearst.*

*Pack burros bring wood for the furnaces of Senator Stewart's twenty-stamp mill, built at Panamint in 1875.*

*Before the boundary line was surveyed, Aurora, Nevada, was the county seat of Mono County, California.*

*Gun-toting ladies of Lundy dress up for this 1885 photo.*

*The massive flywheel for this forty-stamp mill at Mammoth was hauled by mule-team all the way up from Mojave in 1879.*

*Mexican muleteers packing wood by burro into the busy mining community of Bodie.*

*Riding the near wheeler, a teamster guides his freight-laden, ten-horse team into Bodie.*

*Bodie citizenry turn out in Sunday best for Independence Day Celebration.*

# Chapter 19. The Rush in Reverse

INTO THE MOUNTAIN-BOUND mining camp of Grass Valley, California, rode a weary traveler late in June 1859. He had jogged more than 150 miles over the massive Sierra Nevadas from the Washoe country—what would soon be called the Comstock Lode in what would later become the new state of Nevada. With him, mostly as a curiosity, the stranger carried some odd-looking chunks of gold-bearing ore.

Next day Melville Atwood, the local assayer, tested the rock. What he discovered made him doubt his own calculations. Besides the gold content, which ran nearly $1,000 to the ton, the specimens contained a much higher value in silver—over $3,000 per ton!

What was more, the stranger confided, over in Washoe the discoverers were extracting the gold and throwing the rest away! Since California's big strike more than a decade earlier, prospectors had never thought of looking for anything but gold. In fact, an earlier assay of Washoe ore in Nevada City had failed to reveal the silver.

Within hours of Atwood's assay, the neighboring towns of Grass Valley and Nevada City were boiling with excitement. First to learn the news was Judge James Walsh, an old hand in California mining and a friend of the ore-bearing stranger from Washoe. Near midnight he banged frantically on the door of another friend. Quickly they piled provisions on a mule, mounted horse and spurred out of Grass Valley. Not far behind them clambered a desperate party in pursuit—one traveling on borrowed money, another on a borrowed horse. Within two days a clattering column was surging through the pine-forested Sierra—some on horseback, some afoot, all bent forward like hounds on the scent.

By the summer of 1859 Washoe ore was being shipped back over the Sierra—ore so rich that it could be carried 160 miles by muleback and another 80 miles by steamer, and could then be smelted in San Francisco at a fantastic profit. By October the growing shipments were attracting attention as they passed through California's mining region. Early arrivals in Washoe were writing back that the mines were the richest in the country. California newspapers were quoting assay figures of thousands of dollars per ton. Before long, bars of Washoe silver were hauled through the streets of San Francisco and displayed in bank windows before the eyes of gathering crowds. All at once California rang with a new cry: Silver in Washoe!

In fact, only silver could have excited the Californians in 1859. For too long they had followed the call of gold. As the placers had declined in the mid-'50s, they had been quick to heed each rumored strike. Disappointed, many had forsworn the siren call of gold. But against the cry of silver these stalwarts had no immunity. When it burst upon them in the fall of 1859, they were especially vulnerable. It had been a long summer, and in Sierra canyons the placer and hydraulic mines were idle for lack of water. At the end of September one Sacramento man estimated a thousand unemployed were roaming the town. "Never before," he wrote, "have I seen so many people looking for work and can't get it."

To this restless crew the silver call was like a trumpet blast. All at once mules, horses, flour, picks and shovels were in fevered requisition. "From the crack of day to the shades of night," exclaimed one San Franciscan, "nothing is heard but Washoe." It made no difference that the new strike was located in the very desert through which most of them had suffered on their way to California. They could only agree that it was "Forty-nine all over again."

With "Washoe!" thundering like a battle cry, the rabble army converged on the Sierra passes. The favorite route was up the American River canyon; at its foot lay Placerville, which was suddenly overrun with silver-seekers. One of them was the journalist, J. Ross Browne, who later described his attempt to get a night's sleep in a Placerville hotel room. People were rushing through the corridors all night, he wrote, "in and out of every room, banging the doors after them, calling for boots, carpet-sacks, cards, cocktails, and toddies; while amidst the ceaseless din arose ever anon that potent cry of 'Washoe!'. . . ."

In this breathless spirit California marched to the Comstock Lode. And as the line of glory-hunters moved through Placerville's streets each morning—clattering with shovels, picks and wash pans—there rose from the throats of bystanders the inevitable shout, "Go it, Washoe!"

Up into the pines the adventurers thronged, making an unbroken line of men, mules and wagons from Sacramento Valley over the mountains to Carson Valley. As the stagecoach whirled around blind bends the passengers found themselves looking hundreds of feet downward to the churning American River while the wheels dusted the brink. In the steepest stretches they walked and sometimes pushed as the teams struggled upward. Those who hiked or rode muleback suffered worse—slogging in the ruts of freight wagons, jumping out of the trail to avoid being knocked down when a pack train brushed relentlessly past.

Among the worst hazards on the trail were the wayside taverns, where the travelers piled in on one another in frantic quest for board and bed. Typical was Dirty Mike's, where one paid for the privilege of sleeping on the floor in company with numerous other flea-bitten vagabonds, in a room whose only fixtures were a piece of looking glass fastened to the window casing and a common comb and toothbrush dangling by strings nearby. Best stopping place on the route was Strawberry Flat, where hundreds of travelers congregated each night, flooding the barroom and jostling each other for a place near the dining room door. J. Ross Browne thus described the evening meal:

At the first tinkle of the bell the door was burst open with a tremendous crash, and for a moment no battle-scene in Waterloo. . . could have equalled the terrific onslaught of the gallant troops of Strawberry. The whole house actually tottered and trembled at the concussion, as if shaken by an earthquake. Long before the main body had assaulted the table the din of arms was heard above the general uproar: the deafening clatter of plates, knives, and forks, and the dreadful battle-cry of "Waiter! Waiter! Pork and beans! Coffee, waiter! Beefsteak! . . quick, waiter, for God's sake."

Next morning, after a night's sleep in a room with 250 companions and a bracing wash at the horse trough, the silver-hunter was on his way. At Genoa, first settlement reached on the east side of the Sierra, accommodations were even more formidable. Lodgers were packed like stowaways—two and three in a bunk, the unfortunate ones curling up on saloon floors, behind store counters, between packing boxes and even on the tops of nail kegs. At the booming new town of Carson City, last stop before the mines, one weary arrival ate a hearty meal and then told the hotel keeper he was ready to be shown to his room. "Just imagine my surprise," he wrote, "when the landlord informed me that he had no place for me to sleep but on the floor, that is, if I had blankets. . . ."

Early in November a storm struck the Sierra, covering it with the snow and ice that had already brought tragedy to many California-bound emigrants in previous years. But this only deterred the faint-hearted and the sane. While commercial traffic was halted, the most frantic rainbow-hunters floundered upward in the snow, resting at the highest outposts until the weather cleared enough for them to push over the summit. One storm after another raked the Sierra in one of the fiercest winters on record. Snow drifted as deep as 50 feet in the upper canyons. Numberless animals and a few men met death in blizzards and avalanches, but still the most daring pressed on, driven by visions of Washoe silver.

As the spring thaw approached, all of California seemed to rally at the foot of the Sierra. The winter's isolation had left the Comstock so short of supplies that prices were soaring, and between rival freight packers there was a breakneck race to be first across with whisky and other "necessities". As early as February 1860 they laid blankets in the snow for their animals to walk on, taking them up behind the train as it advanced and spreading them on the path ahead. Imaginative freighters tried sleighs, but these were stalled at the frequent patches of windswept granite. Mule trains were the only resort—taking not only merchandise, but offering to deliver passengers in Washoe at $30 per head. By early March even the stages were running again, but passengers had to walk much of the way, holding the coach to keep it from rolling down the mountainside. Above Strawberry Flat they trudged on by foot, braving fierce winds and shoveling a path before them across the summit.

With the first days of spring the Washoe trail was a continuous scar of slush and mud through the Sierra snow. A traveler called it "nothing but one trough of mire from two to three feet deep . . ." Adding further obstruction were the broken wagons, abandoned boxes and dead animals that literally lined the trail for the entire hundred miles across the mountains.

Worse hazards stalked the other Sierra routes opened to accommodate the tide. From California's Northern Mines the adventurers stormed up the tempestuous Yuba River, joined a mule train at Downieville and bent onward along narrow trails that hung hundreds of feet above the foaming river. From the Southern Mines they ventured through giant redwood groves and over Ebbetts Pass to the Carson River. Near the summit of this remote passage some stampeders encountered more than rough trail. Two of them stayed up all night waving firebrands to protect a load of bacon from three grizzly bears which, as one man recalled, "were grumbling and gnashing their teeth."

By April some 150 Californians were arriving in the Washoe country every day. Estimates of its population reached 10,000 in the spring of 1860, with thousands more on the way. Those remaining in California were investing every spare cent in Washoe mining stocks. "The Washoe mania has operated very much against us here," wrote one San Francisco merchant, "diverting men and money from the legitimate channels."

Early in May a savage Indian uprising in the Washoe country knocked the remaining steam out of the first rush. But such setbacks could not down the Lode, which was basically sound to the extent of an estimated one-third of a billion dollars. The tide to the Comstock rose again in the summer of 1860 and ran heavily until '63. Its riches helped to finance the Union side of the Civil War. Through the 1860s and '70s its wealth was the first fact of economics on the Pacific Coast. For the rest of the century its legend inspired the countless prospectors who combed the Great Basin looking for "another Comstock."

---

# Chapter 20. Cerro Gordo: L.A.'s Comstock

MOTORISTS driving through Owens Valley, on the east side of the Sierra, sometimes catch a glint of light high in the Inyo Range on the opposite side of Owens Lake. This is reflected sunlight from a window at the old mining camp of Cerro Gordo, which looks down on the valley from its mountainside perch some 9,000 feet high.

From this abandoned town, now reached by eight miles of steep and winding dirt road, once flowed as much as

$13,000,000 in silver and lead bullion. Between 1868 and 1875 its thriving trade helped to spur a furious boom in the young city of Los Angeles. In its day, Cerro Gordo's traffic was fought for by railroad kings and freightmasters, by every rival trading center from Los Angeles to Visalia. Deserted today, it stands as the greatest silver and lead producer in California history.

Discovered by Mexican prospectors in 1864 or '65, Cerro Gordo belongs to the era of the Comstock and the silver craze. It languished virtually unknown in remote Owens Valley until 1867, when one of its Spanish-speaking pioneers rode into Virginia City, Nevada, gleefully displaying chunks of rich silver ore.

After that the rush was on. Into the new camp on the brow of the Inyo Mountains came a stream of adventurers—miners, teamsters, merchants, gamblers. One of the first arrivals was M. W. Belshaw, a mining engineer from San Francisco. A shrewd and audacious operator, Belshaw quickly recognized that Cerro Gordo was a treasure house, and that it could be controlled by the man who controlled its smelters. Hurriedly he bought an interest in the Union Mine, the one reliable source of the lead ore needed in the smelting process. Then he hauled in machinery for a smelter, built a toll road over the only feasible route into town, and piped water from the only adequate springs nearby. Belshaw was not the man to leave a stone unturned.

Joining him as an owner of the Union Mine was Victor Beaudry, a French Canadian who operated a store at Cerro Gordo. The two would dominate the history of Cerro Gordo for the next decade.

By the fall of 1868 Belshaw and Beaudry were producing silver-lead bullion at a faster rate than the United States had ever seen. The metal bars, each weighing eighty-five pounds and shaped like a long loaf of bread, posed a real shipping problem from this remote camp on the wrong side of California. To haul their output they secured the mule-team

211

freighter, Remi Nadeau—the writer's great, great grandfather. For the next eleven years—except for a few months in 1872-'73—his jingling mule teams hauled the silver-lead shipments of Cerro Gordo.

In the earliest days the wagons rolled for 220 miles around the north side of Owens Lake, southward past Little Lake, across the Mojave Desert, and through Los Angeles to San Pedro. There they were transferred to paddlewheel steamboats for the 400-mile ride up the coast to San Francisco, where a refinery had been specially built for the purpose. The lead went to a local shot tower, the silver to the U.S. Mint. Any excess bullion was shipped around the Horn to the refineries of Swansea, Wales.

Sparked by Belshaw's energy, Cerro Gordo suddenly blossomed from a shanty camp to a full-fledged mining town sprawling up the slope of Buena Vista Peak. Through her rutted streets surged a motley parade of men and animals. Ten- and twelve-mule teams hauled bullion down the precipitous "Yellow Grade" on the first leg of the three-weeks' journey to the coast, and brought back provender and merchandise—everything from baled hay to billiard tables. An unending procession of pack burros along the nearby mountainsides carried in water, charcoal and pinon timbers for the furnaces and mines. By 1870 two six-horse coaches rolled in every day from Owens Valley, where they connected with stage lines to Virginia City, San Francisco, and Los Angeles.

Such feverish activity was always accompanied by lawlessness in Western mining camps—and Cerro Gordo had more than its share. Through the early '70s it was as famous for its shootings as for its silver riches. "Cerro Gordo is a prolific source of the 'man for breakfast' order of items," was the wry comment of an Owens Valley editor at news of the third shooting scrape in two days.

An ambitious young doctor arrived in town, only to leave the same night without his baggage. To the first man he met down the Yellow Grade, he frankly declared himself: "My friend, I came here to buy a stock of drugs and practice medicine, but damn me if I want an interest in a shooting gallery."

Not that Cerro Gordo had no law. One night a pile of wooden poles was stolen—an unforgivable crime in this lumber-shy camp. One inoffensive citizen was dragged before the Justice of the Peace as a suspect. Not a speck of evidence could be found against him, but the worthy magistrate had a duty to perform.

"You may not have stolen the poles," he admitted, "but there has been poles stolen, and I must make an example of somebody, so I fine you twenty-five dollars."

Most of Cerro Gordo's violence was traceable to two establishments, one at each end of town, which were generously termed "dance halls." The object of more than one fatal argument was a charming girl known as "The Fenian", the reigning belle of Cerro Gordo. Possessing a ferocious temper and a weakness for whisky, she was often less than ladylike. While on a sojourn to Los Angeles she beat up a man for calling her an Irish dog, broke an Italian boy's harp for refusing to play an Irish song, and returned to Cerro Gordo by request of the L.A. authorities. One night while staggering among the cabins on the side of Buena Vista Mountain she lost her footing and fell through a roof, causing the Chinese card-players beneath to flee the shack in terror.

By the fall of 1871 the more civic-minded citizens of Cerro Gordo decided to break the evil influence of the gay-gartered troupe led by The Fenian. The honest miner, thought these reformers, must abandon the quick-time of the harp and fiddle for more cultural, high-minded pursuits.

So the "Cerro Gordo Social Union", a literary and debating society, was founded. The largest hall in town was rented for the meetings, and the boys eagerly took up the new diversion. Week after week the debaters played to a full house, the girls found their dance floors deserted, and the club's founders congratulated each other on their success.

Enthusiasm was at its highest one night during a stormy political contest. The town's chief orator was condemning his opponents with such vehemence that he had to pause for a long breath of air. At that moment the sweet strains of the harp and fiddle drifted in the windows.

As one man, the crowd abruptly rose and made for the door. To the nearest dance hall they resolutely marched, while the speaker harangued empty benches. The one man remaining was the club's secretary, who was nursing a lame foot. The Cerro Gordo Social Union had met its inevitable fate.

Excitement also stalked the Cerro Gordo stage road, though most holdups were on the Mojave Desert at a safe distance from town. California's famed bandidos, Tiburcio Vasquez and Cleovaro Chavez, stopped the Cerro Gordo stage in 1874 at Coyote Holes, near the foot of Walker Pass. On the box beside the driver was none other than M. W. Belshaw, who was relieved of a silver watch, $20 in gold and a pair of new boots.

But in 1875 two other robbers rode boldly up the Yellow Grade and sacked Belshaw's toll house, almost within sight of Cerro Gordo. Two weeks later they returned and robbed the upstage two miles below town, making off with the Wells Fargo chest and the U.S. mailbag.

At this outrage, a formidable posse whirled down the Yellow Grade and scoured desert trails for the intruders. When the evil pair held up a freight station and boasted that they would kill Belshaw and Beaudry on sight, word passed through Owens Valley that the bullion kings had Cerro Gordo fortified against attack. But before matters grew worse, one of the outlaws was killed and the other fled to Mexico.

Though a lawless and remote camp, Cerro Gordo nevertheless cut a wide swath in California commerce. Nevada's Comstock Lode, pouring hundreds of millions into the wealth of San Francisco, was then towering over the other Western mining districts. But Cerro Gordo was the Comstock for another California city—Los Angeles. The coming of the bullion teams to Southern California in 1868 had happily coincided with a new influx of farmers. They found a ready-made market for their products—wine, corn and other items for Owens Valley miners, hay and barley for the freight mules. By 1870 all the surplus barley grown in Los Angeles County was consumed by Remi Nadeau's bullion teams.

"To this city," said the *Los Angeles News,* "the Owens River trade is invaluable. What Los Angeles is, is mainly due to it."

Other towns, notably Visalia, Santa Barbara and Ventura, were quick to bid for the trade. For a few months in 1872-'73 Bakersfield drew the traffic, only to lose it again to Los Angeles.

By early 1875 the Southern Pacific had reached past Bakersfield to the foot of the Tehachapis, settling for good the direction of Cerro Gordo traffic. Los Angeles enterprisers tried to build their own railroad to Owens Valley and hold the trade, but before it was well started Nadeau's bullion teams were connecting with the S.P. railhead at Caliente, while tunnels were being built over the Tehachapis.

So steady was Cerro Gordo's production that for years the freight wagons were unable to catch up with the furnace output. More teams were put on the road, the teams themselves were augmented with more mules and wagons, but the metal bars kept piling up at the source. In 1872 a small steamboat, the *Bessie Brady,* began hauling the bullion across Owens Lake to speed the process. But this merely transferred the piles from Cerro Gordo to the south shore of the lake.

During the Bakersfield debacle, 30,000 ingots had accumulated in Owens Valley, and passing miners were building them into temporary cabins. But in 1873 Nadeau insisted that Belshaw and Beaudry join him in financing a new firm, the Cerro Gordo Freighting Company. He built new stations and began dispatching teams on an almost hourly basis like a stage line. Within a few months, using 80 teams of 16 mules and three wagons each, the freighters cleared the furnace output for the first time.

Meanwhile, Belshaw and Beaudry had been fighting to keep their iron control of Cerro Gordo. Since 1869 another company had been operating a smelter at Owens Lake on ore brought down from Cerro Gordo. Belshaw's first reaction was to let his toll road fall into such neglect that the Owens Lake Company could scarcely bring enough ore to the furnace. It answered by trying to build another road, but found it impossible to get around the strategic canyon occupied by Belshaw's toll house. Then when it took the issue to the County Supervisors, Belshaw got himself voted a member at the next election.

But there was more than one way to fight the bullion king. Allies of the Owens Lake Company bought the San Felipe Mine, which held a conflicting claim to Belshaw and Beaudry's great Union Mine. But the pair countered by acquiring the San Felipe mortgage, foreclosing, and buying the property at sheriff's sale. So great was Belshaw's power in Owens Valley that when a San Felipe man arrived from San Francisco to pay off the indebtedness within the six months allowed by law, the undersheriff refused to take his money.

Believing themselves secure, the bullion kings now told the Owens Lake Company that they "owned the whole hill" and ordered it to quit working its mines. The rival outfit then financed a lawsuit to claim ownership of Belshaw and Beaudry's property. During the "big trial" in 1873, an armed clash was barely averted when Belshaw's miners halted an inspection of the disputed property by force.

Finally the decision went to the San Felipe group, but Belshaw and Beaudry kept the issue in the courts for over two years until their enemies settled for a minor interest in the Union Mine.

By this time the Union's fabulous treasure was failing. In December 1876 Belshaw shut down his furnace, and the following year a severe fire dealt the company a final blow. Cerro Gordo was all but deserted when the last mule team carried a load of bullion down the Yellow Grade in October 1879.

Since then, more than one new company has tried to strike a new fortune on Buena Vista Peak. After zinc was discovered in the depths of the mountain, Louis D. Gordon acquired the property in 1914 and built a bucket tramway to carry ore down the side of the Inyo Range to a narrow gage railroad that had its terminus at Owens Lake. From time to time other enterprisers try their hand at reviving the days when Cerro Gordo was L.A.'s Comstock.

## POINTS OF INTEREST

CERRO GORDO. From the little village of Keeler on the east shore of Owens dry lake, a dirt road heads up into the Inyo Range and Cerro Gordo. The last two-thirds of the eight-mile trip are steep and winding. Until recently, in the heat of summer your engine was apt to boil before you reached the town, particularly if you had been experiencing a tailwind on the upward climb. However, the road has been much improved.

As you enter town, the remains of Victor Beaudry's smelter, and part of the chimney, are standing on your left. In the middle of town is the two-story American Hotel, built in 1871. This and other buildings have been preserved by the generous restoration work of many Owens Valley people led by the town's current owner, Jodie Stewart. Over the divide at the head of San Lucas Canyon, which heads northeastward into Saline Valley, is the rock furnace of the Owens Lake Company, its shale chimney built for convenience up the face of the slope. Dominating the town are the rebuilt workings of the Union Mine, while the canyon sides above town are still pocked with the remains of the half-caves, half-shacks where the miners once lived. Even over the Buena Vista Peak, the ground is still pitted with craters marking the caved-in mouths of old mines, which the visitor would do well to avoid for safety's sake. Individual tourists to Cerro Gordo are currently being discouraged due to mining activity there, but group tours can be arranged by phoning (619) 876-4154 or 5178.

SWANSEA. This small locality was the headquarters of Belshaw's rival, the Owens Lake Company. Situated near the old shoreline of Owens Lake a short distance north of Keeler, it is marked today only by the crumbled remains of the brick smelter and by two buildings—one of stone and the other partly adobe—dating from the 1870s.

DARWIN. South of Owens Lake in the Coso Range, rich silver-lead deposits were discovered late in October 1874. By the year's end the town of Darwin—named for an early explorer of the region, Dr. Darwin French—had sprung up at the foot of Mount Ophir. One of the first arrivals was Victor Beaudry, who made haste to buy a nearby spring, lay pipes into Darwin and become "water king" of the new camp. Following him were several hundred stampeders from Cerro Gordo and another current Inyo County mining camp, Panamint. More adventurers from the tough Nevada towns of Pioche, Columbus, and Eureka arrived with a sharp eye for claims not held by right of shotgun. Claim holders soon moved out of town and lived in tents on their locations to hold them against the covetous newcomers.

By the end of 1875 Darwin boasted two smelters, some 20 operating mines, 200 frame houses and more than 700 citizens. Every day two Cerro Gordo Freighting Company teams, each equipped with 16 mules, pulled out of Darwin loaded with silver, skirting Owens Lake to reach the old Cerro Gordo bullion trail at Olancha. Lola Travis took her flock of girls from Cerro Gordo and started a dance hall in Darwin. Heading the 15 saloons was the Centennial, complete with cut-glass chandeliers and a billiard table advertised as "of the same pattern as used in the Palace Hotel in San Francisco."

Darwin reached its peak in 1876 with five furnaces and more than a thousand inhabitants. The town's wealth was not overlooked by California's fraternity of highwaymen, who robbed the Darwin stages repeatedly in 1875 and '76.

Darwin's decline began in August 1876 when the Defiance smelter, largest in town, shut down temporarily. An exodus began which rose to a stampede when Bodie and Mammoth City beckoned two years later. Darwin's light would not flicker out, however, without a labor dispute in 1878, wherein the disagreement turned into a general shooting match by all hands.

Today the ghost of Darwin is a collection of rude shacks—few of of them traceable to the 1870s. The Defiance smelter, with its scattered and rusted machinery, remains the most recognizable landmark of the old town. From time to time, as in Cerro Gordo, a major mining company probes Mt. Ophir for more pay dirt.

OLD COSO. In March 1860 an exploration party from California's Central Valley discovered silver deposits in the Coso Range between Little Lake and what is now Darwin. Reports of the first comers created a modest rush and a new town. Through the summer of 1860 the excitement mounted; the *Visalia Delta* reported, "Parties are leaving almost daily for the mines." Coso was going strong throughout the early 1860s, and when the easiest ores were skimmed by the Americans, Mexican miners experienced in working silver mines arrived in numbers. Through the 1870s Coso was a live camp, though it never numbered more than a few hundred.

Located about seven miles southwest of Darwin, Old Coso is inside the Navy Weapons Center firing range, and therefore inaccessible to the public. Ruins of four or five rock houses, using adobe for mortar, are still standing, while others remain in nearby canyons. Some other foundations, Mexican arrastres, and rusted machinery help to mark this Civil War ghost town.

# CIVIL WAR TOWNS OF OWENS VALLEY

Beginning in 1862 prospectors braved Indian hostilities to make new discoveries in Owens Valley. The first was San Carlos, started in the fall of '62 a few miles north of the present-day Independence, on the east side of Owens River. Two others founded in 1863 were Bend City, three miles south of San Carlos, and Owensville, situated to the north near the present locality of Laws. All were largely adobe or stone walls, which have all but disappeared today. Though they numbered several hundred people between them, they were handicapped by remoteness from the nearest head of "Whoa navigation". Closest stage depots were Visalia in San Joaquin Valley and Aurora in Nevada; from either place you rented a horse and rode on for Owens Valley.

For some two years the excitement lasted. The streets of San Carlos, Bend City, and Owensville rang with the hubbub of mule teams, and occasionally with the staccato of pistol shots. Agitation was begun for a new county seat east of the Sierra and south of Mono County. But by the time it was created by the Legislature in 1866, the mining camps had faded and the farming center of Independence became the seat of Inyo County.

KEARSARGE. In 1863 Secessionists in Owens Valley named their mine (and, later, the Alabama Hills) after the rebel raider, the *Alabama.* In June the U.S.S. *Kearsarge* defeated and sank the *Alabama* off the coast of France. Several Union men, prospecting in the Sierra during the fall of 1864, gave their retort to the Southerners by naming their claim the Kearsarge Mine.

Through the mid-1860s the remote camp of Kearsarge flourished; a 40-stamp mill and a number of log cabins were built on the west side of Kearsarge Peak. On March 1, 1867, it came to an abrupt end when a snow avalanche destroyed most of the buildings. That night the population of Kearsarge moved down to Owens Valley. Mining activity continued, but although good ores were worked, the mine never paid for itself and was finally deserted.

# Chapter 21. Panamint: A California Legend

A FEW MINING CAMPS stand out beyond their historical context as part of Western folklore: Bodie, Deadwood, Tombstone, and, not least, Panamint. Two books have been written about this fabulous ghost town: one a novel, *The Parson of Panamint;* the other a history with frank excursions into the unhistoric, *Silver Stampede.* Panamint is a necessary fragment of the California legend.

Yet this camp rose and fell in the slight space of three years. Its population never exceeded 2,000. As a mineral producer it was a dead loss. And few Californians have any idea where its ghost is located.

The Panamint of history was the California echo of Nevada's Big Bonanza. In 1873 the West Coast was caught in the frenzy over the new silver strike in the Comstock's Con Virginia and California mines. Their owners—Fair, Mackay, Flood and O'Brien—had suddenly become the Bonanza Kings of Western mining. With wild optimism ruling the day, any new silver discovery was hailed as a potential Comstock.

It was on this crisp tinder that the Panamint spark fell. In January 1873, three prospectors poking through the canyons of the Mojave Desert struck silver in the Panamint Range, the western wall of Death Valley. Rock samples showed as-

221

tounding values ranging from $300 to $3000 per ton. But the discovery was made at the head of Surprise Canyon in remote Panamint Valley, 200 miles from the coast. To translate this kind of ore into cash required two things: transportation and capital.

For more than a year the first Panaminters spent more energy pursuing these two necessities than in digging silver. Finally, in the spring of 1874, they found both. The Los Angeles Chamber of Commerce raised money and built a wagon road to Panamint Valley. Capital was provided by the two Nevada Senators, John P. Jones and William M. Stewart.

Panamint's name suddenly skyrocketed from the fame of these two investors. Stewart was the leading lawyer on the Comstock, the man who had written the Nevada Constitution and literally fathered the 36th state. Jones was a mine superintendent who had gained fame as hero of the terrible Yellow Jacket fire of 1869. More recently he had won new popularity among Nevada miners by outsmarting the California banking interests that had dominated Comstock finance. Knowing of a rich new lead in the Crown Point Mine, he quietly bought up its mining stock and made himself one of Nevada's silver kings.

When the West Coast heard of the latest interest of these "Silver Senators", the stampede to Panamint was on. Through the summer and fall of 1874 desert roads were choked with silver-seekers bound for Surprise Canyon. By November no less than seven stages a week were carrying the crowds into Panamint from the direction of Virginia City, San Francisco, Los Angeles and San Bernardino.

In the bottom of Surprise Canyon a rude town was rising from the handiest materials—stone shanties, log cabins built of piñon pines and even frame buildings made from lumber hauled in by mule team at $250 per thousand feet. Of the 50 structures that lined the mile-long street, there were six general stores offering goods at prices ranging from $2 per dozen eggs to $200 per ton of hay; at least twelve saloons, led by the Oriental, whose elegant furnishings were advertised as "the finest on the Coast outside of San Francisco"; a Bank of Panamint; a brewery; a meat market (whose wagon also served as the town hearse) ; and the office of a small but virile newspaper, the *Panamint News*. The sides of the canyon were dotted with the cabins, tents and caves of the miners, but were too steep to permit wheeled traffic. The mule teams, ox trains and stages kept to the main street, which was made livelier by showers of rock from the hills whenever a new blast was set off in the mines.

Panamint was just about as far from law and order as a California town could get, and so were her citizens. Among them was Ned Reddy, proprietor of the Independent Saloon, who had already killed two men in Owens Valley, supposedly in self-defense. Owner of the Oriental Saloon was Dave Neagle, who had arrived after a shooting scrape in Pioche, Nevada; later, as bodyguard to Justice Stephen Field, he would put a violent end to the violent career of Judge David S. Terry.

But Panamint's quickest gunman was Jim Bruce, professional gambler. The claim that Panamint's Boot Hill was his private cemetery was not quite fair. But two Panaminters did bite the dust before his ready trigger. One of them burst in on him in the boudoir of one of the camp's madams, and was promptly chastened with lead. Another prospector had a shooting argument with Bruce in front of the Bank of Panamint and came out second best. A witness to this second duel was one of the founding fathers, Senator Stewart, who discreetly took refuge behind a stone wall while bullets swept the main street.

It remained for two Nevada stage robbers, John Small and John McDonald, to bring the Robin Hood element to Panamint. Living in nearby Wildrose Canyon, they swaggered Panamint's streets unmolested by the law. On one occasion they journeyed to Nevada, robbed the Eureka stage and wounded the messenger, then returned to their Panamint hideout with the loot.

It was this outlaw pair that sold Senator Stewart one of his biggest Panamint mines. According to his reminiscences, they hung about while his giant stamp mill was being built, inquiring pointedly when he would begin shipping bullion. Finally on June 29, 1875, the great monster was fired up and the 20 stamps began grinding up the ore. When the first silver bullion was tapped from the smelter, the bad men were on hand, armed with six-shooters and sheepish grins.

But the crafty Stewart was ready for them. Out of his smelter rolled silver ingots weighing from four to five hundred pounds each. The bandits abruptly lost their smiles.

"Do you think it's right to play that game on *us*?" one of them demanded with injured pride. "And after we sold you the mine, too. Why, we can't haul away one of those boulders!"

It was Stewart's turn to grin.

"You can't expect *me* to be sorry for you, can you?"

So, while the hard-hearted Senator watched, the robbers tried to lift one of the silver pigs. It remained stubbornly in place. Then they got a pack mule and tried to heave the thing on his back. With no stomach for the venture, the animal bucked furiously until the men gave up. What was the use of making off with these impossible objects, anyway? Only Stewart's company could cash them in.

For months Small and McDonald had to suffer the torture of watching these silver balls leaving Panamint regularly by Remi Nadeau's mule teams, lurching down Surprise Canyon and across Panamint Valley. Before the cargo could reach Los Angeles and the steamboats that would carry it to the San Francisco mint, it had to traverse 200 miles of lonely desert under no protection but an unarmed driver. But there was nothing Small and McDonald could do about it. The insult was so deflating that in April 1876 they robbed a general store of $2,300 and left Panamint for good.

But while Stewart was opening production in Panamint, his

Senator partner was on the coast rounding out the enterprise on a grand scale. If Panamint was to be another Comstock, it needed a railroad. And so in September 1874 John P. Jones rode into Los Angeles and put up $220,000 toward a proposed line from tidewater to the silver country—the Los Angeles and Independence Railroad. Then he visited Santa Monica Bay and bought up three-fourths of the Rancho Santa Monica y San Vicente as a sea-going outlet for his tracks. What was more, Jones contacted the Eastern railroad magnate, Jay Gould, and suggested linking up with his Union Pacific line for a transcontinental connection. Gould agreed informally to meet him halfway, and the Panamint venture became national news.

All this did not suit the Big Four directors of the Southern Pacific—Stanford, Crocker, Huntington and Hopkins. They had their eyes on the Panamint traffic, and were miffed when Jones carefully avoided a connection with their Southern California rails. Worse still would be any linkup that would introduce a competing transcontinental line into California. To the Big Four, such a challenge meant action.

The strategic spot in Jones' master plan was Cajon Pass, where a Los Angeles and Independence survey party had already made preliminary explorations. On January 7, 1875, a band of Southern Pacific men rode into the Cajon to drive their stakes and take possession. But the L.A. & I. had an alert construction engineer—young Joseph U. Crawford. Getting wind of the S.P. move, he took his own crew and headed for the pass the same day. Somewhere along the sandy bottom of Cajon Creek they passed the rival S.P. gang. Knowing the ground from his previous reconnaissance, Crawford rode straight for Tollgate Canyon—the one spot too narrow for more than one railroad. His men were driving stakes and running lines when the Southern Pacific men arrived. Jones' railroad had won the first round.

Then Huntington of the Southern Pacific tried to stop the upstart railroad with an act of Congress. On January 8 a bill was introduced to give the S.P an exclusive right-of-way through Cajon Pass. But the Los Angeles people heard of it and deluged Congress with such outraged protest that it dropped the scheme. Huntington soon had to calm his alarmed partners.

"I do not think they will hurt us much," he wrote. "I will ventilate their safe harbor."

But Jones had only begun to fight. In July he founded the town of Santa Monica with a grand auction sale of lots. By December the L.A. & I. rails had reached from the bay 14 miles to Los Angeles. And in Cajon Pass his men were digging a tunnel that would give access to the Mojave Desert—and Panamint.

Then things began to happen that deflated Jones' dream. A financial panic swept California and took with it the leading Los Angeles bank, thus hurting stock sales for the L.A. & I. In the accompanying crash of Comstock mining securities, Jones was badly crippled. Then some of the most promising Panamint mines started running out of ore. In the spring of 1876 Jones and Stewart shut down their mill while their miners explored for more raw material. The Panamint venture had suddenly stalled.

Out of Surprise Canyon now trudged a disconsolate horde—miners, stock promoters, merchants with their goods, even the *Panamint News* editor with his hand press and type cases. Nights in Panamint's roaring saloons suddenly went still. Town lots that had sold as high as $1,000 could not be given away. By May 1877 the last company mines were closed and Panamint was a dead camp.

Today the reckless miners who once inhabited these hillsides are replaced by jackrabbits and ground squirrels. And the shouts of revelry that used to burst from saloon doors now find echo only in the rustle of wind through the sagebrush on Main Street.

BALLARAT. Taking the road to Death Valley through Trona, the traveler crosses the Slate Range into Panamint Valley. A short side road to the east brings one to Ballarat, a ghost town dating from the 1890s, when gold was discovered in the canyons south of Panamint. Named for the famed Australian gold center, this camp served for several decades as a hell-roaring oasis for Mojave Desert prospectors. Today it is marked by a number of picturesque adobe walls that are crumbling under the elements.

PANAMINT. From Ballarat the visitor continues on a dirt road up the great alluvial fan at the mouth of Surprise Canyon. If conditions are favorable, you can get to the mouth of the canyon before having to proceed for the last few miles on foot jor horseback. Though cloudbursts have left little of the Panamint that was, the camp still displays some foundations in the brush-covered bottom of the canyon, and the ruins of the brick stamp mill that was built by Senators John P. Jones and William M. Stewart.

LOOKOUT. Beginning in 1875 the camp of Lookout flourished in the Argus Range. It was connected by pack trail with its neighboring mines, the Minnietta and Modoc (the latter owned by Senator George Hearst, father of William Randolph Hearst).

Today's tourists find a remnant of this silver boom in the rock charcoal kilns of Wildrose Canyon in the Panamint Range; their product was hauled by Remi Nadeau's mule teams across Panamint Valley for the smelters of the Modoc and Minnietta.

For the traveler of today the Modoc and Minnietta may be reached by driving west on a dirt road from the main north-south highway through Panamint Valley. The Minnietta is located on the south side of Lookout Mountain, while the

Modoc is in a deep canyon about a mile away on the east side of the mountain, and requires a short but steep hike from the end of the road.

Reaching Lookout is even wilder, since it is perched on top of the mountain above the mines. It requires either a hike of about three miles up an old mule trail from the Modoc, or a roundabout drive via the back of the mountain if you have a jeep. Located on the north slope of eastern Lookout Mountain, it exhibits the foundations of some forty buildings, a few with walls still standing, and the remains of the Modoc furnace.

MILLSPAUGH. South of Maturango Peak on the western slope of the Argus Range is the site of Millspaugh, a short-lived camp that flared just after the turn of the century during the Tonopah-Goldfield era. Almost nothing is left at the location, which could be reached by dirt road from China Lake through Mountain Springs Canyon to Etcheron Valley, then by a dubious and unpredictable road about two-and-a-half miles east of Carricut Dry Lake into the Argus Mountains. But the site is within the Navy Weapons Center range, which is closed to public travel.

---

# Chapter 22. Bodie: Badman's Roost

"AS SOON AS the local talent get to thinking they're tough," a Comstock undertaker once complained, "they go to try it out in Bodie and Bodie undertakers get the job of burying them."

No doubt about it, Bodie was a bad town. It was gloriously rich; it was remote; and its boom in the late '70s was timed to draw a horde of adventurers from Virginia City and other fading Nevada camps. This combination gave meaning to the standard Western phrase, "Bad man from Bodie." One arrival of 1879 noted six fatal shooting scrapes during his first week in town. The daily *Bodie Standard* of September 5, 1880, mentioned three shootings and two stage holdups—apparently an ordinary day's work. A little girl, whose family was leaving the neighboring town of Aurora for the new camp, ended her nightly prayer with: "Goodbye, God; we're going to Bodie."

According to legend, Bodie owes its discovery to a wounded rabbit and its name to a signpainter's mistake. In 1858 Waterman "Bill" Body, an adventurous Dutchman from New York state, crossed the Sierra from the Mother Lode to reach a new strike at Monoville, a now-forgotten camp near the shore of Mono Lake. The following July, while riding past the townsite of Bodie, he shot and wounded a rabbit. In trying to dig it out of a hole, he discovered something else—gold.

Body never lived to reap the rewards, for he died in a snowstorm while trying to reach his cabin a few months later. But his discovery sparked a mining boom in the Mono country. In August 1860 the rousing town of Aurora was founded across the border in what soon became Nevada. Here it was that a painter is said to have changed Body's name in putting up the sign "Bodie Public Stables." At any rate, Bodie it has been since the early 1860s.

But while Aurora burned brightly during the Civil War, Bodie slumbered. In 1864 one visitor found less than twenty frame and adobe houses in town. Then in the middle '70s two partners paid $950 for what came to be known as the Standard Mine. They barely grubbed out an existence until another accident gave Bodie its tumultuous rebirth. A sudden cave-in exposed a fabulous ore body. The pair took out $37,000 in gold and silver before they sold the mine in 1876 for $67,500.

The buyers were San Franciscans headed by William M. Lent, known throughout the West as a shrewd mining investor. When they poured funds into the Standard Mine and began paying monthly dividends in the fall of 1877, Bodie's first rush was on. Miners who had stampeded to every strike from the Mother Lode to Pike's Peak now turned their feet toward Bodie. By February 1878 the new camp was so overrun that one arrival wrote of the difficulty in finding "even a place to spread one's blankets." Chilling winds, snowstorms and 9,000 feet altitude made Bodie miserable.

Meanwhile, Bill Lent had bought the nearby Bodie Mine, and its stock was languishing around 25 cents a share. In May 1878 his miners discovered a new vein which skyrocketed its real value. Mysteriously, Bodie Mine stock began to rise. When the first run of 1,000 tons of the new ore yielded $600,000, Bodie stock soared to $57 per share. Miners who had taken stock in lieu of wages earned $900 a day; a Chinese launderer came off with $57 for cleaning a shirt.

This news shook the West like an alarm bell in the summer of 1878 and triggered a second, bigger rush to Bodie.

By the end of the 1878, Bodie had 600 frame buildings and some 5,000 heavy-booted, wide-hatted adventurers. Through her bustling streets moved horsemen and pack burros; twenty-mule freight wagons from as far as Mojave on the Southern Pacific Railroad and Wadsworth on the Central Pacific; and daily and weekly stagecoaches from Carson City, Sonora, Mammoth City and Owens Valley.

In its heyday between 1878 and 1881, Bodie ran full blast round the clock, both above and below ground. Underneath, in the shafts of the Standard, the Bodie, and nearly 30 other mines on the side of famed Bodie Bluff, a total of $20,000,000 was being recovered in gold and silver ore. On top, fortunes were also passing across the bars and gaming tables of the hell-roaring Bonanza, Rifle Club, Champion, and the dozen or so other saloons that graced the main street. At its height Bodie boasted two banks, three breweries, half-a-dozen hotels, a sizable red light district, four daily newspapers, a well-populated Boot Hill, a volunteer fire brigade, and what was claimed as the West's biggest Chinatown after San Francisco's. The boys liked to insist that Bodie had "the widest streets of any Western mining town, the wickedest men, and the worst climate out-of-doors."

From the beginning of its big revival, Bodie was tough and proud of it. One of the earliest and most popular sports was claim-jumping. To settle one dispute in August 1879, the adjacent Owyhee and Jupiter Mines joined battle in earnest. From two makeshift forts the rival corps carried on an exchange of fire for two days. Then the Jupiter forces charged the Owyhee dugout. With bullets coming through their roof, the Owyhees lost one man and surrendered. Several hundred armed members of the Bodie Miners Union marched up the hill and set fire to the Jupiter fort.

The Jupiter superintendent and five of his men were tried and exonerated in the death of the Owyhee man, but on orders from the Miners Union they had to leave town.

Apparently the original "Bad man from Bodie" was one "Rough and Tumble Jack," who was described by a Nevada newspaper as "one of the roughest and toughest customers ever known." In January 1878 he was boasting of his physical prowess in a Main Street bar, claiming to be the undisputed "chief" of Bodie. He went outside with one challenger, and the two coolly drew guns at a distance of two feet and unloaded them at each other. Back into the bar reeled Rough and Tumble Jack. The other, with one arm shattered, reloaded his gun by holding it between his knees. A moment later Jack got a second dose which proved sufficient to end the career of Bodie's first bad man.

After that, shootings—usually unpunished—were weekly and sometimes daily occurrences. The camp's better citizens stood the bombardment until New Year's Even, 1879, when one celebrant objected to another dancing with his wife, and got a fatal bullet for his effort. This was too much, even for Bodie. A vigilance committee took the culprit from his jail cell, hustled him down Main Street to the scene of the crime, and hung him on a makeshift gallows. The one voice raised against the affair was that of a prominent attorney. One of the vigilantes cried, "Get a rope and we'll hang you!"

Not that Bodie meant to flout the law. A hearing was held on the lynching—with the jury including the leader of the vigilantes and the one who had applied the noose! Its conclusion: the victim was lynched by parties unknown.

Bodie's one lynching had no noticeable effect on its bad men. In fact, they soon turned their attention to the Concord stages that rocked out of town every day groaning with gold and silver bullion. The cliff-lined canyon through which it passed between Bodie and Aurora was made to order for banditry. During 1880 enterprising road agents stopped the Bodie stage no less than six times.

Wells Fargo Express was getting its fill. It soon began putting on two or more guards when a heavy consignment was shipped, transferring stage passengers to a light wagon following at a safe distance. The company brought in its crack shotgun messenger, Mike Tovey—a Canadian who was shy of manner but not of nerve.

On the afternoon of September 4 the robbers stopped the up-stage coming into Bodie, then waited in the canyon for the down-stage next day. But this time Tovey and a second guard rode the down-stage while the passenger wagon brought up the rear. Near the scene of the earlier robbery, Tovey got out and walked ahead. Undaunted by this precaution, the two robbers fired a volley at the guard. He then retreated to the stage and cut loose at the advancing enemy with a shotgun. One bandit was killed outright and the other was frightened away. But while Tovey went to a nearby house to get a wounded arm dressed, the surviving robber came back and rode off with Wells Fargo's treasure chest.

Successes of the road agents failed to make a dent in Bodie's high prosperity. No extravagance was too great, no celebration too extreme, for this riotous camp. In 1879 someone remembered that old Bill Body's remains lay down the canyon in an unmarked grave. "Poor old Body!" said the boys. Nothing was too good for the town's noble founder! A search was launched forthwith, and his bones were brought back in triumph. For days they were on public exhibit, subject to handling and close scrutiny by every civic-minded citizen. On November 1, 1879, amidst much speech-making (and doubtless elbow-bending), Bill Body's bones were laid to rest in Boot Hill.

What, then, of a suitable monument to Bodie's founder? For months the camp waited while an elaborate headstone was ordered and hauled in by twenty-mule team. But when it arrived the month was September 1881, and Bodie was stunned by news of President Garfield's death by assassination. Nothing was too good for the nation's martyred President! The monument was erected as a memorial, and Bill Body's bones remained in a transplanted, but still forgotten grave. Bodie's heart was big, but it was not always constant.

Meanwhile, boisterous Bodie was about to gain the ultimate feature of all top-notch mining camps—a railroad. Since 1880 the narrow-gauge Carson and Colorado, a branch of the Virginia and Truckee, had been inching southward across Nevada sands. In its march toward California's Owens Valley it would come no nearer to Bodie than some forty miles. This plan was hardly acceptable in that proud camp. Accordingly, another branch was begun in the spring of 1881 to connect Bodie with Benton, a mining town situated next to the Carson and Colorado route. Practical purpose of the road was to supply Bodie's deep-growing mines with timbers from fresh forests south of Mono Lake. But its name was the Bodie and Benton, and the owners also aimed to make rail connection with the outside world.

When the boys found that Chinese laborers were being imported for the work, their enthusiasm suddenly dimmed. Since the 1850s, intolerance of Chinese had been rife on the Coast, particularly since they were a source of cheap labor. At a meeting in the Miners Union Hall, a crowd of workingmen resolved to carry out the popular slogan, "the Chinese must go." Though the miners union itself opposed any action, a rough mob, traveling by wagon, horseback, and foot, moved toward the work camp east of Mono Lake.

But messengers for the railroad had ridden ahead with the warning. Immediately the Chinese were placed in boats and carried to an island in the middle of Mono Lake. When the Bodie bad men arrived, they found the camp deserted and their intended victims protected by several miles of inhospitable brine. The unholy crusade thereupon collapsed. For the next full day the ragged army was dragging back into town after a 40-mile round trip. Thereafter the Mono fiasco was a moot subject in Bodie.

As for the railroad, its Chinese workmen went back on the job undisturbed. By November 1881 they completed 31½ miles to the Mono timber stands, which is as far as the road ever got. Over its rugged grades, sometimes as steep as six percent, soon chugged quaint little engines with quaint little names—"Mono", "Inyo", "Tybo", and of course, "Bodie".

Bodie had its railroad, but its halcyon days were numbered. When a rumor reached the Mono County Supervisors that Bodie's mines might falter, they decided that there was no time to lose in building the new courthouse at Bridgeport, the county seat. With a stiff 6½% tax levied on all property (chief of which was Bodie's Standard Mine), they erected the new building in 1881. The elegant Victorian structure, carefully maintained ever since, stands today as the most picturesque courthouse in California—a monument to the Standard Mine.

By 1882 Bodie's noontide had passed, and the boys were

soon deserting her for new silver strikes in Arizona and Colorado. After Bodie mining stocks crashed the following year, the town faded fast. The Standard was merged with the Bodie in 1887 and continued to run intermittently, but the truth was that the camp's underground treasure was largely exhausted. It was the old familiar saga—a rich strike, an uproarious stampede, an hour of frenzied triumph, and afterward the shell of a town standing in ghostly silence.

One man who would not believe that the camp was dead was Jim Cain, an original arrival of the late '70s. Living in Bodie with his family, he gradually bought up the mines and buildings until he virtually owned the town. For years he opened the Bank of Bodie every day at 10 am—when the only possible customers were the ground squirrels scampering across the grass on Main Street. When surfaced highways brought Bodie within the reach of motorists in the 1920s, old Jim Cain showed off his ghost town to wondering tourists, always assuring them that Bodie would come back. This writer remembers visiting Bodie as a boy just before the fire of 1932, marveling at the rows of false front buildings "right out of a Western movie", and meeting Jim Cain—tall and nattily dressed, with a gold watch chain across his vest—as he showed us glittering ore samples in his bank.

### POINTS OF INTEREST

BODIE. Until that year, when the fire swept away two-thirds of the business district, this was probably the best preserved wooden ghost town in the Far West. Enough buildings remain to make Bodie well worth the 13-mile side trip (the last three unsurfaced) from Highway 395 south of Bridgeport.

Among the buildings of interest are, on the west side of Main Street south of Green Street, the U.S. Post Office and later the Dechambeau Hotel (1879), the Odd Fellows Hall (1880), and the Miners Union Hall (1878), now the Visitor Center and Museum. The Bodie Firehouse is further north on the east side of Main. On Green Street west of Main is the Boone Store (1879), while further west is the Methodist Church (1882). On Green east of Main are the Wheaton & Hollis Hotel and U.S. Land Office (about 1885), the Bodie schoolhouse (1879), and the power station where the first use of hydroelecticity to drive a motor by means of long-distance transmission lines (13 miles) began in 1892. The Kirkwood Livery Stable (about 1879) and the town jail are on King Street west of Main. The Red Light District was on Bonanza Street north of King, while Chinatown was located further west. The cemetery is on the hill southwest of town.

The workings of the Standard Mine, located on the slope of Bodie Bluff, are fenced off from sightseers because of the danger of falling down one of the many shafts in the area. But on weekends, visitors can tour the stamp mill.

The California Department of Parks and Recreation now maintains the townsite as a State Historical Monument, and rangers are available to answer questions about this ghost-town prototype. Due to their efforts, Bodie has been preserved from further decay. Today, from her warped board walks to her sagging false fronts, Bodie still keeps her reckless and truculent air.

MASONIC. A mile north of Bridgeport, a dirt road branches northeastward through Rock Spring Canyon to Sonoma in Nevada. On the way is the small camp of Masonic, nine miles from pavement in California, seven miles from pavement in Nevada. It was located in three clusters of population along the road on the north slope of Masonic Mountain. While the district had previously been prospected for a number of years, the first big discovery was not made until 1902, and substantial production of gold ore began in 1907. A few wooden shacks and the cable for a tramway are all that is left.

CAMERON. This old gold camp, which was at its height in 1882-'83, is located twelve miles north of Bridgeport via

Highway 22 and four miles west on a poor and unpredictable dirt road through part of Frying Pan Canyon. Almost nothing remains standing. Other nearby camps, even more obscure today, are Star City, located a mile-and-a-half northwest of Cameron by trail; Clinton, three miles north of Cameron near the mouth of Ferris Canyon (also accessible by trail); and Belfort, located in Boulder Flat about two-and-a-half miles west of Star City by trail.

DOGTOWN. On Highway 395, six-tenths of a mile south of the dirt turnoff to Bodie, one reaches the nearest auto point to Dogtown, located a few hundred yards off the road. In 1857 Mormons found gold here and started the first mining excitement in Mono County. Fortune-seekers came in from the Mother Lode and founded a town that today is marked by little more than piles of sand placered in Dogtown Creek.

MONOVILLE. Near the foot of the Conway Grade, a big canyon to the east reveals the general site of Monoville, where gold was discovered by a miner from Dogtown in 1859. A small rush from the Southern Mines set in over Tioga and Sonora Passes, bringing seven hundred men to Monoville within a few months. The town never became big and boisterous like some of its neighbors, but the excitement led to demands by the new population for another county separate from Calaveras County. As a result, Mono County was created in 1861. However, the population dwindled to 430 by the census of 1870, and Mono County had to wait for the Bodie stampede to regain a respectable population. Little remains to show the site of Monoville excepting the Sinnamon Cut, where a golden fortune was mined by hydraulic monitors.

AURORA. The dedicated ghost towner may want to attempt a 14-mile drive on a generally-bad road east of Bodie to the historic old town of Aurora. Located inside Nevada, Aurora could conceivably be classed among California mining camps, since it was the seat of Mono County until a boundary survey proved it to be outside of California. Founded in 1860, Aurora had two newspapers, a population of several thousand, and a dramatic vigilance committee episode. For a time Mark Twain stayed here and describes the Esmeralda County scene in his *Roughing It*.

When first visited by the author and his wife in 1947 while honeymooning at Mammoth Lakes, Aurora was easily one of the best ghost towns in the West. But since then it has vanished under the destructive work of commercial operators who were allowed to haul all of the bricks away. Only one cement wall, a few foundations and the ruins of a reduction works remain. Even the old cemetery, dating to Civil War days, has been desecrated by souvenir hunters. They have stolen the gravestones and headboards of loved ones whose children and grandchildren still live in California and Nevada.

---

# Chapter 23. Mammoth: Timberline Treasure

LOST MINES hold a fond place in Western tradition, and California has contributed more than its share. Of these, none has surpassed the famous "Lost Cement Mine", which sent a small army of prospectors combing the Mono country for over two decades. They never fulfilled their quest, but in the process they founded several roaring camps in the High Sierra and opened up a scenic wonderland—Mammoth Lakes.

Like most legends, the story of the Lost Cement Mine has several versions. Mark Twain's account, recorded in *Roughing It*, is as good as any. In the early '50s three

238

German brothers joined the Gold Rush and reached the Sierra somewhere in the Mono country. While resting in a canyon they found a vein of cement "shot full of lumps of dull yellow metal". It was two-thirds pure gold! Loading themselves with rock samples, they covered up the vein, made a map of the location and struck on again over the mountains. Two of them died on the gruelling trek, and the third reached the Mother Lode settlements so worn out that he never ventured back to find his mine. But he gave his map and the samples to a miner named Whiteman, who journeyed over the mountains and spent the rest of his life searching for the cement mine.

Mark Twain came to Nevada's Esmeralda mines, across the state border from the Mono country, in the early 1860s. In the mining camp of Aurora he got "one accidental glimpse" of Whiteman, who displayed a chunk of cement given him by the German. "Lumps of virgin gold," wrote Mark, "were as thick in it as raisins in a slice of fruit cake."

From time to time, word went through town that Whiteman had appeared—in disguise, of course—and the camp would be thrown into a frenzy. The universal object was to follow him and his map to the lost mine. Wrote Mark: "I have known it reported at eleven at night, in a large mining camp, that Whiteman had just passed through, and in two hours the streets, so quiet before, would be swarming with men and animals. Every individual would be trying to be very secret, but yet venturing to whisper to just one neighbor that W. had passed through. And long before daylight—this in the dead of winter—the stampede would be complete, the camp deserted, and the whole population gone chasing after W."

This, if we may believe Mark, was the state of mind in the border country south of Lake Tahoe in the '60s and '70s.

In June 1877 a group led by James A. Parker discovered a wide ledge of silver-gold ore on Gold or Red Mountain east of Lake Mary. According to custom, they announced it as "the largest bonanza outside of Virginia City." By August a Comstock company had optioned it for $40,000, and before the snows melted in the spring of 1878, had sent in a crew of miners and ordered a 40-stamp mill.

This kind of news sent a miner's heart leaping, and the stampede was on. From the mining camp of Benton, on the route between Owens Valley and Bodie, a wagon road was hurriedly built to the Mammoth mines. Another branch was constructed from Bishop Creek to the lake country by J. L. C. Sherwin, and the famous highway switchbacks over the toughest part of this route are still known as the Sherwin Grade. By April 1878 an upper Owens Valley resident described the passing traffic: "Men bound for the lake district. . . pass through here daily. Some go afoot, others horseback while a few navigate by vehicles."

One of the earliest to arrive was General George S. Dodge, a noted California mining investor. Owners of one of the mines showed him their property, offered ore samples and quoted assay figures. Dodge sat down on a pine stump in the main street and looked up a thousand feet to the Mammoth outcroppings.

"I don't want to know how rich they are," he answered. "They'll do for a deal anyhow."

With this bold optimism, General Dodge bought the mine for $30,000 in cash and mining stock, giving another spurt to the Mammoth boom. For the next two years the district rode high on California's wave of mining excitement. In the spring of 1878, lots were occupied and fenced for a mile up the single street, with at least 20 log houses under construction. By 1879 it had two newspapers, two breweries, six hotels, six general stores and 22 saloons. A thousand people had arrived, and town lots of 25-foot frontage were selling at $1,500.

In April 1879 the Mammoth mine reached ore that was said to be "half gold," and excitement raged still higher. Mammoth Mine stock jumped from $3 to $15 a share. Reported one newcomer:

"The main street here is a jam of men and teams coming in from all parts and loaded with every conceivable article."

Travel into this remote camp was by three methods, each from a different direction. Freight arrived by Remi Nadeau's twenty-mule teams over a wearisome trek of 220 miles from Mojave, on the Southern Pacific Railroad. Passengers came by a tri-weekly coach from Benton, which connected with stages from Nevada's Carson City, 150 miles away. Californians who cared to rough it by a more direct route could leave the stage at Fresno Flats (now Oakhurst), south of Yosemite, and take the saddle train 55 miles over the ridge of the Sierra. This approach was not recommended for those with bad nerves or a short temper.

But for at least four months of the year, Mammoth was completely snowbound. In this grim season most houses were buried in snow, with entry made by burrowing down to the front door. All travel was by skis, which the Mammothites called "snowshoes". There were no horses in camp, and as one resident put it, "we couldn't use them if they were here."

To add to this handicap, Mammoth was dogged with bad luck. In hauling in machinery for the stamp mill, the huge boiler offered the toughest problem. It was carried by rail from San Francisco to Mojave, then carefully transferred to one of Nadeau's twenty-mule team freight wagons. Then for 10 or 12 days it was pulled across the Mojave Desert and through Owens Valley.

Finally, the plodding animals reached the Sherwin Grade—a day's haul from Mammoth City. As they labored upward to the tune of cracking blacksnake and jingling chains, the wagon toppled over and the boiler crashed into the canyon below. No amount of straining and swearing could haul the stubborn object back up to the road, and at last report it lay there still.

Mammoth finished its stamp mill—after further delay. But an even bigger problem was getting the ore from the mine down the dizzy 3,500-foot decline to the mill. The miners built a trestle, which blew down in the first heavy wind. Next came a chute lined with sheet-iron, but the first carload smashed it to splinters. Then then erected a covered tramway. On the starting ride, the car jumped the track at the first curve and cracked up. The structure was remodeled, but soon a car got out of control on an icy track and almost killed the brakeman. Mule power was installed on a more level section of the route, but another Sierra breeze blew the mule from the track. After that it was reported that mountain storms were slowing production. Apparently the reason was that whenever a wind rose in the canyon the mule laid down until it passed.

Under such misfortunes, the Mammoth company had spent some $385,000 by early 1880, and had produced an estimated $200,000 in silver and gold. This was less than satisfactory to the stockholders, and the whole works shut down for good. A snowshoe army marched out of Mammoth, and by the spring of 1881 the camp was deserted. Nobody has yet found the mine with gold as thick as raisins in a fruit cake.

**POINTS OF INTEREST**

MAMMOTH CITY. At first glance, little remains of Mammoth City as one drives down the old Mammoth Road from Twin Lakes. But high on the side of Gold Mountain one can see the tailings of the Mammoth Mine. Beyond the willow thicket that lines the road are the remains of a small mill built by a later investor in the 1890s. Alongside the road on the south there remained, until a few years ago, the ruins of two log cabins, both of them containing a few of the cut nails (along with many wire nails of later vintage) that indicate construction prior to about 1885-90. On the north side of the road are the real remains of the town. Among the pines and up the slope, hidden by thick manzanita, are many stone foundations. Only a hike among these ruins can give any idea of the size of Mammoth city in its heyday.

MILL CITY. About half-a-mile below Mammoth City, the road winds among the pines and goes by a camp ground on the left. Entering the campground and driving to its south-western corner, one may go a little farther among some summer houses before the road ends. A short walk on a plain trail beyond this point brings one into a clearing—the site of Mill City.

Dominating the scene are the remains of the Mammoth Mining Company's 40-stamp mill, including the stone foundation and a huge flywheel perhaps 20 feet in diameter. Painted on the wheel in two places are the faint letters: "M.M. Co., Care of C.G.F. Co., Mojave." This forwarding address, marked there by a Southern Pacific Railroad freight agent, may be translated: "Mammoth Mining Company, Care of Cerro Gordo Freighting Company, Mojave,"—the latter being the freighting outfit operated by Remi Nadeau, with headquarters at Mojave after the Southern Pacific line was finished from San Francisco to Los Angeles. Among the aspens and pines on the hill above the millsite are the sunken foundations of other houses that made up Mill City.

BENTON. A silver camp, Benton dates from the 1860s and played an important role in Mono County mining life during the bonanza heyday of Bodie and Mammoth. From Bishop, take U.S. Highway 6 north for 34 miles to Benton Station, once a depot on the old Carson and Colorado Railroad from Nevada. Then turn west four miles to Benton itself, now a sleepy village in striking contrast to its turbulent past. Still remaining are a few historic buildings and the cemetery, which can be pointed out to the visitor from the town's general store.

LUNDY. In 1879, gold was discovered near the west end of Lundy Lake, a few miles from Mono Lake, in what became the Homer Mining District. Here sprang the mining camp of Lundy, famous for its timberline mines, snow avalanches and a hilarious newspaper, the *Homer Mining Index*.

The latter was edited by a character known as "Lying Jim"

Townsend, said to have been the inspiration for Bret Harte's "Truthful James". He specialized in puffing up the size of the town for the benefit of British mine investors. Lundy was small, even for the Sierra camps, but the *Mining Index* carried ads for two banks, a railroad timetable and writeups of sparkling first nights at the theater.

But there was nothing imaginary about Lundy's snowslides. Two resolute miners had their cabin buried by avalanches in two successive winters. Six feet of snow fell on Lundy in March 1882, starting a whole series of slides. One mountain of snow dropped several thousand feet and covered three cabins, whose occupants were later rescued. Another miner lay in bed one night worrying over warnings from friends in town; he rose and started for Lundy, and was scarcely out of the way when a snowslide buried his shack.

Located at the west end of Lundy Lake, the old camp today includes several old stone and frame buildings—a few of early vintage—and a number of rock foundations. The May Lundy Mine, which is said to have produced $2,000,000 in gold before it was shut down in 1898, may be seen high up on the mountainside to the south.

TIOGA (Bennettville). Near the top on the west side of Mt. Excelsior, north of Tioga Pass, is the Sierra ghost town of Tioga or Bennettville. Its mining history dates to 1860, when the first silver claim was made by some adventurer who strayed off the beaten paths of the California Gold Rush. In 1878 the Tioga Mining District was organized, eastern capital was soon forthcoming, and a crude town sprang up at an altitude of nearly 12,000 feet.

But though the silver ore was there for the taking, the trick was to get it refined and transported from its remote Sierra perch. Milling machinery was sledded in from Lundy to the east. A road was built over the Sierra from the Southern Mines. A long tunnel was driven to tap the silver ledge. But the eastern capital ran out and in July 1884 the whole operation was shut down. Picks were left in the tunnel and miners' plates abandoned at the table in the mess hall. Tioga was a mining town that never mined an ounce of silver. But it did spark the first road over Tioga Pass—one that was later taken over by the National Park Service for the benefit of vacationers bound to Tuolumne Meadows.

SILVER MOUNTAIN. One of the first real strikes made in the High Sierra was at Silver Mountain, located east of Ebbetts Pass near the headwaters of the Carson River. In 1863, when the main Silver Mountain discovery was made, the Comstock boom was at its height and California was ready to believe any new silver strike a potential bonanza. Miners from the Mother Lode stampeded over the old Ebbetts Pass emigrant road, paralleling the Stanislaus River. Soon stages began running from the Southern Mines as far as Silver Valley, west of the summit, whence a saddle train carried passengers the remaining miles to Silver Mountain.

"As we descend the canyon from the summit," wrote an early arrival of August 1863, "suddenly a bright new town bursts into view. There are perhaps forty houses, all new. . . .This log shanty has a sign up, *Variety Store;* the next, a board shanty the size of a hogpen, is *Wholesale & Retail Grocery;* that shanty without a window, with a canvas door, has a large sign of *Law Office;* and so on to the end. . . . Tunnels and drifts are being sunk, and every few minutes the booming sound of a blast comes to the ear like a distant leisurely bombardment."

In these first days the camp was seized with silver fever. Hundreds of miners were "scampering like a nest of disturbed ants"; mining terms"—"lodes", "indications", "rich rock"—were heard on all sides. Speculation was raging in town lots. "Nearly everyone," observed the visitor, "is, in his belief, in the incipient stage of immense wealth."

Despite such bursting confidence, Silver Mountain never rivaled Virginia City. But together with the neighboring camp of Monitor, it drew enough population to form the new county of Alpine in 1864. By 1875 the county seat had shifted from Silver Mountain to Markleeville. It remained big enough to support a newspaper, the *Alpine Chronicle*, through the late 1870s. But by the mid-'80s the old camp was deserted.

Today the remains of Silver Mountain lie along the bank of Silver Creek on a remote dirt road a few miles south of Markleeville. The most substantial ruins are the old jail and the home of "Lord" Lewis Chalmers, a Scottish mine developer who threw in his lot with Silver Mountain in her palmiest days. Climbing in these, as in other tempting ruins, can be dangerous.

MONITOR. Six miles southeast of Markleeville, Highway 89 goes eastward over Monitor Pass to meet U.S. Highway 395. On Monitor Creek west of the pass is a locality called Loope on the maps, but is actually the site of the old mining town of Monitor. Flourishing throughout the 1860s and '70s, Monitor was big enough to support a weekly newspaper, first the *Alpine Miner,* then the *Monitor Argus.* Today practically nothing is left of the old camp. Two miles up Loope Canyon is the site of Mogul, another mining town of the same period. The mines of the Monitor-Mogul district produced silver and copper, with some gold.

# PART VI. GHOST CAMPS OF THE SOUTH

THE MINING TOWNS of *Southern California, not to be confused with the Southern Mines of the Mother Lode, spanned almost the entire mineral era of California. In fact, from the first Kern River excitement in 1854 to the Death Valley camps of the early 1900s, they covered nearly the whole period of the nation's mining frontier.*

*Moreover, they were located in scattered spots throughout the region—in the southern Sierra, the Sierra Madres, the Colorado and Mojave Deserts—even in the Coast Range, which was singularly barren through most of California. They simply proved, again, that "gold is where you find it."*

*For these reasons the Southern California camps fall into no neat category. But in their entirety they represent the whole saga of Western gold and silver mining. Most of them rose and fell like a flash flood in a desert canyon. More than in the North, they are today abandoned—all except a very few, such as Julian, that turned to other activities.*

*Due to neglect and the ravages of wind, sun, and rainstorm, most of them are nearly obliterated. In the piñon pines and the sagebrush of Southern California, cracked and rusted ruins remain as monuments to the jackass prospector—the man with sand in his boots and the sun in his eyes.*

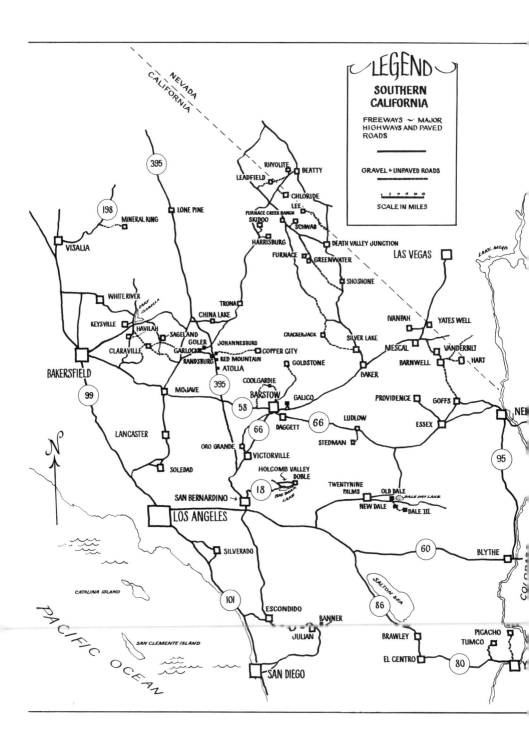

*Long mule-team loading ore at the Silver King Mine, Calico, in the 1880's.*

*Faded, rare old photograph of Julian City in the 1870's.*

*Sprawling on the side of Rand Mountain in the 1890's, Randsburg was Southern California's biggest gold strike.*

Courtesy of Los Angeles County Museum, Historical Photo Archives

*With its false front buildings and board walks, Randsburg was a model for later Western movie sets.*

*Randsburg miners had champagne tastes and champagne pockets to match. Helping to celebrate Flag Day in 1896 is the discoverer of the Yellow Aster Mine, F. M. Mooers, fourth from left.*

*In 1907 all roads led to Skidoo—California's
last big gold rush.*

*Lonely, desolate Borate, center of the Calico Mountain
borax excitement of the late 1880's.*

*From birth to death in 10 short years was the fate of Skidoo
—Southern California's Coloma of the early 1900's.*

*Located near the Mexican border was Tumco—California's southernmost mining town.*

# Chapter 24. The Kern River Camps

LITTLE REMAINS in the Kern River country to show for the early days of gold. Much of what there was is now under water backed up by Isabella Dam, southern anchor in the Central Valley Project. But the sites of the old camps of Keysville and Havilah are still accessible over bumpy dirt roads for the true ghost town hunter.

Today the Kern County empire, with its capital at Bakersfield, is made up largely of cotton and oil. But in the gold era the valley was a worthless plain, and population in the thousands inhabited the mountain section of Kern River and its South Fork. For the Kern was Southern California's first mining rush. In one brief moment it was the biggest mining news in a state that was gloriously and proudly gold-crazy.

It began in the summer of 1854, when California was suffering the first setback after the high tide of the Gold Rush. The placers were failing, the shift to quartz mining had only begun, and depression was creeping over the state. Southern California, which had boomed as the supplier of beef cattle for the mines, was returning to the pre-Yankee spirit of *poco tiempo.*

At this receptive moment came the cry of gold from Kern River. A party of Argonauts had found it near the junction of the Kern and its South Fork. By August 130 men were on the ground, taking out from $10 to $25 apiece per day. One of them picked up a 2½-pound nugget. As if this news was not enough, the report passed through the Mother Lode that a Mexican from Kern River had flourished a bag of nuggets on the streets of Mariposa and told his listeners of hills "yellow with outcroppings."

Quickly, Southern California editors seized on Kern River as proof of the mineral wealth which they had long claimed for the neglected South. In December the matter was settled when an Angeleno wrote from Kern River that "there is no doubt of there being a plenty of gold here. . . .The only difficulty is that we have no provisions."

Provisions? L.A.'s merchants saw their signal. Here was the end of Southern California's doldrums. A second Gold Rush—and Los Angeles was to be its San Francisco!

In 1854 there was no wagon road directly north from Los Angeles. This didn't stop the Angelenos. The dynamic Phineas Banning, local stage and freight king, drove a coach out of Los Angeles to prove the route was feasible. The first obstacle was the formidable Frémont Pass, just beyond San Fernando Valley. Here his passengers got out and walked while Banning's horses fought their way to the top. Down the other side plunged a rugged brush-covered gulch at a near-perpendicular angle.

Against the pleas of his comrades, according to pioneer author Horace Bell, Banning urged his team over the edge with the retort that a driver who couldn't negotiate that hill "should confine himself to ox teaming in the valley." Over they toppled, crashing headlong at the bottom of the pass. Feverishly the passengers scrambled down and pulled Banning from the wreckage.

"Didn't I tell you," beamed the stageman. "A beautiful descent, far less difficult than I had anticipated."

In this spirit, Los Angeles got through to Kern River. Her merchants raised money to fix the worst spots in a new road that led over Frémont Pass, up San Francisquito Canyon, past the Army fort at Tejon Pass, and as far as the mouth of Kern River Canyon where it emerges into San Joaquin Valley. From this point a pack trail led through the rugged Kern River gorge for the last thirty miles to the mines. By early February 1855, Banning was sending regular six-horse stages and ten-mule freight wagons to Kern River. Accompanying them were two express lines and a virtual horde of gold-seekers.

For Southern California had now caught the fever. Raising

dust through the streets of Santa Barbara, Los Angeles and San Bernardino were miners and storekeepers, wagon trains and pack burros, herds of cattle and bands of sheep.

"Picks, pork, shovels, hard bread and pans are at a premium," wrote a Santa Barbara citizen.

"Our public houses are crowded with strangers," cried the *Los Angeles Star*, "although every kind of conveyance is called into requisition to get to the diggings."

"Through the entire distance." observed one Argonaut, "one cannot lose sight of men, teams and cattle."

By early March the editor of the Los Angeles *Southern Californian* lost his head in the frenzy.

"Stop the Press!" he wrote. "Glorious News from Kern River! Bring out the Big Guns! There are a thousand gulches rich with gold and room for ten thousand miners."

Northern California kept its head until steamers from the South began bringing news of the mining craze. On February 12 the *Goliah* reached San Francisco with word the miners were making up to $50 per day. Over 2,000 men were on the ground and more were on the way from as far as Sonora, Mexico.

The skeptical North could hold itself no longer. Next day the *Goliah* pulled out of San Francisco jammed with rainbow-hunters. A party of riders left the Bay the same day by the overland route. By early March river steamers—some of them decked with huge signs, "Kern River"—were puffing out of Sacramento and other northern points loaded to the guards. Then they descended on Stockton, head of navigation on the San Joaquin. Into this bustling center—her streets and stores suddenly alive with men—converged steamboats, freight wagons and stagecoaches. It was Forty-nine all over again. "Ho! for Kern River!" shouted the men of '55. "Kern River or Bust!"

South from Stockton the crowds took a wagon road that entered the Sierra by way of White River and came to an end at Posey Flat. In the last 30 miles over Greenhorn Mountain they pressed on by foot or horseback.

Life in this new Kern country of rocky hills and scrub junipers followed the Mother Lode pattern. At the main settlement of "Forks of the Kern", miners slept in tents, worked all day carrying ore to be washed at the river in their long toms, paid exorbitant prices for food and tools. Living far from ordered society, they observed no law but their own consciences. One storekeeper was shot and killed, according to the report, "because he refused to sell a man a pair of pants on credit." When foreign miners—French, Spaniards and Mexicans—arrived, the hostile Americans refused to let them stake out the best ground.

But by early spring it was apparent that nobody was going to gain a fortune on Kern River. Gold was there, though not in quantities that made the trip worthwhile. Denouncing the whole excitement as a Los Angeles promotion scheme, disheartened miners drifted back into the settlements and dampened the Kern River fever. By May only a few hundred men remained where as many as 5,000 had crowded in scarcely a month before. One eyewitness summed up the dismal scene: "Provisions, tools, bad whisky and vicious rattlesnakes . . . in all directions."

The Los Angeles papers tried to bolster the gold boom by fairly pleading with the miners to stay on the Kern. "Two or even one dollar per day," urged the *Star*, "is far better employment than to come back here and loaf around our grog shops." But it was no use; Southern California's dream of mining glory had vanished. The Kern River "humbug" became a laughing stock in the Northern gold fields. A stray horse wandering through Sacramento had a derisive sign tied to his rear: "Bound for Kern River."

Still, the Kern country's golden days were not over. A rich ledge that was one of the sources of the gold placers had been discovered in a side ravine by one Captain Richard Keys as early as 1854. Near his Keys Mine grew a rustic frontier town named Keysville, first American community in what is now

260

Kern County. Without formal streets, its rough wooden stores were scattered at random over the hillslope, while miner's cabins dotted the mountainside above.

Through the late '50s this was one of the most remote settlements in California—110 miles to the nearest town of Visalia in one direction, 140 miles to Los Angeles in another. Most supplies came in over the northern route, and were packed over Greenhorn Mountain until 1856. The first wagons on the trail from Posey Flat had to follow the ridges and canyon bottoms while one teamster went ahead and chopped down trees with an axe. Teams were doubled going up the steepest mountains, while wagons were held back on the downhill run by dragging trees behind. First wagon to arrive in the Kern mining country was lowered by rope down the mountainside into Keysville. One visitor called it "the hardest wagon road I have ever seen that was much traveled."

In 1856 this far-off settlement found itself in the midst of an Indian war. The tribes of San Joaquin Valley had taken the warpath, and most of Keysville's able-bodied men rode out to help put down the uprising. Just over Greenhorn Mountain a party of miners killed five Indians in cold blood; the infuriated natives then proclaimed war on all the whites in the Southern Sierra—of which Keysville was the chief settlement. Around May 1 its people heard that some 500 Indians had gathered at the mouth of the Kern to attack the town.

Keysville was thrown into panic. With most of her men away, she was left with only 60 defenders. Wielding picks and shovels, they hurriedly dug an earth "fort" on a prominent knoll near the lower edge of town. To the commander of Fort Tejon and the Los Angeles sheriff they sent riders in quest of arms, ammunition and reinforcements.

"We have fortified ourselves and will defend ourselves if they make an appearance," ran one message.

From Fort Tejon came a troop of cavalry, which found no Indians on the Kern, but came on anyway and occupied Keysville. In Los Angeles the citizens held a meeting to raise a rescue company, but before they could act the Indian scare had subsided.

In April 1863, when Indian fighting was intense in Owens Valley, a relief company of cavalry was sent over Walker Pass. On the way the troopers stopped at Keysville and learned that a party of Indians was encamped several miles to the north. Advancing in the dark, they surrounded and captured the village, separated 35 of the grown males, and then coolly murdered them. It later turned out that the victims of this foul massacre were peaceable Indians who had refused to war against the whites. Reported the captain, proudly, "Not a soldier injured."

As early as 1860 Kern mining was branching out beyond Keysville. A miner bearing the unenviable name of "Lovely" Rogers struck out from Keysville on a prospecting trip and lost his mule. In the tradition of half the mining strikes in the West, he found the animal in a remote canyon, picked up a rock to throw at him, and found it was rich in gold. His discovery led to development of the famed Big Blue Mine and the new Kern River town of Quartzburg.

The newest Kern camp grew in wealth and wickedness until the temperance element gained power and turned the town dry. Saloonkeepers thereupon moved a mile down the river and founded their own town—with the obvious name of Whisky Flat. In 1864 the new camp made a concession to respectability by changing its name to Kernville. Through the early 1860s these rival towns were the center of population in the Kern country.

Into this backwoods center in 1864 came the genial showman, Asbury Harpending, a Confederate sympathizer in search of refuge. From Kernville he pushed on with three companions into the Tehachapi Mountains south of the river. In this wild country they made a rich new strike, organized a mining district, and named their camp Havilah—after the locality in Genesis "where there is gold."

This pine-shaded camp promptly boomed in the fashion of

Kern mining excitements. Men flocked in by the hundreds, town lots sold as high as $20 a front foot, pack trains and stage coaches were arriving regularly from Kernville and Los Angeles.

From the beginning Havilah was known as a hotbed of secessionists, of whom Harpending later claimed to be the leader. Suspicion against the place grew so strong that a cavalry troop was sent from San Joaquin Valley to bring Havilah into line.

But the camp was warned of the invasion and laid its own strategy. When the bluecoats reached the outskirts of town, they were immediately surrounded by a small army of well-heeled miners. Harpending, according to his own account, then stepped forward and, with a mock salute, told the officer in charge that they were "just in time for breakfast."

Heeding his sense of discretion, the officer thereupon accepted the offer, and Havilah was left alone—at least according to Harpending.

In fact, by the end of the Civil War the Kern mining community was demanding its place under the California sun. In 1866 Kern County was formed, with Havilah as the seat of government. Through the early 1870s the influx of real mining capital kept the Kern camps thriving. Havilah boasted two newspapers, while Kernville and Quartzburg supported nearly a dozen stamp mills. In 1875 one of Nevada's silver senators, John P. Jones, came through and in his familiar offhand manner bought up the Big Blue and most of the neighboring mines. Then he built a tremendous 80-stamp quartz mill, and for several years the Kern camps hummed with full production. But fire blackened the Big Blue installations in 1883, and the heyday of Kern River mining was over.

### POINTS OF INTEREST

Much of the cradle of Kern County settlement—including the original townsites of Kernville and Quartzburg—is under

263

water at the bottom of Lake Isabella.

KEYSVILLE. Reached by a dirt road, this pioneer mining camp of Kern County is marked only by a few houses of comparatively recent vintage. But on a small knoll at the lower edge of town the visitor may still see the outlines of the circular trench and shoulder-high breastworks of the fort built to defend Keysville against Indians. In a gulch to the north of town is the entrance to the Keys Mine, discovered in 1854.

HAVILAH. The pioneer cemetery is the only important old landmark remaining at what was once the seat of Kern County. However, replicas have been built of the old schoolhouse and the county courthouse. There are also the rock ruins of an old store, and an air of sweet nostalgia, to mark Havilah, "where there is gold."

CLARAVILLE. Near the base of Piute Mountain, reached by dirt roads from several directions, is the site of Claraville, founded early in 1866. While no building of early date remains on the actual site of Claraville, there are many rock foundations and boards with cut nails hidden from view among the sagebrush on the north side of the road just west of Landers Meadow. Beyond where the road crosses Kelso Creek, the pine-covered slopes to the north are pocked with the remains of mining shafts, and there is a well-defined ditch dug by the miners to carry snow water to their workings for a long distance along the contour of the mountainside.

SAGELAND. Of somewhat later vintage is Sageland, located just north of Kelso Valley and marked today by two or three houses that do not date to its pioneer days. Across a hillside to the northwest are the remains of old ore workings, while on a ridge to the northeast is the original cemetery. Here a number of weathered picket boards, with the typical carved points of the Victorian cemetery fence, are scattered about in somewhat pathetic reminiscence of lives long departed. The cut nails abounding on the knoll date it at least as far back as the 1880s.

MINERAL KING. North of the Kern country, tucked in a sharp indentation of the Sequoia National Park boundary, is Mineral King, a mining camp of the 1870s. From the main highway entering Sequoia, a dirt road branches east at Hammond and follows along the East Fork of the Kaweah River. Crossing the river at Oak Grove, it hugs the north side of the canyon, crosses a spur of the park boundary, and after 25 tortuous miles arrives at Mineral King in the Sequoia National Game Refuge.

In 1873 a party of spiritualists discovered silver here and founded the town. Two years later the toll road was built and a modest rush of miners followed. But the deposits were never rich, and an end to the mining era was written by a snowslide that buried part of the workings in 1888.

Today Mineral King is a resort for summer homes and a starting-point for pack trips in the Sierra country. On the old road four miles short of Mineral King is another old camp, Silver City, which also has a pack station and summer homes.

WHITE RIVER. The little village of White River, ten miles east of Delano, was founded as a gold camp in the 1850s. First called Dogtown, it soon went by the wonderful name of Tailholt, which was later changed to the more respectable title of White River. Among the points of interest are two cemeteries—one north of the river for regular citizens, and a small one south of the river for the town toughs who died violently.

# Chapter 25. Julian City: Southland Bonanza

EARLY-DAY CALIFORNIA had hundreds of rancho grants and hundreds of gold mines, but the two claims clashed at only two points. One was on Colonel Frémont's Mariposa Rancho, near Yosemite. The other was at San Diego County's one bonanza, Julian City.

San Diego in mid-19th Century was a town with a magnificent harbor, a delightful climate, and little else. California's earliest settlement, it had watched with envy the spectacular rise of Northern California cities during the Gold Rush. Then in 1867 Alonzo Horton arrived and took charge. Near the old San Diego community clustering beneath the mission, he subdivided an entirely new town, placing San Diego on the high tide of a Southern California boom.

Meanwhile, placer mining on a small scale had begun in the late 1850s high in the San Diego Mountains, west of the old Santa Ysabel chapel. In January 1869 the first trace of gold was discovered on the ranch lands of Mike Julian, a former San Diegan. This activity was not lost on San Diego newspaper editors, who had long claimed that golden treasure in the mountains behind the city only awaited exploration.

This was the situation early in 1870, when several prospecting parties were combing the San Diego Mountains. On February 20 a party including N. C. Bickers was camped on the Julian lands. Since this was Sunday, they were taking their leisure. Bickers was returning to camp from a walk when he accidentally kicked over a piece of quartz. According to miner's habit he picked it up, and saw specks of free gold. Excitedly he raced back to his friends, but the consensus was that nothing could be done about it on the Sabbath. One disciplinarian even refused to look at the rock on Sunday.

But next day, in the teeth of a rainstorm, the prospectors descended on Bickers' discovery. On Tuesday, February 22, they took out half a ton of the rich ore. Convinced that they had a mine, they consulted their calendar and christened it the George Washington.

At first the miners of the Julian country tried to keep the secret. The new owners of the Rancho Cuyamaca, lying to the south, were trying to confirm their boundaries with a survey. If they heard of the gold discovery, they might try to "float" their grant northward to include the mines.

But one miner broadcast the story. The Julian men held a meeting to decide their course. They first went to the Cuyamaca surveyor and asked him where he was finding the boundary. He was noncommittal. Then, since the news was out, they decided to make the most of it. Down to San Diego went Bickers and a companion, carrying nearly a ton of rock samples. Part of it was left in a San Diego show window and the rest shipped to San Francisco for refining.

Within minutes the streets of San Diego fairly hummed. Reported the *San Diego Bulletin:* "The news flew like wildfire, and soon the whole town was agog to learn the particulars." Quick estimates of the ore's value ranged from $50 to $10,000 per ton. At this, many San Diegans struck out at once, pausing only long enough to get provisions, tools, and directions.

In San Francisco the excitement was almost as intense. Results of the ore tests showed values from $75 to $200 per ton. The *Alta California,* usually conservative where mining discoveries were concerned, published a glowing letter from a gold-struck San Diegan. That was enough. On only 12 hours' notice, the steamer *Oriflamme* churned out of the Golden Gate jammed to the rails with 150 Argonauts. At San Diego most of them stopped only long enough to inquire the route to the diggings.

This was the Julian rush, California's big mining excitement of 1870. From Northern California the gold-hunters came by sea. From the Southland they converged along roads through Los Angeles and San Bernardino. San Diego, convinced at last that gold prosperity had reached its door, prepared to harvest the mining trade. It started a line of stages to the mines via Poway (fare, $8), and began building a new road to shorten the distance to 44 miles. Los Angeles, sending freight teams and stages to the diggings, loomed as a competitor.

"There will be an immense crowd of gold seekers," the *Los Angeles News* told its readers. "They must naturally be skinned. Fellow citizens, let us prepare to do the skinning."

Center of excitement, however, was the Julian mine. Within days of the George Washington strike, a town named after Mike Julian was laid out, and lots were selling at from $50 to $180 apiece. By mid-March, 800 gold seekers were on the ground. Wrote one:

"The people here are positively wild. Such a thing as a sober thought is unknown. The rumor comes that Tom, Dick, or Harry has 'struck it' and forthwith the whole camp rushes pell mell for the 'new diggin's'. People don't sleep here at all (or if they do they are more lucky than I). All night long the ferocious prospectors make the hills resound with their stories of the day's adventures. Talk of Babel!"

At first, Julian was a tent city, with a handful of log cabins. Then, as lumber arrived by mule team from San Diego, frame buildings rose along the main street. Two stamp mills were under construction, preparing to work ores from such mines as the Washington, Golden Chariot, Ready Relief, Stonewall and—of all names—Lady's Leg.

But this booming camp had its troubles. Rains and chilling weather made life miserable for the treasure-hunters, most of whom slept on the ground and cooked by campfire. The first April wind blew down every tent and knocked over the general store. "Gunn's express matter," reported one resident, "was distributed among the hills and gulches gratis."

Then there were the bad men. By June 1870 Julian City had two shooting scrapes and a vigilance court. An *hombre* named Trask shot a Chinese citizen for pure entertainment, and then had to ride for the brush under a hail of bullets from

Julian's outraged population.

Late in April the Julianites began to notice an unusual amount of missing horses. One Bob Crawford, whose reputation as a horse thief had accompanied him from Montana, was discovered with a stolen saddle. The miners formed a vigilance committee, took Crawford to the nearest tree and hoisted him up to a limb "once or twice." Under this gentle persuasion he confessed to stealing both saddle and horses and was promptly banished from camp. Before it adjourned, the committee resolved "to hang the first man who shall commit a murder here." The threat was not invoked until 1874, when an Indian was hanged for attacking a woman near Julian.

Still, Julian City was not a lawless town. Its greatest test came when a few landowners tried to jump the whole mining camp. There was talk of gunplay, but the Julian men chose to fight it out in the courts.

The Rancho Cuyamaca, one of the last Mexican grants in California, had been given in 1845 to Augustin Olvera, the Spanish pioneer for whom Olvera Street in Los Angeles is named. In the early 1850s a U.S. Land Commission took up the task of settling all California property titles. It rejected Olvera's claim, for the reason that he submitted no map, no boundary description and no clue to show where in San Diego County his rancho existed.

Olvera then appealed, and won the second round in the Southern California District Court. The government next appealed the case to Washington but failed to press the suit until it was too late. In the 1860s drought and poor markets forced most Southern California ranchos into the hands of mortgage holders, and Cuyamaca was no exception. The new owners got the title suit dismissed and asked for an official boundary survey of their property.

It was in the midst of this survey that the Julian gold strike was made. True to the miners' fears, the Cuyamaca people moved in. Within a few weeks of the discovery, two of them appeared in Julian and announced that the mines were on Cuyamaca land. They were willing to let the men continue exploration, and if the mines proved permanent they would settle for a royalty on all ores.

This demand threw the bustling camp into sudden paralysis. Work on the main stamp mill was halted; word was dispatched to San Francisco to stop delivery of the machinery. The men left their mines, called a meeting in Julian, and sent a delegation to the Cuyamaca people asking the terms. They got them: royalty figures which left the miners less than half the returns after paying milling costs on the ore.

As one man put it, this amounted to a "prohibition". The miners resolved to fight, and at another mass meeting attended by more than 500, picked a delegation to seek help in San Diego.

Incensed at this threat to its new mining trade, the harbor city responded with a huge meeting of its own on May 28, 1870. For the first time San Diegans heard details of the conflict. They learned that the Cuyamaca people had presented a letter supposedly written in 1846 by General Ortega, then owner of the neighboring Rancho Santa Ysabel, saying that his property was bounded on the south by the Cuyamaca. This evidence was too little and too late, said one aroused speaker.

"But if the Ortega letter is to guide the surveyor," he concluded, "and the Santa Ysabel Rancho forms one of the boundaries of the grant, then the mines will be gobbled up by the land-sharks. . . ."

San Diego promised to help, but another setback came when the surveyors reported in favor of the Cuyamaca claim. The miners, fired for battle, took the case to court. For years they held their stand, financing the litigation through the yield from the mines. Still, the steam had been knocked out of the Julian stampede. In 1873 the town made a strong bid for the county seat, but its population probably never exceeded a thousand. When the Tombstone excitement flared in the late

'70s, most of Julian's remaining population packed off for Arizona. By 1887 it was a quiet village of two stores and a tri-weekly mail.

Then the few miners who had remained won their reward. The boundary case was settled, and the northern Cuyamaca line was established seven miles south of Julian City. The town, together with its neighboring community of Banner, gained new life. By 1890 four quartz mills were running and a fifth was under construction. Six years later there were a thousand men in the district and Julian City boasted hotels, churches and schools.

But by this time a new attraction had invaded the Julian country. The pleasant valley had become a stockman's range, supporting some 16,000 horses and cattle and about 10,000 sheep. Pioneer farmers arrived, and soon Julian became known for choice apples, pears and honey. Though its gold production reached an estimated total of $5,000,000, Julian is today a reformed mining camp with an agricultural basis—and a clear title. As for San Diego, it got its commerce and its population—but never another mining frenzy like Julian.

### POINTS OF INTEREST

JULIAN. No ghost town, Julian today breathes the spirit of its gold days in its bustling streets, with the difference that mule teams and stage coaches are replaced by autos and pickup trucks. Frame buildings of false fronts and wooden awnings complete the nostalgic look of this authentic old gold camp. The Julian Pioneer Museum is at Fourth and Washington streets. Some of the earliest buildings are the Wilcox Store (1870) on the east side of Main near B Street; the Bailey House (1870), west side of Main north of A Street; the Brewery (1876), Washington Street west of Fourth; and the grammar school (1878), west side of Second Street between B and C streets. Others are the Deluca Store (1880), west side of Main between Washington and B streets; the Witch

Creek School (1880), west side of Fourth; and Mark's Building (1886), southeast corner of Main and Washington.

BANNER. Six miles east of Julian on Highway 78 is the location of Banner, a companion camp to Julian. Its discovery dates to February 1871, but little remains at its original site on a public campground under the shadow of Volcan Mountain.

CUYAMACA. Another camp of the Julian-Banner era is Cuyamaca, once located nine miles south of Julian on Highway 79.

PICACHO. In Imperial County, up the Colorado some 25 miles from Yuma, is the site of Picacho, located on the California bank in one of the few sections where the river flows from west to east. Mexicans located the first placers here in 1862, and a pueblo of Spanish atmosphere—complete with bullfights and fiestas—flourished in the early years. Later, the Picacho Mine and other deposits were opened in the hills near Picacho Peak. With construction of big stamp mills at the turn of the century, the town became a center of hardrock mining and took on an American character. A five-mile railroad was built connecting the Picacho Mine with one of the mills. Today Picacho has been largely obliterated by floods, although a rock house and some mill ruins remain. In many places the roadbed of the old railroad is still visible. Much of the old townsite is under Colorado River water.

TUMCO. At the turn of the century Tumco (also known as Hedges) boomed as a mining town in the Cargo Muchacho Mountains that border Imperial Valley on the east. Today, a few walls and some mining structures are still to be seen at the townsite. Take a dirt road at Ogilby Station on the Southern Pacific Railroad, go two miles northwest paralleling the railroad, then branch north on a road that leads into the hills for three-and-a half miles to Tumco.

SILVERADO. One of the few mining towns in coastal Southern California is Silverado, easily reached by paved road in the Santa Ana Mountains of northeastern Orange County. A boom town in 1878, it flourished until 1881. Today Silverado Canyon is lined with homes, and there is little or no evidence of the old mining town.

SOLEDAD. Beginning in the 1860s a small gold-mining town existed in Soledad Canyon, north of Los Angeles. Only assured early-day remains are some evidences of mining activity on the hillsides across the canyon from Ravenna Station on the Southern Pacific Railroad.

---

# Chapter 26. Calico: Model Ghost Town

AT LEAST one desert camp—Calico—is apt to be more famous as a ghost than it ever was in real life. For Walter Knott, of Knott's Berry Farm, champion collector of Californiana, added Calico to his treasury of keepsakes. Later turned over to San Bernardino County, it is a mining town made to order for tourists.

Calico first leaped onto the California stage in 1881—just in time to take up where the fading camp of Bodie left off. Two prospectors first located the famed Silver King Mine in April, but the ore was mediocre. Then in June a third miner associated with the others climbed to the top of the ledge, stuck his knife into the ore, and found it was like "cutting into a lead bullet." Feverishly he scrambled down and raced back to camp.

"Look here," he shouted to his partners, "pure horn silver!"

Soon Silver King ore was in a San Francisco smelter, where it returned a value of $400 to $500 per ton. Later shipments were reported to include chunks of pure silver the size of two fists. When this news struck the California mining world, the stampede was on.

Busy gateway to the mines was San Bernardino, where, as one observer put it, "everybody in town was carrying specimens in his pockets."

"The road from this town to the mine is alive with men and teams," he added. "There is now more travel through the Cajon than ever before."

On a narrow shelf of land below the King mine sprang the new town, which at first consisted of two stores, one boarding house, two assay offices, and the remarkable combination of boot and shoe shop with adjoining bar. But within a year the camp was bursting with 2,000 men and a long, single street lined with canvas and adobe buildings—wearing the characteristic pink hue of the Calico hills.

In the rugged canyons behind the town appeared new mines of picturesque names—Dragon, Snow Bird, Four Aces, Burning Moscow and Jersey Lily (named for the currently-popular Lily Langtry). From these mines a line of twenty-mule teams hauled ore through the streets of Calico on their way to the nearby mill at Oro Grande, an earlier mining camp located on the Mojave River.

In those first flush days Calico's optimism had no limits. One newcomer recalled that judging by talk in the restaurants, "half the diners were wealthy men to whom a few thousands of dollars were a mere bagatelle. While we ate, mills and roads were planned, railroads laid out and new camps started as though such things were mere incidents of the day's work."

Calico was clearly named for the hills at its back; their kaleidoscopic hues of green and rose had already earned the name of "Calico Mountains." But at least one version of the town's christening deserves repeating. A notable "man about town in Calico" was Joe Joiner, whose outstanding attire included a swallowtail coat and a beard that hung to his knees. When "Buena Vista" or some other fine-sounding Spanish name was suggested, Joe rebelled.

"It ain't gonna be no Boona Vista, nor nothin' o' the sort," he snorted. "Look at the colors in them rocks! I say call her Calico!"

Joe may have named the town, but his fun-loving neighbors had the last word. They were especially attracted to those magnificent whiskers, which were said to be such an "awful nuisance" when the wind blew that Joe wore 'em in braids or stuffed 'em in his trousers. One night Joe lingered too long at the brass rail and on his way home fell asleep in the main street. As one of the Calico muleskinners described it, Joe Joiner awoke next morning to find that the boys had cut off "the haw side of his beard" and the "gee tail of his coat"—a humiliation which thereafter kept the "man about town" off the camp's main street.

But Calico had an ample supply of characters. One of the first was irrepressible John Overshiner, who came up from San Diego to found the town's newspaper. Its name, the *Calico Print,* was as inspired as that of another mining camp newspaper, the *Tombstone Epitaph.* In fact, when the *Epitaph* commented that the *Calico Print* smacked of petticoats, Overshiner was equal to the challenge: "It overshines a graveyard inscription, anyhow."

Another prize Calico native was Bill Harpold, who kept an abominable hotel known as the Hyena House, which consisted of barrel staves on the outside and holes-in-the-rocks on the inside. When the Calico stage rolled in, Bill was on hand with a wheelbarrow and the commanding yell: "Here y'are, gentlemen! Right this way for Hyena House, best hotel in all Calico!" Bill's breakfasts were simple and straightforward: chili beans and whisky. When Hyena House caved in after a storm, Bill was unconcerned as he dragged out his two guests. He was sorry, he said, for the leaky roof.

Calico's best-loved character was Jack, a black-and-white shepherd which earned fame as the only four-legged mail carrier in the United States. For three years Jack (also known as Dorsey) delivered Uncle Sam's cargo from Calico to the nearby Bismarck mines. He was usually a playful dog, but once the mail sacks were on his back, Jack was strictly business. Touching him was considered tampering with the U.S. mails. Jack's master, a Bismarck miner, once refused a $500 offer with the reply, "I'd sooner sell a grandson."

Tradition has it that Calico was never a tough town, and the story goes that there was only one killing in the first two years. Editor Overshiner insisted that "there are no more orderly and law abiding people living anywhere than in Calico."

If so, Calico had a powerful lot of bad luck. It was probably the only mining town in California where the brothels were in the middle of the business district, rather than on the outskirts. They were undisturbed until they started robbing the patrons, one of whom was bold enough to protest and bring down the full force of the law.

And was Calico particularly gun shy? Early in 1885 a dispute arose over one of the Occidental group of mines. It was so rich that ore under $100 per ton was thrown away. Opposing sides, armed with rifles and shotguns, squared off for a battle royal. At the last moment the deputy sheriff arrived and won a grudging agreement to settle the case in court.

Ordinarily, law and order were less triumphant. Whenever things got especially dull in Calico—which was seldom—the town roughs marched over to the east end and raided Chinatown. Life was hectic for Calico's Oriental population until the year the Chinese decided to fight back. At the next invasion, they counterattacked with laundry paddles and hot irons, forcing the raiders into ignominious retreat. Thereafter, Chinatown was unmolested.

But Calico's roughs had plenty of diversion. Their idea of an April Fool's joke was to stuff a dummy and then shoot it

276

full of holes in a mock battle on Main Street. The "shooting spirit" fairly penetrated the Calico community. In the mid-'80s its residents seized a sudden fad for fencing vacant lots. One stranger came upon some young boys driving stakes and stretching wire near the edge of town, and asked what they were doing.

"Fencing in a lot," was the stout answer.

"But you boys are not of age and you can't hold any real estate."

"You bet we can," retorted one. "If anybody tries to jump my lot, I'll shoot him!"

By 1885 Calico began to look almost civilized. It had a schoolhouse, church services, temperance lectures, a literary society, even a dancing school.

The social triumph of the year came on May 1, when the Calico ladies held their "May Day Ball and Ice Cream and Strawberry Festival" in the town hall. Festive events included a maypole dance, crowning of a Queen of the May and other good fun until two in the morning. At that time James Patterson, superintendent of the Occidental Mine, was called outside. He and two friends appeared on the front steps to be greeted by a shower of raw eggs, with maybe a brickbat thrown in. Some uninvited guests from a rival mine were expressing their disappointment, Calico style.

This naturally called for war. One of Patterson's friends drew his gun and fired away. The attackers retreated—except one, who dashed up the steps and ran right through the May Day Ball and Ice Cream and Strawberry Festival. Right behind him sprinted an Occidental man, shooting at his quarry while the party was thrown into panic and several women fainted. Nobody was hurt, but by the time the deputy sheriff arrived, the festival was over. Most of Calico thought this was going a mite too far. Growled the *Calico Print:* "a disgraceful and outrageous assault." It might have passed on the Fourth of July, but on May Day!

Calico had already had a new spurt to its boom when the

Iron Horse came by its front door. As the Santa Fe Railroad reached across Arizona to the California border, the Southern Pacific moved to block entry. It started a new line from Mojave to Needles on the Colorado River, and the construction train passed a few miles south of Calico by late 1882.

To the camp this meant a sizable drop in shipping costs, and the mines were soon disgorging lower-grade ores that were previously ignored. At the nearest point on the railroad grew the town of Daggett, bustling depot for Calico. For years Daggett, its streets filled with fourteen-mule teams, was the busiest and toughest whistle stop on the Mojave Desert. Crowded with gamblers and bunco artists, it was modestly called "the worst place between Mojave and New York." Meanwhile, the stampede to Calico was renewed—this time by rail.

"Every day people were arriving on the trains from both east and west," wrote one visitor; "others came along via the ties; and across the desert from Cajon Pass straggled a long procession. . . .Some were in wagons with their scant household goods, and others on foot, unencumbered by any earthly possession beyond blankets and canteens."

From Daggett, train passengers were whisked onward by the Calico Stage Line, which advertised "a new, Light-running, Easy-riding Concord Coach." It also gave special assurance to the timid: "Children and nervous persons taken forcibly and efffectually."

Calico was still flush with silver when a new kind of boom struck camp. Borax had been found in the Calico Mountains as early as 1883, but it was several years later that huge ledges of a more valuable product—calcium borate—were discovered in the hills just east of Calico town. By 1898 a railroad was built between Daggett and the Calico Mountains to tap not only the silver ore but the borax. The district eventually turned out almost as much wealth in borax as in silver.

Through the 1890s, however, Calico went into its silver decline. By the turn of the century the price of silver had dropped from $1.31 to 63 cents an ounce, and Calico's great days were over. Today it enjoys a third boom in the tourist business—but it's a mining town without paying mines, without miners and without May Day balls that turn into shooting scrapes.

## POINTS OF INTEREST

CALICO. When the writer first visited Calico in the late 1930s it consisted of a number of adobe walls and roofless buildings made of the dark pink soil typical of the Calico Mountains. In the early 1950s it was acquired by Walter Knott of Knott's Berry Farm and was later turned over to the County of San Bernardino. With the old walls as a nucleus, a commercial ghost town was built and is operated as a family attraction.

BORATE. Center for the borax excitement in the Calico Mountains was Borate, whose site can be reached by leaving Highway 91 four miles east of Yermo, going north on a dirt road for another four miles, then turning east on a dim and dubious road into the mountains for about three miles.

ORO GRANDE. This small community on the Mojave River, now marked chiefly by a large cement plant, began in 1878 when gold was discovered in the Old Silver Mountains and Granite Mountains. Like Calico, it boomed in the early 1880s.

COOLGARDIE. One of the few placer districts on the desert, Coolgardie was discovered about 1900 and enjoyed a short rush of miners. The desolate site is located 19 miles north of Barstow.

GOLDSTONE. While its mining history goes back to 1881, the Goldstone district boomed with the gold discovery of

December 1915. Within a few months it was practically covered with claims. A few structures remain in various stages of collapse at the townsite south of Goldstone Lake and 33 miles northeast of Barstow.

VICTORVILLE. First called Mormon Crossing, Victorville was a mining town in the early 1880s, even before it was a railroad town.

STEDMAN. In some reddish hills eight miles south of Ludlow (on the Santa Fe Railroad) are a few frame headworks that are shown on maps as the Pacific Mine. These deposits were first discovered about 1898 by John Suter, roadmaster for that section of the railroad, while searching for a source of water to serve the trains. The town that sprang up was first called Rochester, then Stedman. A railroad going by the impressive name of Ludlow and Southern was built the eight miles from Ludlow to Stedman between 1899 and 1901. The Bagdad Chase Mine, located just south of the town, produced more than half the total recorded gold production of San Bernardino County. In the early 1960s vandals destroyed the remaining houses in Stedman.

THE HOLCOMB VALLEY CAMPS. In the next valley north of Big Bear Lake, high in the San Bernardino Mountains, "Uncle Billy" Holcomb discovered gold in May 1860. Within weeks a rush of miners came by way of the Santa Ana River headwaters and over the top of the mountains by mule path. Another road was soon built from the Cajon Pass summit along the rim of the Mojave Desert to reach the west end of Holcomb Valley.

During the Civil War, Holcomb Valley was a secessionist stronghold; terrorized by the rebels, Union men were afraid to express their sentiments. In July 1861 one person was killed and several wounded in a shooting affray between Unionists and secessionists. A plea for troops was sent to San Francisco by the Unionists, and one of them hastened there by stage to make a personal plea. Four companies of infantry and a detachment of cavalry were quickly dispatched, and according to one Holcomb Valley Unionist, "the troops barely got here in time." For the rest of the war, Holcomb Valley continued to erupt with rebel conspiracy, and was a rallying point for parties escaping to the Confederacy.

Today, little of interest remains in the valley, though the pine-forested setting is attractive. For the best way to visit it, start at the U.S. Forest Service Big Bear ranger station on Highway 38 on the north side of Big Bear Lake. There you can get a description of the history and points of interest, with a small map of an 11-mile loop trip through the valley. Start at the Polique Canyon road (2NO9) a mile west of the station. The dirt roads in and out of the valley are rocky in parts and not recommended for a conventional car that you cherish. It is certainly passable for four-wheelers, but in the worst spots, the motto is, "slow".

After 5.2 miles you reach the Last Chance Placer area (all sights are marked by Forest Service signs), which like much of the valley displays the mounds and ditches that reveal intensive placer mining. Another mile takes you to a side loop northward and the log remains of Two-Gun Bill's Saloon. Another seven-tenths of a mile on this side loop brings you to the Hangman's Tree, the supposed scene of several summary executions. Completing the side loop back to the "main" dirt road, you pass the original 1860 discovery spot and reach the site of Belleville, the principal settlement of the gold excitement. Today it is marked by the remains of an arrastre and a lone log cabin of uncertain vintage.

DOBLE. Leaving Holcomb Valley to the east and coming out on a view of Baldwin Dry Lake, you reach the timber remains of E. J. "Lucky" Baldwin's stamp mill and cyanide works, used to reduce the ore from the nearby Gold Mountain Mine that he purchased in 1876 for an alleged $6,000,000. In the valley below, just before you join the surfaced road northwest of Baldwin Lake, was the small town of Doble, serving the Baldwin mine and mill. Nothing is left but the remains of a cemetery.

PALM CITY (TWENTY-NINE PALMS). Beginning in 1873 Twenty-Nine Palms (then often called Palm City) became the supply center for a number of mines in the hills northeast of the Little San Bernardino Mountains.

DALE. Located near the Pinto Mountains 19 miles east of Twenty-Nine Palms, gold mines at Old Dale were first discovered in the early 1880s. It came into prominence with discovery of the Virginia Dale Mine in 1885, and was active until the turn of the century. At that time most of the activity was transferred a few miles away to New Dale, six miles southeast overlooking the Pinto Basin. Dale the Third was situated on a nearby ridge. All three localities were virtually abandoned by 1916, although there was a small revival of activity at New Dale in the 1930s. A few rock walls and frame houses remain at the sites, particularly at what has been termed Dale the Third.

PROVIDENCE. Evidence of early mining activity abounds in the Providence Mountains, located in the eastern Mojave Desert between the Santa Fe and Union Pacific railroad lines. Richest mine of all was the Bonanza King, discovered in the 1870s and extensively developed in the 1880s. According to one report, it produced nearly $1,000,000 in eighteen months alone.

Here stands the town of Providence—mainly a company town for the Bonanza King Mine, though serving as a commercial center for the Silver King and other mines in the Providence Mountains. It was built largely of white softstone sawed from a nearby ledge. The old stamp mill and a few buildings still stand in various stages of decomposition to mark the town and its main street.

Providence may be reached by a 25-mile road (surfaced for about twelve miles) that goes northwest from Essex on Highway 66 to Mitchell Caverns State Park. A little less than 20 miles from Essex, a sign marked 7IL Ranch indicates a branch road going north that ends at Providence and the Bonanza King Mine. The last mile or more may be in disrepair, but like other desert roads may be negotiated by very slow driving and some occasional shovel work.

HART. Northeast of Essex on the Santa Fe line is Goffs, where a dirt road heads north 37 miles to an agricultural ghost town called Barnwell. From here a dirt road goes east nine miles to the Castle Mountains and the townsite of Hart, located less than five miles from the Nevada border. Gold was discovered here about 1907, in the same general excitement that swept the desert after Tonopah and Goldfield, but only a few ruins remain of the little town of Hart.

---

# Chapter 27. Randsburg: Gay 90s Stampede

EXCEPT IN COLORADO, the West's mining excitements seemed to have faded by the 1890s. In the California and Nevada deserts, exhaustion of underground treasure and the poor price of silver brought mining stagnation. To cap it all, a depression seized the nation in 1893 and made the Gay Nineties less than gay.

Then came Randsburg. Together with its neighbor camps springing up in the Mojave Desert, it broke the spell for

California mining. Of the thousands who stampeded to the side of Rand Mountain, few made their fortune. But they had the time of their lives in California's one big mining boom of the 1890s.

First strike of the new gold diggings came in 1893 at Goler, between Red Rock Canyon and Randsburg. This was enough to create a town, a stage line from Mojave, and an eager population which prospected the nearby hills. Next year two miners found placer gold on the slope of Rand Mountain. One of them, Frederic M. Mooers, took two others back in the spring of 1895 to find the source of this surface color. Near the top of the mountain they broke a chunk off a rock outcropping and found it heavy with gold.

"Boys, we needn't look any further," shouted Mooers; "we've struck it rich."

The jubilant miners located their first claims on April 25, labeling them with the one name, Rand Mine—after the famous gold district opened a decade earlier in Transvaal, South Africa. When stock promoters began putting the Rand label on everything they sold, the name was changed to Yellow Aster—the big mine of Randsburg.

Meanwhile, the first rush for the Rand had begun. From Mojave to Panamint Valley, desert prospectors flocked to the new ground. But with a fortune under foot, Mooers and his partners were too broke to develop it. They almost sold half the mine to one newcomer, but soon the wife of one of them—a San Bernardino woman doctor named Rose Burcham—arrived to halt any talk of sale. Next, a mining expert examined the ground and clinched the case.

"Boys, you have a good thing," he told them. "Get a 100-stamp mill and shovel in the entire mountain, for it's all ore."

Randsburg would eventually get its 100-stamp mill, making it one of the few mining booms to enrich the discoverers. From the beginning, in fact, this was a "poor man's camp". Locators of the Butte Mine were so destitute that they would have had to break camp the next day out of sheer hunger. As it was, they had to grind out enough gold dust from the first ore to raise the $1.60 fee for recording the claim.

For a full year the Randsburg boom was strictly local. Mojave prospectors continued to locate new mines, and to give them such picturesque names as Big Norse, King Solomon, Monkey Wrench, Minnehaha, Bully Boy, Napoleon and Gold Coin. By the end of 1895 the camp had only 13 buildings—some of them part canvas.

But in the summer of '96, miner Si Drouillard found the St. Elmo Mine more than five miles east of the Rand Mine on the open desert. Added to the growing roster of rich lodes, it showed that the Rand deposits comprised "one of nature's great treasure houses." Randsburg's big rush was on.

From out of Southern California and Nevada came a horde of fortune-seekers in the fall of '96 and winter of '97. Randsburg mushroomed to some 300 buildings and tents, its population to some 2,500 by early 1897—with 40 or 50 more arriving every day. Through its surging streets walked Argonauts from as far off as Australia and South Africa. Under foot, they believed, was another Comstock Lode.

The Randsburg stampede converged along two general routes. From San Bernardino and points east, gold hunters took the Santa Fe Railroad through Barstow to the nearest station, Kramer. Over the last 28 miles to Randsburg, three stages a day delivered Randsburg's population.

From Los Angeles the Argonauts rode the Southern Pacific to Mojave, then took one of the four daily stages for the mines. Just below Red Rock Canyon the coaches veered eastward through Garlock, adding an extra pair to the four-horse team for the sandy, uphill pull into Randsburg. Wrote one passenger:

"All along the road from Mojave to Randsburg we passed dozens of team and freighting wagons, some of the latter having sixteen horses; also three or four stages returning to Mojave; many private conveyances, burro prospecting outfits,

285

and miners and tenderfeet, with packs on their backs, going on foot to the new El Dorado."

Another newcomer described his stagecoach companions: "miscellaneous load of capitalists, carpenters, prospectors, miners, drummers [traveling salesmen], fakers, newspaper correspondents, and perhaps a traveling company of barn-stormers."

When the stageload rocked into camp, Randsburg's welcome was exuberant and typical. The whole population turned out to greet newcomers, and to line up at the post office for mail. In the crowd, according to one arrival, were "sturdy Cornishmen from the mines, tramp-like prospectors from the hills and desert, keen dealers in mines that others have found, gamblers, actors, mule-punchers, and the general riff-raff that gathers whenever gold clinks and moral restraints are lax. The deputy sheriff is there," the eyewitness continues, "with a fierce black mustache, a slouchy sombrero, a long, black frock coat, high boots, and protruding pistol. There are women in the crowd, but the most prominent are not the most worthy."

Randsburg was rowdy, but not particularly lawless. By March of '97 it had witnessed three or four shooting scrapes. A band of toughs, proudly calling itself the "Dirty Dozen", tried to run things in true mining camp style. At this, peace-able Randsburgers formed a citizens' committee "to enforce the laws," and posted a pointed notice.

"Ten Deputy Constables have been appointed," it warned, "and any riotous and threatening conduct will be suppressed and punished."

The Dirty Dozen were properly cowed, and though Randsburg flourished in the farthest corner of huge Kern County, it shunned a tough reputation. Good clean fun, however, was something else again. Randsburg was quick to acquire a brass band, a volunteer fire company, an Orpheus Theater—and a full complement of saloons. In her streets, complete with boardwalks and false fronts in the best mining camp tradition, the entire population met every night in social confab. It was the custom for everybody, whether imbibing or not, to make the rounds of the bars and dance halls each evening and mix with the crowd.

With Randsburg it was anything for a joke or a celebration. Its riotous Fourths of July included sack races, grand balls—and dynamite salutes that rattled every building in camp. Once a stage driver, swinging an empty coach through town, turned too short at the end of the street and overturned the vehicle. When a wisecracking bystander bet him drinks for the crowd that he couldn't do it twice, the driver wheeled down the street and capsized his stage again. The boys were just as prompt to collect the bet.

By 1897 Randsburg mining was big business. The neighboring town of Johannesburg had been founded over the divide a mile away. The Yellow Aster Mine had yielded its owners $250,000 in ore, catapulting them from prospectors to mining magnates. Most of this had been hauled by twenty-mule team to the stamp mill at Garlock, but by '97 both Randsburg and "Joburg" had small mills of their own. The first of Randsburg's $8 million gold yield was on its way.

At the same time Randsburg was rising to that upper class of mining camps sporting a railroad. From the Santa Fe line at Kramer, tracklayers were spiking steel across the desert for the standard-gauge Randsburg Railroad. When the Iron Horse reached Rand Mountain, the giant ore bodies would find their proper market, and Randsburg its proper place as a second Comstock.

On December 23, 1897, the rail crews laid track over the hill into Johannesburg. This naturally called for a celebration, Randsburg style. That afternoon, all of Joburg and half the population of Randsburg turned out to cheer the first Iron Horse. Finally the expected train chugged over the hill and stopped in the midst of the shouting crowd.

"The locomotive blew a long blast," described one eyewitness, "and everything that could make a noise chimed in."

287

But the Rand District had just begun to celebrate. "Tonight," wrote a news correspondent, "the two towns of Randsburg and Johannesburg are painting things vermillion." It was an understatement. Just before midnight, in the midst of the carnival, fire broke out in a gasoline storehouse at Randsburg. The fire company swiftly arrived with its new "chemical engine". It was greeted by exploding drums of gas and oil that sent burning liquid to other buildings hundreds of feet away.

"The fire was a magnificent spectacle," said one gleeful celebrant. "'The black smoke, intermingled with flame, rolled up hundreds of feet, to fall back in showers of sparks on the roofs of adjoining buildings. Each explosion of oil added to the terror of the situation, and red-hot drums flew through the air in all directions, but, miraculously, no one was killed."

Randsburg was equal to the moment. Despite explosions that knocked several men down, the Randsburgers joined their firemen in attacking the blaze. They blew up several structures in the path of the flames, and checked the fire before it had consumed more than three buildings. Randsburg went home, but it was not through celebrating. Next night the firemen held their Christmas Eve Ball, with proceeds going to pay for their new engine that had received a premature baptism of fire.

The fire boys, in fact, had only begun to fight. Less than a month later, in the early morning of January 19, flames broke out in the Mojave Saloon and spread rapidly up Rand Street. The close-packed wooden buildings kindled like tinder, and soon the town was spouting smoke 1,000 feet high. The St. Elmo, main hotel in town, was consumed early, the guests escaping only with their clothes.

"Men, women and children filled the streets," recorded one citizen. "Everybody near the fire was intent on saving their houses or furniture."

The one hope of rescuing part of the town was to keep the flames from jumping Broadway. When the Broadway Hotel was threatened men climbed to the roofs of nearby buildings and tore loose burning boards with their bare hands. Two or three fell from exhaustion before the fire was controlled. But half of Randsburg lay in smoking cinders.

All of this was part of mining camp life, and Randsburg turned cheerfully to the job of rebuilding. Less than five months later another fire took care of the other half.

Yet it would take more than fires to down the Rand District. Randsburg's gold output had scarcely begun to fade when rich deposits of tungsten were found on Rand Mountain. The nearby town of Atolia was born, and the whole Rand District boomed again.

Then in 1919, discovery of the Big Silver Mine near Atolia gave the district its third mining excitement. Here was founded the silver town of Red Mountain, "where every night is Saturday night, and Saturday night is the Fourth of July." Today the Rand District is quieter, but the old-timers will tell you it's just resting between booms.

### POINTS OF INTEREST

GOLER. At Goler Canyon in the east end of the El Paso Mountains, the rough camp of Goler flourished from 1893 to the Rand discovery in 1895. Little but miners' diggings mark the site today.

GARLOCK. Located on the present Southern Pacific line that skirts the southern slope of the El Paso Mountains, Garlock was founded in the fall of 1895 when an eight-stamp mill was installed there to work ores from Rand Mountain and other nearby districts. By 1899 it was a fairly sizable town with several hundred population and a number of frame buildings along its main street. Today Garlock is marked by the railroad siding and the remains of a rock-and-adobe structure, a Mexican arrastre and several frame buildings, mostly of more recent vintage than the old town.

RANDSBURG. One of the best-preserved mining towns on the desert, Randsburg still gives evidence of its once-large size. A relatively few inhabitants operate a handful of enterprises on the main street in old buildings, many of them dating to the turn of the century. Starting place for visitors is the Desert Museum, on the south side of Butte Avenue.

Entering Randsburg from Highway 395, you first encounter the old jail on your left. On the right just before the big curve in the road is an old-time bar and dance hall, while on your left inside the curve is Peterson's Corner, which successively served as an ice house, meat market and bar. On Butte Avenue, the Rand (or Parker's) mercantile store is on the left, and beyond it, the White House saloon and dance hall. Across Butte Avenue are the old U.S. Post Office and the general store. Further along the main street are other old structures including, on the north side, the Juvell Commercial Company buildings and the American Legion Hall, part of which is known as the McGinnis Opera House. The old Catholic Church is propped up with telephone poles.

Up the canyon to the south are the remains of giant workings of the Yellow Aster Mine. Beyond the east end of town, the Big Butte Mine is on the hillside to the north.

Throughout this district, old mine shafts—complete with ladders and sometimes with windlasses—beckon the inquisitive explorer. But dropping a rock down the hole often reveals a startling depth. Be careful of your ground near the mouth of mines, trust no old timbers, stay out of the shafts, and better yet, don't get near their edges.

JOHANNESBURG. Founded shortly after Randsburg, "Joburg" was smaller and less rambunctious. But it did boast a railroad, which continued to operate until it was shut down and the rails removed in the early 1930s. So many houses of more recent vintage have been built, and so many pioneer buildings torn down, that Joburg today gives little impression of its boom era.

ATOLIA. In 1905 rich tungsten ore was discovered five miles southeast of Randsburg, and by 1907 the town of Atolia was founded there. The demand for tungsten during World War I created a boom that sent Atolia's population to 2,000 by 1915.

RED MOUNTAIN. Less than a mile south of Joburg is Red Mountain, which was born with the rich silver strike of 1919 that became known as the Big Silver Mine. One of the richest silver deposits in California, the Big Silver produced more than $7,000,000 in its first four years. The town of Red Mountain, first called Osdick after two brothers who owned a stamp mill nearby, was for many years the rip-roaring trading center for miners and prospectors who came in from miles around.

---

# Chapter 28. The Death Valley Camps

POPULATION FOR MOST of California has always zoomed steadily upward, but Death Valley's census reached its peak at the century's turn. Between 1905 and '08, several thousand miners, promoters, gamblers, prostitutes, and other fragments of humanity poured into this "white heart of the Mojave" and then poured out again. Overnight were born the wild and raucous camps of Greenwater, Harrisburg, and—of all names—Skidoo. Then, as though blown by a hot desert wind, they faded—leaving little but great piles of tin cans and empty bottles.

This was the tail end of the West's last big gold rush. It started in the early 1900s, when the riotous Nevada towns of Tonopah and Goldfield aroused the mining world by producing a cool $250,000,000. It drew near to Death Valley when the Mojave Desert's greatest prospector, Shorty Harris, made his Bullfrog strike in August 1904. On the barren hills just inside the Nevada border sprang Rhyolite, which brought 7,000 people and two railroads racing across the desert.

From Rhyolite the excitement leaped to California and the very rim of Death Valley. Arthur Kunze, a miner who had strayed south from Tonopah, had already found promising copper ore in the Black Mountains near the southern end of the valley. But Nevada was then wild over gold, and Death Valley was considered too remote to make a copper mine pay. Kunze and his partners spent two years trying to sell their claims. But by the spring of 1906 Rhyolite and its railroads brought the valley closer to civilization. Kunze sold out to various mining magnates, among them Charles M. Schwab, president of Bethlehem Steel.

In those days, the Schwab touch was all that was needed to launch a new stampede. And when Nevada heard that one of Kunze's partners had sold his share for $40,000 cash, the rush to Death Valley was on.

Out of Goldfield stormed a host of men—by horseback, foot, and chugging auto. Over the last miles this motley crew came up a ravine so steep and gruelling in the desert sun that it earned the grim name of Dead Horse Canyon. Within a month a thousand adventurers were on the ground looking for copper—and excitement. In less than five months, claim stakes and rock monuments peppered the ridge of the Black Mountains for thirty miles.

Thus was born Greenwater, farthest outpost of the desert mining frenzy in the 1900s. Her saga will forever serve to show what can be done by the combination of two ingredients—excitement and publicity. Before 1906 there was nothing on these brush-covered slopes but a dismal spring whose water was an unappetizing green. Within a year Greenwater had 2,000 people, a $100,000 bank, two newspapers, a magazine glorying in the name of *Death Valley Chuckwalla,* and a boundless future. It was, claimed the boys, "the world's biggest copper deposit." When it attracted mining capital from Butte, Montana, the copper center of the world, they knew it would be "bigger than Butte."

This kind of city would certainly need room for growth. At first the camp lay in a ravine near the main claims, but this hardly afforded room for another Butte. So after Christmas of 1906 the whole camp pulled stakes and moved two miles to the new Greenwater, on a broad slope just east of Death Valley's rim. Over the rugged route marched a procession of miners and merchants, carrying their possessions with them and looking like refugees from a desert cloudburst. Along the road an enterprising barkeeper dropped his inventory and began catering to the parade. So did a Greenwater butcher. Pausing for a shot or a steak, the trekkers pushed on with new zest.

"Saloons and boarding-houses, stores and brokerage firms are doing business on the run," wrote one observer," and trying to be on both sides of the mountain at the same time. . . Those who remain in the old camp are walking two miles to the new to get their eggs for breakfast. Those who journeyed to the new are walking two miles to the old to get their mail."

All this was a mere lark for wild and reckless Greenwater. Though technically out of bounds, it followed the wide open tradition of Nevada camps. Gambling was illegal in California, but at Greenwater faro, roulette and poker roared round the clock. So did the other customary mining camp vices.

But while the copper camp had no peace officers during most of its career, it had a form of miner's justice. Greenwater could tolerate a lot, but as in other desert camps, it was sometimes necessary for a citizens' committee to collar a particularly obstreperous character and hand him a canteen. This was a silent but effective invitation to start walking.

293

When four robbers were caught in Greenwater they were ordered to be on the street at nine the next morning. At the appointed hour, Greenwater's entire body politic met them and served notice that they had half an hour to settle matters before their departure. One optimist asked for an hour, but was soon convinced that he could make it on time if he tried. Within the half hour the four outcasts and their canteens were heading toward Dead Horse Canyon.

Greenwater was stern, but it could also be sentimental—on occasion. When Billy, one of the town hangers-on, died in a bout with Demon Rum, Greenwater resolved to bury him in style. For the padding of the coffin one saloonkeeper offered the packing from a barrel of bottled beer. Another contributed some respectable street clothes for Billy's last public appearance. On the night before the service, the improvised mortuary was visited by the belle of the camp, Tiger Lil. She surveyed the undertaker's work and was especially pleased at the way he had placed Billy's right hand on the chest—"just the way he held a poker hand." Still, something was missing.

Next day Greenwater turned out in its best attire and followed the hearse over a bumpy half mile to the town cemetery. Tiger Lil rode beside the driver, taking a particular interest in the proceedings. A young man who had studied for the ministry performed the service, and his wife closed by singing *Nearer, My God, to Thee*.

Those who had seen the open coffin knew the secret: close to his vest Billy's fingers held a poker hand. The cards? Tiger Lil had sent him off in style with five aces.

By mid 1907 Greenwater was on the crest of its boom. From the nearest railroad 35 miles away lurched one of the earliest auto stages in the West—the Death Valley Chug Line. The fearless driver on this hair-raising ride was Alkali Bill; according to the *Greenwater Times*, "He generally goes out empty and comes back loaded." Greenwater was, in fact, the first mining area in California reached by auto—and when you got there gasoline was an outrageous $1.00 a gallon.

Among the other luxuries in this parched country was water. Hauled in from wells 30 miles away, it sold as high as 12 cents a gallon retail. Mule teams freighting in water drank up half their cargo en route. With water this scarce, fire was the dread of Greenwater. When flames broke out in the office of the *Greenwater Miner,* its editors had to let it burn to the ground; water to put it out would have cost more than the plant was worth.

Meanwhile, other discoveries were contributing to Death Valley's big mining boom. In the summer of 1905 Shorty Harris left Rhyolite, the Nevada town sprung from his gold discovery. In a drunken spree he had sold his original Bullfrog claim for $900, and had promptly dissipated that as well—according to the custom of desert prospectors. Now he headed across Death Valley in search of a new strike.

On the way he met Pete Aguereberry, another famed Death Valley prospector. What happened next is in dispute; each man claims he made the discovery. But one of them found an outcropping of high grade at what is now Harrisburg Flats, next to Emigrant Canyon.

"They beat me out of Bullfrog," shouted Shorty, "but now I'm going to show 'em."

"You take one side and I'll take the other," said Pete.

So the two miners followed the outcrop up the mountainside, putting up locations for themselves and some friends. That night when they met other prospectors at Wildrose Springs, the secret was out. The rush came so fast it caught the discoverers by surprise. Pete Aguereberry had to go down to Ballarat, the gold camp in the south end of Panamint Valley. When he got back a few days later, the flats were overrun with gold-seekers; his own claim stakes had been pulled up and men were occupying the ground. Shorty Harris was also away, but Pete lost no time in identifying himself as French Pete, the discoverer.

"Before I would let anybody take it away from me," he boomed, "I would fight and either leave my bones or another man's on the ground."

His listeners pulled up their stakes and Pete put back his.

Harrisburg, as the camp came to be called, was never a big excitement. Its population got no further than 300. But it led to the discovery of the one Death Valley camp that paid for itself. In the rush to Harrisburg, two miners were going up Emigrant Canyon and got lost in a fog—one of the few recorded on the Mojave Desert. They strayed up the side of Tucki Mountain, north of Harrisburg Flats, and made the gold strike that founded the town of Skidoo.

One of them was Harry Ramsey, famous in the mining world as one who had grubstaked the discoverers of Goldfield. Ramsey and his partner now sold out to Bob Montgomery, who had owned the main mine in Rhyolite, for $60,000. Then Charles M. Schwab invested some money in Montgomery's mine. When these big movements were broadcast, all roads led to Skidoo.

"Follow Schwab to Skidoo, the New Gold Camp of 1907," advertised one mining stock company.

Winter and summer, the gold hunters trekked out of Rhyolite and across Death Valley. It was then that Stovepipe Wells sprang up as a stopping place on the weary route. In the summer of 1907 at least 16 men died trying to cross the blistering valley on the way to Skidoo.

There are two versions on just how Skidoo got its wonderful name. One is that it was first discovered on the 23rd of the month—calling to someone's mind the popular remark which then covered any situation—"Twenty-three Skidoo" (meaning "beat it"). The other is that Bob Montgomery announced he would bring water into camp from Telescope Peak, 23 miles away— causing the same wisecrack.

In any case, Skidoo it was, and the new camp promptly gained a bank, a newspaper, a red light district, a row of saloons, 700 citizens, and a telephone line all the way across Death Valley to Rhyolite.

Skidoovians, as they were called, were somewhat touchy

about murder, there being no jail in camp. One rough character, a saloonkeeper named Joe Simpson, had recently shot up a hotel in Independence while on his way to Skidoo. In April 1908 he went on a prolonged jag; running out of money, he decided to get it by the direct process of robbing the bank. But when he presented his gun at the teller's window, he was overpowered by several men and thrown out by the manager, Jim Arnold. Sometime later Joe got another gun and went storming back into the bank.

"Have you got anything against me, Jim?" he demanded.

"No, Joe, I've got nothing against you."

"Yes, you have," Joe insisted dramatically. "Your end has come—prepare to die."

He thereupon shot Arnold in the chest—a mortal wound. The constable came running up and wrestled with Simpson, who was wildly emptying his gun. He was placed under guard, but three days later the aroused Skidoovians took action. Overpowering the officer, they took Simpson and hanged him to a telephone pole. Skidoo was so excited that night over the big event—the first lynching in California mines for years—that one man claimed he was awakened and told the news 23 times. "I was surprised every time," he added. One of the town ne'er-do-wells, hearing of it, skidooed out of camp. He was reported still running when he passed Stovepipe Wells next morning.

As for the lynchers, no one thought of punishing them. Reported the coroner's jury, "He died by strangulation by persons unknown." Headlined the *Skidoo News,* **"MURDERER LYNCHED WITH GENERAL APPROVAL."** The rest of California sent out news photographers who reached remote Skidoo somewhat late. Joe was already buried. But Skidoo was not a town to hide its light under a bushel. Joe was obligingly dug up and rehanged for the benefit of the press cameras.

Skidoo, like Greenwater, had already been waning fast since the panic of autumn, 1907. Investment money suddenly disappeared, and without more capital coming in, the Death Valley camps collapsed. Greenwater's death was abrupt and complete; her mines had run out of ore at two hundred feet. Practically the only shipments ever made were rock from the claim monuments—hauled away in the camp's dying hour. This was the end of California's "second Butte."

Skidoo was harder to kill. For another decade it continued to yield gold and silver ore—perhaps as much as $3,000,000. But when the pipeline to Telescope Peak was sold for metal in World War I, Skidoo died of thirst.

Death Valley mining flared again in 1926 when the quack promoter, C. C. Julian, founded the town of Leadfield at the head of Titus Canyon. But Julian was even then under investigation by state officials. Like Greenwater before it, Leadfield mined more stockholder's pockets than mountains.

### POINTS OF INTEREST

GREENWATER. To reach the site of Greenwater, take the road from Furnace Creek toward Shoshone, turning southwest at a dirt road 5.8 miles south of the turnoff to Dante's View. The town was located 1.8 miles along this dirt road; little is there now but some stone foundations among the sagebrush. If you want to see the ghost of Greenwater, don't go to its site. The lumber from its shacks was hauled to the little Amargosa River town of Shoshone.

FURNACE. A contemporary of Greenwater was the copper camp of Furnace, located 1.4 miles on a dirt road paralleling the Greenwater road and branching from the Furnace Creek-Shoshone road 2.8 miles south of the Dante's View turnoff.

SCHWAB. Two miles east of Furnace Creek Junction, a bad dirt road goes nine miles up Echo Canyon to the site of Schwab, a small camp dating from the Greenwater era and named for the noted financier. Little more than a few piles of boards mark the spot.

**LEE.** Another small town of the same period was Lee, which was located in the Funeral Mountains just inside the California border. Its site, which contains only a few remains, may be reached by driving north from Death Valley Junction to a point half-a-mile inside Nevada. There a dirt road turns west and goes in and out of California and Nevada for 21 miles to what was once Lee. It is hardly worth the trip, as the road gradually worsens and becomes negotiable only for jeep-type traffic.

**RHYOLITE.** Not a California town, but nevertheless a "must" for the Death Valley tourist, is Rhyolite, one of the big excitements of the Tonopah-Goldfield boom. Once served by two railroads, Rhyolite is deserted today and fast vanishing under the desert elements. The bottle house and the railroad station are the principal points of interest.

**CHLORIDE CITY** Still another camp of the Rhyolite gold boom is Chloride City, located in a small basin in the Funeral Range. From a point on the Rhyolite road 2.6 miles west of the Nevada border, take a dirt road southeast 4.7 miles; then turn right (south) on a short branch that leads into the little valley and townsite. The shell of the Chloride Cliff Mine works is all that remains.

**LEADFIELD.** C. C. Julian's old town at the top of Titus Canyon is reached by a dirt road branching from Nevada Highway 58 about 2.4 miles west of the Rhyolite turnoff. Leadfield is 14.5 miles along this road, and while the remains are not imposing the drive is made additionally worthwhile by the rugged desert scenery on down Titus Canyon. The road is one-way only, and should not be attempted without first inquiring about conditions at ranger headquarters in Death Valley.

HARRISBURG. Just over a mile north of Emigrant Pass in the Panamint Range, a dirt road goes 1.8 miles east to the site of Harrisburg, where practically nothing exists today. An additional five-mile drive takes one to Aguereberry Point, the best view of Death Valley from the west.

SKIDOO. Little more than two miles north of the Harrisburg road, another winds seven miles to the site of Skidoo, where little is left but the cemetery, the remains of the stamp mill, and several mines.

SILVER LAKE. Just over eight miles north of Baker, the traveler drives through the remains of adobe walls that stir the imagination. These are what is left of Silver Lake, a town on the old Tonopah and Tidewater Railroad. Flourishing in 1910, it served as a center for many mines in the nearby mountaiins.

CRACKERJACK. From Silver Lake a dirt road leads west 24 miles to Avawatz Pass, which divides the Avawatz Mountains. West of the road going north through the pass, and about two miles southwest of Cave Springs, are the scant remains of Crackerjack. This gold camp reached its height in 1907-8 and was deserted by 1918.

IVANPAH. In 1869 silver was struck on the east slope of Clark Mountain, which is north of Mountain Pass and Interstate Highway 15, just west of the Nevada border. It became a thriving camp in the early 1870s, when machinery was hauled in for stamp mills. For a time it was the big silver excitement of the Mojave, and stampeders came from all directions. It yielded $3-4 million before it died about 1885. In 1872, nearby discoveries by Mat Palen added to the region's riches.

Today Ivanpah may be reached by taking the overpass at Yates Well, just south of Ivanpah Dry Lake, and going west a short distance on a paved road. Here you intersect a dirt road (it was once the main paved highway, but has been covered with sand). Turn north for two miles to a dirt road leading west through the sagebrush up the alluvial slope toward Clark Mountain. After eleven miles, turn left and park next to a cattle corral and two cottonwood trees. Walk west across a ravine and you find yourself in a shallow canyon that was the site of Ivanpah. The remains of two mills, a smelter, and about a dozen rock and adobe buildings are easily found.

VANDERBILT. Southeast from Mountain Pass is Ivanpah Station or South Ivanpah (not to be confused with the old mining camp of Ivanpah) on the Union Pacific line. By driving east about four miles on an old railroad bed (the tracks have been torn up) into the New York Mountains, you reach the old camp of Vanderbilt. The gold and silver mines here were discovered in the 1870s and reached a peak of activity in the 1890s. Still present are the remains of a few frame buildings.

MESCAL. Launched in 1887, this old silver town is one mile south of Interstate 15 on a dirt road west of Mountain Pass.

# Post Script: Other California Mining Towns

CAMBRIA. Started as a mining camp during California's copper craze of 1863, Cambria was later a center for quicksilver mining in the Santa Lucia Range. The attractive coastal town is located on California Highway 1 between Morrow Bay and San Simeon.

KLAU. This mining town on a road from Cambria to Paso Robles was the center for several quicksilver mines dating from the 1870s.

LOS BURROS AND GORDA. On the coast side of the Santa Lucia Range west of Jolon, in Monterey County, is a small gold mining district first worked by the Spanish. Activity began in earnest with the discovery of the Last Chance Mine on Alder Creek in 1887. Two very small settlements—Los Burros and Gorda—were reported active as late as 1916.

NEW IDRIA. First operated in 1850, the famous New Idria Mine of San Benito County is second only to New Almaden in the production of California quicksilver. Named for the Idria quicksilver district in Austria, the mine and the town are located in the Diablo Range 66 miles southeast of Hollister by paved road.

NEW ALMADEN. Fourteen miles south of San Jose on the east side of the Santa Cruz Mountains are the oldest mine and mining town in California—New Almaden—named for the famed Almaden quicksilver center in Spain. First extracted by the Indians for warpaint and other uses, the cinnabar deposits were known to the Spanish-speaking Californians as early as 1824. The mine was officially located by Andres Castillero in

302

1845—first as a silver and gold mine, and then for its more important content, quicksilver. But the mine soon became the prize in a celebrated dispute that rocked the courts for many years. The issue was intensified when California's Gold Rush put a premium on quicksilver for its value in smelting gold-bearing ores.

One of the longest producers among American mines, New Almaden has turned out a sizable proportion of the nation's quicksilver. The remaining relics of older times are a tumbledown schoolhouse, a powder magazine, and some old cemeteries (largely vandalized).

THE MOUNT DIABLO COAL TOWNS. For some 30 years starting in the mid-1850s, several coal mining towns— Somersville, Nortonville, Judsonville, and Stewartville— flourished on the northeast approach to Mt. Diablo in Contra Costa County. But when they closed in the 1880s most of the buildings were torn up and transported elsewhere.

# Bibliography

## NEWSPAPERS

Auburn *Placer Herald*, Jan.-Mar., 1853

Aurora *Esmeralda Union*, Nov. 23, 1867-Sept. 12, 1868

Bakersfield *Kern County Courier*, Jan. 21, 1871-Sept. 9, 1876; *Southern Californian*, July 3, 1873-July 1876; *Kern County Gazette*, Nov. 13, 1875-Oct. 14, 1876

*Bishop Creek Times*, Nov. 1, 1881-Feb. 1882

*Bodie Standard*, Sept. 5, 1880

Boston *California Bulletin*, Mar. 6, Apr. 5, 19, 1849

*Calico Print*, Oct. 10, 1886

*Columbia Gazette*, Feb. 12-Mar. 5, 1853, Mar. 15, 1856

Darwin *Coso Mining News*, Nov. 6, 1875-Nov. 10,1877 (incomplete)

Downieville *Mountain Echo*, June 19, 1852-June 1853

*Grass Valley National*, Oct. 5, 1853 (Extra)

*Havilah Miner*, June 29, 1872-May 1874

Honolulu *Polynesian*, June 24-Nov. 4, 1848; *Sandwich Island News*, June 22-Oct. 5, 1848

Independence (Calif.) *Inyo Independent*, July 9, 1870-Feb. 1882

*Julian Sentinel*, May 9-16, 1890, July 23-Dec. 1891

Kanesville (Council Bluffs, Ia.) *Frontier Guardian*, Feb.-June 1849

*London Times*, Dec. 22, 1848-Jan. 15, 1849

Los Angeles *News* (scattered issues), Apr. 1866-Nov. 1872; *Southern Californian*, July 20, 1854-June 20,1855; *Star*, June 1853-July 1856, June 1868-Jan. 1871, Apr. 1874-Dec. 1875

*Mariposa Chronicle*, Jan. 20, 1854; *Democrat*, Aug. 5, 1856; *Gazette*, July 14,1858

*Marysville Herald*, Aug. 6-Dec. 1850

Mokelumne Hill *Calaveras Chronicle*, Mar. 19-26, 1853

New Orleans *Picayune*, Jan. 26-Feb. 21, 1849

*New York Tribune*, Nov. 25, 1848-Jan. 15, 1849
*Panama Star*, Mar. 17, Nov. 10,1849
*Panamint News*, Nov. 26,1874-May 18, 1875 (inc.)
Philadelphia *Public Ledger*, Dec. 1, 1848-Jan. 11, 1849
*Quincy* (Calif.) *Prospector*, Mar. 3-Nov. 17, 1855
*Randsburg Miner*, July 2, 1898, Mar.17, 1900 (copies)
*Rhyolite Herald*, Feb. 8, 1907
Sacramento *Placer Times*, Ap. 28, 1849-June 7,1850; *Union*,
   Jan.-Mar. 1853, July-Oct. 1859, Mar.-Oct. 1860
*St. Joseph* (Mo.) *Gazette*, Ap.-June 1849; *Adventure*, Mar.
   16-Ap. 20, 1849
Salt Lake City *Deseret News*, June 29, July 6, 1850
*San Bernardino Argus*, Sept. 14, 1874- Feb. 8, 1875 (inc.);
*Guardian*, Mar. 21, 1874-May 22, 1875; *Telegram*, June
   1881-May 1885
*San Diego Bulletin*, Sept. 1869-Dec. 2, 1871 (inc.); *Union*,
   Dec. 30, 1869-1871 (inc.)
San Francisco *Alta California*, Feb. 1849-Dec. 1850, Dec.
   1852-Aug. 1853, July-Oct. 1859, Ap.-Oct. 1860;
   *Bulletin*, Oct. 13-31, 1859, Jan.-Ap. 2, 1860; *The Californ-
   ian*, Mar. 15-Aug. 14, 1848; *The California Star*, Mar. 18-
   10, 1848; *The California Star and Californian*, Nov. 18-
   Dec. 9, 1848; *Call*, July-Oct. 1859, Mar.-Oct.1860; *Herald*,
   Ap.18, May 9, 1853; *Pacific News*, Aug. 1849-Jan. 1850.
*Santa Barbara Gazette*, May 24,1855-Dec. 1856
Silver Mountain *Silver Miner*, June 30, 1868
*Sonora Herald*, July 4-13, 27, Dec. 28, 1850-Feb. 1, 1851
Stockton *San Joaquin Republican*, May 14, 1851-Aug. 1853;
   *Times*, Mar. 1850-Ap. 1851, Dec. 1852-Aug. 1853
*Visalia Delta*, Nov. 20, 1867-June 27, 1872.
Weaverville *Trinity Journal*, Oct. 16, 1858


LETTERS, DIARIES, MEMOIRS (manuscript)
Baker, Isaac W, *Journals, 1849-52*. Bancroft Library,
   Berkeley
Bertheau, Cesar, *Journal of Voyage, 1849*. State Library,

Sacramento

Blake, Seth B., *Diary, 1849-50.* Sac.

Bradford, John S., *Diary, 1849, Illinois to California.* Sac.

Buffum, Joseph Curtis, *Diary, 1847-55.* Sac.

Carder, James B., *Journal on board the ship Hopewell, 1849.*
Bancroft

Chamberlin, William E., *Diary, April 11-Aug. 20, 1849.* Sac.

Child, Sophia A., *Correspondence, 1849-51.* Ban.

Clark, Sterling B. E, *Diary, Crossing the Plains, 1849.* Sac.

Counts, George, *Copy of Diary March 23-May 4, 1849.* Ban.

Crackbon, Joseph, *Narrative of a Voyage from Boston to
California, 1849.* Sac.

Dimmick, Kimball Hale, *Diary, San Francisco April 16-Oct.
26, 1848.* Huntington Library, San Marino

Dwinnelle, John Whipple, *Diary, 1849.* Ban.

Emerson, William Henry, *The Diary of, 1849.* Sac.

Farrar, Jarvis G., *Diary of, 1849-1852.* Sac.

Fitch, John R., *Letters and journal, 1848-52.* Hunt.

Fletcher, Warren, *Papers, including journal, Jan. 2-July 15,
1849.* Ban.

Gould, Charles, *Diary as member of Boston and Newton
Association, 1849.* Ban.

Hall, O. J. *The Diary of a '49er.* Sac.

Hittell, John S., *Letters concerning the discovery . . . at
Sutter's Mill.* Ban.

Hyde, Henry Hovy, Jr., *Journal of a Voyage. . .1849.* Sac.

Jordan, Dr. David, *Diary, 1849, from Ohio to Calif.* Sac.

Josselyn, Amos P., *Journal of, 1849.* Sac.

Kirkpatrick, Charles A., *Journal of, 1849.* Ban.

Larkin, Thomas O. *Letters and papers, June 1-Sept. 10,
1848.* Ban.

Lindsay, Tipton, *A Journal of a trip to Calif., 1849.* Ban.

McCrackan, John, *Letters of, 1849-53.* Ban.

Meredith, Griffith, *Journal from NewYork in 1849 via Cape
Horn to San Francisco.* Sac.

Miller, Reuben G. *Journal, 1849.* Hunt.

Nusbaumer, Louis, *Adventures of a Trip to the Gold fields, 1849-50.* Sac.

Reynolds, W P, *Letter, San Francisco., Dec. 27, 1848.* Hunt.

Richardson, Henry P, *Letter, San Francisco, July 9, 1848.* In Stearns Papers, Hunt.

Rogers, John Page, *Five Letters to Wife while en route from Oregon and in the Mines, Sept. 23,1848-Jan. 3,1849.* Sac.

Smith, Azariah, *Diary, Sutter's Mill, Jan.-April 1848.* Photostat at Ban.

Snow, Joseph Chester, *Diary and Papers, 1849-53.* Ban.

Taylor, Augustus E, *Diary 1849, of a trip to Calif.* Ban.

Taylor, John, *Journal of a voyage, New York to San Francisco, 1849.* Ban.

Tuttle, Charles Albion, *Correspondence with his wife and misc. papers.* Ban.

Winchester, Jonas, *Letters from a Gold Hunter, Feb. 27-Dec. 8, 1849.* Sac.


LETTERS, DIARIES, MEMOIRS (Published)

Ayers, Col. James J., *Gold and Sunshine.* Boston, 1922

Bari, Valeska (ed.), *The Course of Empire.* N.Y, 1931

Bell, Horace, *Reminiscences of a Ranger.* Los Angeles, 1881

Bidwell, John, *Echoes of the Past.* Ed., Milo M. Quaife, Chicago, 1922

Bigler, Henry W., "Diary of, in 1847 and 1848", *Overland,* Sept. 1887; "Reminiscence of Gold Discovery", *Q. of Soc. of Calif. Pioneers,* S.F., Vol. 1, No. 3

Borthwick, J. D., *Three Years in California.* Edinburgh & London, 1857

Brewer, William H., *Up and Down California in 1860-64.* New Haven, 1930

Brooks, J. T, *Four Months Among the Gold Finders.* London & N.Y, 1849

Browne, J. Ross, *A Peep at Washoe and Washoe Revisited.* Balboa Island, 1959

Bruff, J. Goldsborough, *Gold Rush,* 2 Vols. N.Y, 1944

Buck, Franklin A., *A Yankee Trader in the Gold Rush.* Boston, 1930

Buffum, E. Gould, *Six Months in the Gold Mines.* Phila., 1850

Burnett, Peter H., *Recollections and Opinions of an Old Pioneer.* N.Y, 1880

Carson, J. H., *Early Recollections of the Mines.* Stockton, 1852

Christman, Enos, *One Man's Gold,* Ed. by Florence M. Christman. N.Y, 1930

Clappe, Louise A. K. S., *California in 1851.* S.F., 1933

Cordua, Theodor, "Memoirs", Ed. and Trans. by E. D. Gudde, *California Historical Society Quarterly,* Vol. 12, No. 4

Coke, Henry John, *A Ride over the Rocky Mountains.* London, 1852

Colton, Rev. Walter, *Three Years in California.* New York, 1850

Crosby, Elisha O., *Memoirs,* Ed. by Charles A. Barker. San Marino, 1945

Delano, Alonzo, *Life on the Plains and at the Diggings.* Auburn & Buffalo, 1854

Downie, William, *Hunting for Gold.* S.F., 1893

Eaton, Henry G., "Bodie Was a Swell Town!" *L. A. Times Sun. Mag.,* July 31, 1932

Ferguson, Charles D., *The California Gold Fields.* Oakland, 1948

Frémont, Elizabeth Benton, *Recollections.* N.Y, 1912

Frémont, Jesse Benton, *Far West Sketches.* Boston, 1890

Gerstaeker, Friedrich, *California Gold Mines.* Oakland, 1946

Gillis, William R., *Gold Rush Days with Mark Twain.* N.Y, 1930

Greeley, Horace, *An Overland Journey.* N.Y, 1860

Gregson, Mrs. Eliza and James, *The Gregson Memoirs.* S.F., 1940

Gwin, William M., "Memoirs", *California Hist. Soc. Quarter-*

*ly, Vol.* 19

Hafen, LeRoy R., *Journals of the Forty-Niners.* Glendale, 1954

Hancock, Samuel, *The Narrative of Samuel Hancock, 1845-60.* N.Y., 1927

Harpending, Asbury, *The Great Diamond Hoax.* S.F., 1913

Hollingsworth, John McHenry, *The Journal of, 1846-49.* S.F., 1923

Ingalls, John, *California Letters.* Worcester, Mass., 1938

Johnson, Theodore T, *Sights in the Gold Region.* N.Y, 1849

Keller, George A., *A Trip Across the Plains.* Oakland, 1855

Kelly, William, *An Excursion to California*, 2 vols. London, 1851

Leinhard, Heinrich, *A Pioneer at Sutter's Fort, 1846-50.* Trans. and ed. by Marguerite Eyer Wilbur. Los Angeles, 1941

Leuba, Edmond, "A Frenchman in the Panamints", *Calif. Hist. Soc. Q.*, v. 17, Sept., 1938

Lynch, James, *With Stevenson to California.* San Luis Obispo, 1896

Lyman, Chester S., *Around the Horn to the Sandwich Islands and California, 1845-50,* Ed. by F. J. Taggart. New Haven, 1924; "Letters of, Sept.-Nov. 1848, in San Francisco". *Cal. Hist. Soc. Q.* June 1934

Marryatt, Frank, *Mountains and Molehills.* N.Y, 1855

Marshall, James, "The Discovery of Gold in California," *Hutching's California Magazine,* Nov. 1857

Megquier, Mary Jane, *Apron Full of Gold*, Ed. by Robert G. Cleland, San Marino, 1949

Mellen, Herman E, "Reminiscences of Old Calico", *Historical Society of Southern California Quarterly,* June, Sept., Dec., 1952

Miller, Joaquin, *California Diary, 1855-57,* Ed. John S. Richards. Seattle, 1936

Moerenhout, Jacques Antoine, *The Inside Story of the Gold Rush,* Trans. and ed. by Abraham P. Nasatir. S.F, 1935

Pritchard, James A., *Overland Diary*, Ed. by Dale L. Morgan. Denver, 1959

Revere, Joseph Warren, *A Tour of Duty in California*. N.Y, 1849

Royce, Sarah, *A Frontier Lady*. New Haven, 1932

Russ, Carolyn Hale, *The Log of a Forty-Niner*. Boston, 1923

Ryan, William R., *Personal Adventures in. . . California.* London, 1852

*San Felipe Mining Co. vs. Belshaw et al.* Calif. Supreme Court Records, v. 289

Sawyer, Lorenzo, *Way Sketches*. N.Y, 1926

Shaw, Reuben Cole, *Across the Plains in '49*. Farmland, Indiana, 1896

Sherman, William T, *Memoirs,* Vol. 1. N.Y, 1891

Stewart, William M., *Reminiscences of,* Ed. by G. R. Brown. N.Y and Wash., 1908

Sutter, John A., *New Helvetia Diary, 1845-48,* S.F, 1939; *Sutter's Own Story*, Ed. by E. G. Gudde, N.Y, 1936; *The Diary of,* S.F, 1932; "The Discovery of Gold in California", *Hutchings' California Magazine,* vol. 4, No. 5, Nov., 1857

Taylor, Bayard, *Eldorado,* 2 vols. N.Y, 1850

Thornton, J. Quinn, *California in 1848,* 2 vols. N.Y, 1849

Twain, Mark, *Roughing It*. Hartford, 1872

War Dept., U.S., *The War of the Rebellion*, v. 50, Parts 1 and 2. Wash., 1899

Wells, Fargo & Co., *Scrapbook, Posters and other papers relating to Robberies, 1871-75; Robber's Record,* S.F, 1885 (includes reports of detectives James B. Hume and John Thacker, 1870-1885).

## SECONDARY WORKS

Bancroft, Hubert Howe, *History of California,* v. 6 & 7, S.F, 1888 & 1890; *California Pastoral,* v. 34 of Works, S.F, 1888; *California Inter Pocula,* v. 35, S.F, 1888; *Popular Tribunals,* v. 36 & 37, S.F, 1887; *History of Oregon,* v. 2, S.F., 1888

Beattie, George W and Helen P, *Heritage of the Valley.*
Pasadena, 1939

Browne, J. Ross, *Report on Mineral Resources of the U.S.*
Wash., 1867

Bucklee, Edna Bryan, *The Saga of Old Tuolumne.* N.Y, 1935

Cain, Ella M., *The Story of Bodie.* S.F. & Sonora, 1956; *The
Story of Early Mono County.* S.F, 1961

California State Division of Mines, *Annual Reports of the
State Mineralogist.* Sacramento, 1882-1918; 1954-1956.

Caruthers, William, *Loafing Along Death Valley Trails.*
Ontario, Calif., 1951

Chalfant, Willie A., *The Story of Inyo*, Chicago, 1922;
*Outposts of Civilization*, Boston, 1928; *Tales of the Pio-
neers*, Stanford, 1942; *Gold, Guns, and Ghost Towns*,
Stanford, 1947; "Cerro Gordo", *Hist. Soc. of So. Calif.
Pubs.*, v. 22, 1940

Coy, Owen C., *Gold Days.* Los Angeles, 1929

Dane, George Ezra, in collab. with Beatrice Dane, *Ghost
Town*, N.Y., 1941

Davis, Sam P. (ed.) *The History of Nevada.* Reno and L.A.,
1913

Dryer, Marjorie, "Old Dale Diggings", *Westways*, Oct. 1957

Dudley, Aaron, and Fickwirth, Alvin, "Ghost Town of the
Mojave", *Westways*, Nov. 1941

Fairfield, Asa Merrill, *Fairfield's Pioneer History of Lassen
County*, S.F., 191

Fisk, O. J., "Ghosts of Greenwater," *Westways*, Nov., 1940

Glasscock, C. B., *Gold in Them Hills*, Indianapolis, 1932; *A
Golden Highway*, Indianapolis, 1934; *Here's Death
Valley*, N.Y., 1940

Greene, Charles L., "The California Rand," *Overland*, May
1897

Gudde, Edwin G., *California Place Names*, Berkeley, 1960

Guinn, James M., "The Sonoran Immigration," *Hist. Soc. of
So. Calif. Pubs.*, v. 8, 1909-10

Holland, Henrietta, "George Washington's Birthday, 1870",

*Westways,* Feb. 1948

Hoover, Mildred B., Rensch, Hero L. and Ethel G., *Historic Spots in California,* Revised by Ruth Teiser. Stanford, 1948

Hungerford, Edward, *Wells Fargo,* N.Y, 1949

Hunt, Rockwell D., *John Bidwell.* Caldwell, Idaho, 1942

Jackson, Joseph Henry, *Anybody's Gold,* NY, 1941; *Bad Company,* NY, 1949

Jenkins, Olaf P, *Geologic Guidebook Along Highway 49.* S.F.,1948

Johnston, Philip, "Epitaph for Ivanpah," *Westways,* Jan. 1942

Kneiss, Gilbert H., *Bonanza Railroads,* Stanford, 1954

*Land of Sunshine,* "Randsburg, the Great New Mining Camp of Southern California," March, 1897

Lord, Eliot, *Comstock Mining and Miners.* Wash., 1883

Page, Elizabeth, *Wagons West.* N.Y, 1930

Parsons, George F, *The Life and Adventures of James W. Marshall.* S.F., 1935

Rickard, Thomas A., *The Romance of Mining,* Toronto, 1945

Rourke, Constance, *Troupers of the Gold Coast.* N.Y, 1928

Royce, Josiah, *California.* Cambridge, Mass., 1886

Russell, C. P, "The Bodie that Was", *Touring Topics,* Nov. 1929; "Early Mining Excitements East of Yosemite", *Sierra Club Bulletin,* v. 13, no. 1.

Shinn, Charles H., *Mining Camps,* N.Y, 1885; *Story of the Mine,* N.Y, 1896

*Sunset,* Editors of, *Gold Rush Country.* Menlo Park, Calif., 1957 & 1963

Thompson, David G., *The Mojave Desert Region: A Geographic, Geologic, and Hydrologic Reconnaissance.* Wash., 1922

Tinsley, H. G., "A Desert Mining Town," *Harper's Weekly,* March 6, 1897

Walker, Franklin D., *San Francisco's Literary Frontier.* N.Y., 1939

Wilson, Neill C., *Treasure Express: Epic Days of Wells*

*Fargo.* N.Y, 1936

Winther, Oscar O., *Express and Stagecoach Days in California*, Stanford, 1936; *Via Western Express and Stagecoach*, Stanford, 1945

Wynn, Marcia Rittenhouse, *Desert Bonanza.* Culver City, Calif., 1949

## LOCAL GUIDES AND MAPS

*Amador City Historic Tour Guide*, Gold Pan Merchants Association, 1988

*Visitors Guide to Amador County*, Amador County Chamber of Commerce, 1991

*Old Town Auburn*, Historic Auburn Merchants Council, n.d.

*Big Oak Flat and Groveland: Gold Rush Gateway to Yosemite*, Southern Tuolumne County Historical Society, n.d.

*Bodie State Historical Park*, California Department of Parks and Recreation, 1988

*The Gold Discovery: James Marshall and the California Gold Rush*, by William C. Dillinger. California Department of Parks and Recreation, 1990

*Coulterville: A Gold Rush Town Map and Historical Descriptions*, Mariposa County Chamber of Commerce, North County Office, n.d.

*Downieville Walking Tour Map*, Downieville Chamber of Commerce, 1992

*Grass Valley Points of Historical Interest*, Grass Valley and Nevada County Chamber of Commerce and City of Grass Valley, n.d.

*Larry Cenoto's Historical Jackson Guide Book*, 1986

*Discover Julian*, Julian Chamber of Commerce, n.d.

*Historical Site Markers - Kern County*, by William G. Hample. Kern County Historical Society, 1991

*Historic Points of Interest in Mariposa*, Mariposa Mercantile, n.d.

*Murphys*, by Bradford Evans and Lawrence Pugno, n.d.

*Nevada City Walking Tour*, Nevada City Chamber of

Commerce, 1991

*The Compleat Pedestrian's Partially Illustrated Guide to Greater Nevada City*, Fourth Edition, by Robert M. Wyckoff, 1991

*Placerville: A Walk Through the Gold Rush*, Gold Rush California Publications, 1987

*Greater Oroville Spring/Summer Visitor's Guide, 1992*, Ad Ventures Publishing Co.

*Randsburg Gazette*, Vol. 1, No. 1, Special Edition, n.d.

*The Little Town of Rough and Ready, California*, Rough and Ready Chamber of Commerce, n.d.

*Tour of Historic San Andreas*, with map supplement, Calaveras County Museum and Archives, n.d.

*Gold Fever Trail Self-Guided Tour, San Bernardino National Forest*, United States Forest Service, 1991

*Shasta State Historic Park: Brief History and Tour Guide*, California Department of Parks and Recreation, 1985

*Siskiyou County Museum* (folder), Yreka, n.d.

*Sonora. . .A Guide to Yesterday*, Tuolumne County Historical Society, n.d.

*The Walker's Tour Guide Map of Volcano*, by Morgan, 1984

*Walking Tour of Historic Weaverville*, Weaverville Chamber of Commerce, Trinity County Chamber of Commerce and Trinity County Historical Society, n.d.

*A Guide to the Historical District of Yreka*, Siskiyou County Museum and Yreka Chamber of Commerce, n.d.

*Historic Walking Tour, Yreka, California*, with supplement, Yreka Historic District & Landmarks Commission, n.d.

# Index

(Photo page nos. in **bold**)

Mariposas, Rancho Las, 119, 122, 126, 266
Markleeville, 246
Marshall, James, 10ff., 35, 45ff., 148, 163
Martell, 91
Marysville, 62, 130, 156, 163-7, 175
Mason, Gov. Richard B., 12-3, 22-3
Masonic, 236
McDonald, John (bandit), 223-4
Merced Mining Company, 122ff.
Merced River, 120, 128
Mescal, 301
Mexicans, 68, 84, 92ff., 102, 111ff., 127, 141, 168, 174, 211, 219, 257-60, 272
Michigan Bluff, **44**, 67
Mill City, **201**, 242-3
Miller, Joaquin, 188
Millspaugh, 228
Mineral King, 265
Minnietta Mine, 227
Missouri Bar, 165
Modoc Mine, **198**, 227-8
Mogul, 246
Mojave, **201**, 241, 243, 278, 284-5
Mojave River, 274, 279
Mokelumne Hill, 79ff.
Mokelumne River, 94-5, 102
Monitor, 246
*Monitor Argus*, 246
Monk, Hank, 55
Mono County, **199**, 220, 234, 237-8, 243
Mono Lake, 229, 233-4, 243
Monoville, 229, 237
Monterey County, 302
Montez, Lola, **136**, 144ff.
Montgomery, Bob (Skidoo), 296-7
Mooers, Frederic M. (Randsburg),

**253**, 284
Mormon Bar, 126
Mormon Battalion, 17
Mormon Island, 14, 21, 45, 47
*Mrs. Skaggs' Husband*, 100
Mt. Bullion, 119, 128
Mt. Diablo Coal Towns, 303
Murieta, Joaquin (bandit), 91ff., 103
Murphy's, 103
Murphy, Dan and John, 103

Nadeau, Remi, 212, 215, 224, 227, 241, 243
Nataqua, Territory of, 171
Navy Weapons Center, 219, 228
Neagle, Dave, 223
Nevada City, 61-2, **132**, **137-8**, 141ff., 205
Nevada County, 62, 147, 153-4
New Almaden, 302-3
New Idria, 302
*New York Tribune*, 23, 79
Nicholas, Pete, 108-9
Nicolaus, 60-1
North Bloomfield, 155
North San Juan, 152, 155
Nusbaumer, Louis, 33

Oakhurst, 241
Olancha, 218
Old Coso, 219
Olvera, Augustin, 269
Orange County, 273
Oregon City, 170
*Oriflamme* (steamer), 267
Orleans Bar, 194
Oro Grande, 274, 279
Oroville, 165ff.
Oroville Dam, 169
Ortega, General (Rancho Santa Ysabel), 270

320

Ott, James J. (Nevada City), 155
Overshiner, John (Calico), 275-6
Owens Lake, 210, 212, 216-8
Owens River, 215, 220
Owensville, 220

Palen, Mat (Ivanpah), 300
Panamint, **199**, 218, 221ff.
*Panamint News*, 223, 226
Panic of 1855, 61
Paradise, 170
Parker, James A. (Mammoth), 239
Parks and Recreation, Dep't of,
    110, 163, 236
Parote, John, 108
*Parson of Panamint, The*, 221
Patterson, James (Calico), 277
Pellet, Sarah (Downieville), 161
Peralta, Luis, 19
Picacho, 272
Pine Log, 108-9
Pine Tree Mine (Mariposa Co.),
    122ff.
Pit River, 189-90
Placer County, 60ff.
Placerita Canyon, 10
Placerville & Sacramento Valley
    RR, 58
Placerville, 50, 59ff., 206-7
Plumas County, 171
Plymouth, 84
Posey Flat, 259, 261
Poway, 268
Prescot (Quartzburg), 96
Prices, 21, 45-6, 54, 88, 167,
    172- 3, 222, 240, 263, 295
Providence, 282

Quartzburg (Mariposa Co.), 96,
    127
Quartzburg (Kern Co.), 262-3
Quicksilver mining, 302-3

Railroads, 58, 64-5, 191, 215, 217,
    225, 233-4, 243, 272, 278, 280,
    282, 285, 287, 291-2, 299, 300
Ramirez, Jesus (Sonora), 115
Ramsey, Harry (Skidoo), 296
Randsburg, **251-3**, 283ff.
Randsburg RR, 287
Rattlesnake Bar, 62
Reading's Bar, 172
Reading, Pierson B., 172
Red Mountain, 289, 291
Reddy, Ned, 2230
Rhyolite, 292, 295-6, 298-9
Rich Bar (Calaveras River), 95
Rich Bar (Feather River), 165ff.
Ridge, John Rollin, 93, 97
Robbins, Jared, 189-90
Rogers, "Lovely" (Kern Co.), 262
Roop, Isaac, 171
Rose's Bar, 156
Rough and Ready, 147
*Roughing It*, 238
"Rough and Tumble Jack" (Bodie),
    231

Sacramento, 11 *et passim*
Sacramento River, 15, 18, 173, 175
*Sacramento Union*, 189
Sacramento Valley Railroad, 64-6
Sageland, 264
Salmon River, 193
San Andreas, 86, 91ff.
San Benito County, 155, 302
San Bernardino, 222, 259, 267,
    274, 284-5
San Bernardino County, 273,
    279-80
San Carlos, 220
San Diego, 266-8, 271
*San Diego Bulletin*, 267
San Diego County, 266, 269